to Naomi and Donna...
Thank You!
Love,
Linda
2008

Bon Appetite
Steven A. Yeanel

OLEY VALLEY INN

A Culinary Journey

by Chef Steve Yeanish

401 Main Street
Oley, Pennsylvania 19547
(610) 987-6400
www.oleyvalleyinn.com

Copyright 2008 © Steven A. Yeanish

Book design copyright 2008 © Tudor Gate Press

All rights reserved, including the right of reproduction, in whole or in part, in any form.

ISBN 978-0-9801660-0-2

www.tudorgatepress.com

DEDICATIONS

IN LOVING MEMORY OF MY MOTHER,
MY FIRST TEACHER AND THE BEST
COOK THAT I HAVE EVER KNOWN

TO BARRIE, WHO HAS BEEN WITH
ME FOR MOST OF THIS JOURNEY

TO MY DEAR SISTERS RUTH ANN AND JAYNE,
WHO HAVE BEEN AN INSPIRATION TO ME SINCE I WAS A KID

FOREWARD

I met Steve more than 20 years ago when we were both young, but established in our chosen careers. I was assigned as an attorney to represent Steve buying his own restaurant. He had been the executive chef at a country club where my law firm had lunch every day. Some doubted he could translate his skills to his own business.

Steve and I hit it off immediately. We shared much experience in the restaurant business, as I had put myself through school as a hostess, waitress and short order cook. When I saw the Inn in its original condition, I knew Steve could transform the Inn into a first rate restaurant, even though it was in deplorable condition and located in an out of way small town. Steve's passion and great talent in culinary arts, interior and floral design, growing his own herbs and edible flowers, keen eye for displaying local artists' work, wicked sense of humor and compassion for all drew loyal clients from his country club clientele and new patrons from New York to Washington, DC, from Lancaster to Atlantic City and beyond. He built a loyal and professional staff and expanded the Inn to include al fresco dining, a beautiful private party room and charming bed and breakfast.

Steve's passion, creativity and compassion have never waned. Over the years, he remembered that one of our law firm's secretaries could only eat whipped potatoes and steamed vegetables. He made a birthday cake for my four year-old daughter, exactly replicating her favorite storybook picture. He donated a special Christmas luncheon for the employees of a daycare for indigent children–the first such holiday celebration they had ever had.

Celebrating the Inn's 20th anniversary was also a celebration of the close friendship we have forged over these years. He is a *mensch*. I call him my friend and family. I hope to enjoy my valued relationship and close friendship with this special man for the rest of my life.

Thea Magee Block

Introduction

This book began seven years ago, when my left foot was completely reconstructed using bone grafts, a steel plate and eight titanium screws. An ordinary recovery would have been a long, slow, boring ordeal, but I also had three serious bone infections and one complication after another. Finally, a specially-molded custom boot was made to immobilize my foot. This was resoled three times because every chance I had, I was back working in the kitchen again as soon as possible.

Eventually a new doctor successfully performed corrective surgery, but once again I was admonished to, *"STAY off your feet and OUT OF THE KITCHEN!"* This time it was serious. I literally had to stay off my feet to save my foot, but the prospect of several months of sitting around waiting while my foot healed was exasperating at best.

Cooking while on crutches is impossible. Not cooking for several months was the hardest blow of all. What was I going to do with myself? I've always been active and used to going 24/7. My dear friends Thea and Natalie enjoyed reading my Oley Valley Inn newsletter for many years. They encouraged me to continue writing and tell the story of how the Inn came to be. Once I got started, writing became a very therapeutic way to pass the time. Eventually, as the story evolved and turned into a book, I began to realize what a very fortunate individual I was to have the opportunities and support of family and friends. Looking back I can say it really has been quite an adventure. I'm living my dream—and it's not over yet!

The Oley Valley Inn's atmosphere is elegant, but unstuffy and gracious without being stiff or formal. The food we serve reflects my passion for what I call "real food." My love of comfort and ethnic foods will never end. A freshly-baked loaf of bread and a good, hearty soup is sometimes as good as it gets for me. I am sharing these recipes with you because they have worked for me and have made many people very happy.

Over the years I have adopted, and adapted, many recipes to suit my own tastes. That's what good cooking is all about. Recipes and ideas about food are continually evolving. As you try these recipes, give them your own special "tweak" to make them your own.

What may seem like trade secrets to some are my gift to you. I feel it is a Chef's obligation, not only to teach, but also to inspire the next generation. As my mother always said to me, "Stevie, you'll never get poor from giving." I've even had a good time to boot!

Chef Steve Yeanish

Where is Oley, Pennsylvania?

Latitude: 40.387N
Longitude: -75.79W

Oley is a township in Berks County.
The largest city nearby is Reading.
Philadelphia is about one hour away.
Washington D.C. is about three hours.
New York City is about two hours away.

DIRECTIONS FROM READING:
Take US 422 West, to Route 12 East, to Route 73 East.
Turn right on Route 73 East.
Go 3 miles to first traffic light, turn left (Friedensburg Road).
Go about two and a half blocks.
The Oley Valley Inn is straight ahead.

DIRECTIONS FROM ALLENTOWN:
Take US 222 South to Route 73 East.
Go 6 miles to third traffic light.
Turn left (Friedensburg Road).
The Oley Valley Inn is straight ahead.

DIRECTIONS FROM PHILADELPHIA:
Take I-76 West (Schuylkill Expressway) to Paoli exit (US 202 South).
Take an immediate exit to Pottstown (US 422 West).
Travel 30 miles to Douglassville.
Take Route 662 north for 10 miles to Route 73.
Turn left (73 West) for ¼ mile.
At the traffic light, turn right (Friedensburg Road).
The Oley Valley Inn is straight ahead.

Contact us at:
(610) 987-6400
www.oleyvalleyinn.com
OleyInn@aol.com

TABLE OF CONTENTS

Index ....pages 184 to 190

List of Recipes by Title ....pages 193 to 197

Chef Steve's Stories by Title ....pages 199 to 201

Photo Credits ....page 202

May 26, 2005 started like any normal Thursday at the Oley Valley Inn. We were busy getting ready for our 18th Memorial Day weekend, but we had no way of knowing it would almost be our last. Incredibly, by morning we would be lucky to be alive.

We were busy all day as extra food deliveries arrived for the holiday. I baked Sticky Buns, which freeze well.

Our entire garden was starting to burst into life after the spring thaw. We planted delphiniums, hollyhocks, foxgloves, Asiatic lilies, and many shades of hostas in window boxes and flower beds. Then, we created baskets for the patio and Boston ferns were hung around the front porch, portico, the entrance and under the pergola.

All day long we puttered around the Inn getting ready for the season, making finishing touches and doing last-minute jobs like putting a stained finish on the new wood floor.

By evening, white lights decorated arbors where clematis and Japanese wisteria would soon climb the pergola. This was a magical place at night with the sounds of fountains and gently splashing water. Paddle fans created a breeze and accent lights made the arbor an intimate spot for dining. Our koi fish in the pond swam gracefully.

It wasn't particularly busy in the dining room that evening, so I did some baking for the weekend, while the other chefs cooked dinners. Our friend Barbara was staying in the Newport Room of our bed and breakfast on the second floor. Barrie and I were in our apartment up on the top floor. We were all really tired that night, so we retired early, around 11 P.M.

We were sound asleep when the telephone rang. I sleep lightly, so I heard it. Our answering service picks up on the fourth ring. The phone rang again, so I finally got up to answer it, but no one was there.

I happened to glance out the side window and noticed a dull, yellow glow. Then I realized, to my horror, that flames were leaping up through the roof of our kitchen. I stared in shocked disbelief. Fire fighters were everywhere, dousing the roof with water and we had slept through it all!

Fortunately, a neighbor had seen the flames and called in the alarm. The Fire Company is only a few blocks away, so they were on the scene immediately.

We had to get out of the building, so I ran down the steps to the Newport Room. I banged on Barbara's door to wake her, and yelled for her to exit by the front stairs. Then I rushed upstairs to get Barrie and we grabbed Calli, our chocolate Lab, her leash, some clothes and shoes, then flew down the stairs.

We met Barbara on the first floor and gasped, coughing as we got our first lung-searing dose of smoke, then covered our mouths, and groped our way to the side entrance.

John, one of our local policemen, met us at the door looking relieved. From the look on his face it was clear that the fire was still not under control. Luckily we had rushed downstairs when we did. Firemen from a Mt. Penn Fire Company ladder truck were just about to go into the building to look for us.

We were all fine, but badly shaken, so we were sent to the ambulance to get oxygen. Our dog, Calli, had some too.

By midnight we were still in shock, but had regained some composure. It took at least another hour for the blaze to get under control. By the end of the night, eleven fire companies had been called to the scene and ninety firemen and rescue people responded. We were lucky to be alive!

The Oley Valley Inn

Ninety heroic Firemen and Rescue Personnel from eleven Fire Companies fought the blaze.

Surveying the Damage

It was impossible to figure out the extent of the damage, because I couldn't even get near the building. Our gas and electric services had been disconnected.

By the time the fire was finally out, the whole back corner of the Inn was completely destroyed. The fire had spread all the way to the original brick building and it even scorched the sitting room of the Montreal Suite in our bed and breakfast. As the fire smoldered, the weary men sprayed foam over the whole area to stop hot spots from erupting into flame. Fortunately, the firemen were able to get up to our third floor apartment and open the windows. They found our two cats scared to death, but safely hiding under the beds.

Our bakeshop was gutted. The flat, rubber-surfaced roof had burned up in a flash. The walk-in refrigerator loaded with $4,000 worth of food was completely destroyed. Our computer was a melted blob. A set of professional cake pans that Mom gave me for graduation was welded into a solid lump. Our whole storage area was completely destroyed. Anything plastic melted from the heat. Two freezers, all our catering equipment, paper and cleaning supplies, glassware, china, you name it, all of it was lost. All of the refrigerators were ruined. Microwave ovens melted. An entire cooler of beer and wine was destroyed. The damage in our main kitchen was not quite as bad, but all the equipment, every single item in it, was completely covered with black soot.

The Fire Chief was a very helpful guy. He took us to his rescue truck, started the paper work, then called someone to help me secure the building. Before I knew it, I was signing a paper to allow a guy to secure our doors with sheets of plywood. I was living a nightmare.

Dead koi from our pond.

We were eventually allowed to go back to our apartment and grab a few personal things. Then we went to a friend's house for the rest of the sleepless night.

At first light, I couldn't stand the suspense any longer, so I drove back to the Inn in a daze and walked around to the patio. As the sun rose, it illuminated the full extent of the damage. The building was charred, the siding was melted and the outdoor dining area, which had looked so beautiful the day before, was completely gone. Firefighter's foam covered the surface of our koi pond and our beautiful fish were gasping at the surface desperate for oxygen. In the eerie silence I tried to save the fish, but it was too late. I tried not to despair as I faced that depressing sight.

Then I was absolutely stunned speechless as it finally hit me—my entire life's work was in ruins. Scores of professional cook books had turned to ashes. All my baking recipes were gone and even my professional portfolio of prize-winning competition entries was destroyed. What to do? Give up? Not likely. I'd been a professional chef since I was sixteen, and a passionate foodie before that. Most of the recipes were in my head and my favorite ones were in my heart, generously shared, or carefully taught, by family and friends. The Chinese say the longest journey starts with a single step. Well, that's what I'd have to do. Rebuild my repertoire with the help of family and friends one dish at a time.

The Oley Valley Inn

This was once the storage area.

The ruins of our bakeshop.

Looking into the wreckage from the green door.

A Culinary Journey with Chef Steve Yeanish

Some of the Wreckage

All my professional baking equipment melted, including my present from Mom.

After 34 years of faithful service, and only one repair, my KitchenAid® mixer was destroyed by the fire.

Hess Brothers Department Store in Allentown was no ordinary store. Max Hess, one of the owners, had an eye for the interesting and unique, although half the fun of shopping there was looking at the outrageous price tags! There was a gourmet shop on one of the upper floors displaying huge glass jars layered with vegetables and olives in mosaic designs and an amazing cheese department. That's where I found my ultimate dream mixer, a Kitchen Aid 5-quart mixer with a bowl that cranked up and down. I bought it at Hess's for $149 in 1972 and used it continuously for the next 34 years, with only one repair. I used it at home, then during my country club chef days, and finally here at the Oley Valley Inn. I have no doubt that it would still be going strong if the kitchen fire in May 2005 hadn't destroyed it. It was like losing an old friend.

By my senior year of high school, I was already planning to go to culinary school. Mom found a classified ad for a complete set of professional quality baking pans. The owner had suffered a nervous breakdown and decided to stop baking, so Mom purchased all the equipment as a graduation present for me.

There were two complete sets of tin and steel, round and square tiered cake pans with high sides. Also included were Wilton of Illinois cake decorating tools, pans and books.

This was just the encouragement I needed to pursue my dream. I started baking at home, after school, in the evenings and on weekends. In my free time, I practiced making flowers and borders out of icing; then I'd scrape the icing up and reuse it over and over again until I got it right. Soon I was confident enough to have some business cards printed: *Cakes For All Ocassions*. My first commission was a wedding cake for a classmate. I remember it well—a three-tiered pound cake decorated in yellow roses. Unfortunately, Mom's Sunbeam Mixmaster soon died an untimely death. I had worn it out perfecting my baking. When I left home, I bought Mom a brand new Kitchen Aid mixer.

The Oley Valley Inn

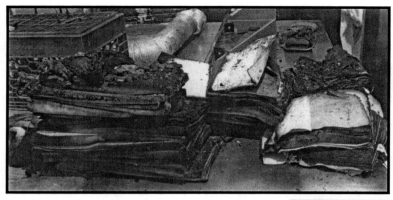

Some of the remains of my cherished cookbook collection.

This used to be the stove.

This was a room-to-room air conditioner that was purchased the day before the fire!

A Culinary Journey with Chef Steve Yeanish

My Family

My grandparents Ray "Pappie" and Louise Yeanish in their soda fountain and confectionery store in Slatington, Pennsylvania.

I'm one of seven children and my father is, too. My particular culinary journey began on a warm June day in 1954 in Pottstown, Pennsylvania when Dr. Ivan Hess delivered me, a whopping 10 lb., 1oz. baby boy to proud parents, Ruth and Jay Yeanish. I was the sixth of their seven children, four boys and three girls: Ray, Mary Lou, John, Charles, Ruth Ann, me and Jayne (pronounced Jay-nee).

There has always been a debate over the origin of our name Yeanish, which rhymes with Danish. After much research, Aunt Joan located our name on tombstones in Columbia, Lancaster County. Then she traced the family back to their homeland in Germany. If they arrived in America unable to speak English, the phonetic spelling of their German name Jehnish would be Yeanish in English. There was also rumored to be some Native American Indian blood in the family.

Dad was born and raised in Slatington, Pennsylvania, a small slate-mining town on the ridge of the Blue Mountain Range, near the Lehigh River. His parents, Ray and Louise, ran a soda fountain and confectionery store on the main street of town. They vented the exhaust from their peanut roaster out onto the street so the mouth-watering aroma would attract hungry customers. They sold all sorts of candy, from Hershey's chocolates to Campfire marshmallows, and I am fortunate to have several candy tins from their store.

We called my grandfather Pappie. During the holidays, he molded special hollow chocolates in all sizes. Pappie made a special large, very ornately decorated Easter egg for my mom when my parents were dating. Fortunately, I have several of these molds which were given to me by my Uncle Bert. These are still being used today.

The seven Yeanish kids: Ray, Mary Lou, John, Charles, Ruth Ann, Steve and Jayne.

My mom, Ruth was called "Little Red" and my dad, Jay, was known as "The Big Chief." This photo was taken during their courting days. Dad, who was nearly six and a half feet tall, was a gifted athlete.

Our Pappie Yeanish was definitely not a typical turn-of-the century kind of guy. Albert, his father, and my great-grandfather, had been a train conductor on the Berksy, a train which ran through Berks County alongside the Maiden Creek. Pappie bought a plot of land at the base of a wooded hill beside the Maiden Creek in Lenhartsville, a small farming community. My father and his six younger siblings grew up during the Great Depression, so nothing was ever wasted. They worked together and recycled lumber, windows and other remnants of railroad passenger cars to build a small frame building. This once-secluded spot was our destination for summer holidays and vacations while we were growing up. The Yeanish Clan called it the Bungalow and we always enjoyed our adventures there. It continues to be the hub of many Yeanish family gatherings.

Dad's mother, Louise, was a workhorse of a woman, and a good cook in her own right. The family often had to live off the land during the Great Depression. Chores were done for neighbors in exchange for food. They spent summers at the Bungalow in Lenhartsville, where the children could swim and fish the day away. Dad described the fish they caught as dinner, as well as sport. Times were tough, but they made it as much fun as possible. Groundhog was also considered fair game for the dinner table.

A Culinary Journey with Chef Steve Yeanish

Thanksgiving Feasts at the Bungalow

Fortunately, while I was growing up the Bungalow was only about an hour away from our home in Schwenksville. The halfway point of the trip to Lenhartsville was the small town of Oley, which would eventually become my home many years later. Dad usually took the by-pass around Oley to avoid the slower speed limit through the village, but I always enjoyed driving down Main Street.

The Bungalow had one large room with a wood-fired stove, a wooden icebox and two small bedrooms. Directly behind the Bungalow was an outdoor pavilion with a fireplace built at one end. During the summer, most of the cooking was done in that fireplace, and there was a long table outside, which we used for eating and food preparation.

Our water came from a hand-dug well that was all of about 20 feet deep. This was fed by springs in the side of the mountain above the cabin. A working cast iron pump supplied incredibly pure, cold water, even in the middle of summer, until recent development took its toll and the well dried up.

There was no indoor plumbing at the Bungalow, but it had what seemed to be the biggest outhouse we kids had ever seen. Old tools, cabinets, cans, fishing rods and nets were stored in there, even though it was just a one-seater. I honestly believe you could have parked a car in there. It was painted an old-fashioned shade of light green.

Everything seemed bigger when we were kids. The outhouse was only about ten feet away from the Bungalow, but the walk seemed considerably longer, especially in the dark. That was one scary place at nighttime, but there was safety in numbers, if we travelled together with a flashlight, or even a kerosene lamp.

We were fascinated by an old poster tacked to the angular ceiling, which showed an orchestra of about twenty-five minstrel musicians. We'd shine a light on the ceiling to light up their faces then we'd start scaring each other silly. As time went by, our shrieks became more traditional than fearful.

Many years later, I found that old poster and had it professionally framed, then gave it to my father for Christmas. Aunt Joan told us it was an advertisement for a show our grandfather Pappie had appeared in. It turns out he was quite the amateur actor. Unfortunately, I never got to see Pappie as he died years before I was born. I do have a photograph of my grandmother and me fishing by the Maiden Creek, which was taken just before she passed away.

My Dad and his six brothers and sisters inherited the Bungalow. Eventually, the rest of the family stopped going to the Bungalow, so Dad purchased it from his siblings. Every year several generations of the family still have a traditional Yeanish clan reunion.

We always had bread filling with our Thanksgiving turkey. Mom's was always made days ahead and was a meal in itself. Turkey backs provided both stock and meat. Mom often used day-old whole wheat bread which imparted a sweetness I love to this day. The bread filling was loaded with chestnuts. Peeling chestnuts is a labor of love and Mom spent hours doing it. With some good giblet gravy and cranberry sauce, you could eat the bread filling alone and still feel like you had a good, tasty Thanksgiving Dinner.

The Oley Valley Inn

Turkey and Chestnut Stuffing

*You need some good, rich turkey broth to make this stuffing.
Add the pieces of meat that have been pulled off the bones.*

1 pound or more **chestnuts** *cooked or roasted, peeled, cleaned and coarsely chopped*
½ cup **turkey or chicken fat, or butter**
2 cups **onion** *finely chopped*
2 cups **celery** *finely chopped*
2 Tbs **parsley** *chopped, (preferably flat-leaf)*
4 **eggs** *slightly beaten*
2 tsp **salt**
½ tsp **pepper**
3 tsp **Bell's Seasoning®** *(or substitute ground sage)*
1 loaf **whole wheat bread** *cut into cubes*
1 loaf **good quality white bread** *cut into cubes (Pepperidge Farms® or Arnold® bread are good)*

Place cut bread on baking sheet.
Bake in 300 degree oven until toasted.
Pour bread croutons into large mixing bowl or pan.
Sauté onions and celery slowly in fat until they are brown.
Place the sautéed vegetables over the bread.
Add parsley, the seasonings, eggs, chestnuts, and
any cooked, chopped turkey meat you have.
Toss the ingredients to blend.
Add slightly warm turkey broth to the mixture.
Stir until mixture is damp, but not wet. I like it to just hold together.
Taste for seasoning.
Place in Pyrex dish to bake. I like to use paper towels that have been soaked in turkey fat or melted butter to cover the dish as it bakes.
Bake in 350 degree oven for 45 minutes.
This stuffing can be used inside the bird,
but it *must* be heated to at least 170 degrees with an instant read thermometer.

Cranberry Relish

1 pound **fresh cranberries**
2 **apples** *quartered, and cored*
2 **oranges** *quartered, seeds removed*
1 **whole lemon** *quartered and seeded*
½ cup **chopped walnuts**
1 cup **granulated sugar**
2 Tbs **brandy**

*Mom always made her own relish,
but we had the jellied kind, too.*

Place all ingredients in a food processor,
then pulse to relish consistency.

A Culinary Journey with Chef Steve Yeanish

Dad

My Dad was the pride of his family. As an eighth-grader he played George Washington, so his Aunt Emma, a wealthy widow, had a portrait of him made wearing Colonial costume. That photograph now hangs in the hall of the Oley Valley Inn.

Dad went to Moravian College in Bethlehem, Pennsylvania to study dentistry. He was active in both sports and music. Standing 6'5," he was quite the basketball star and even played semi-professionally for a while. He played saxophone in the orchestra and sang with the Glee Club, which toured all over the East Coast. He spoke with great pride of performing in the Grand Court of the old Wanamaker's Department Store in downtown Philadelphia.

Before World War II, Dad worked in the laboratory of Bethlehem Steel. While working he slipped on a freshly-waxed floor and was seriously burned by an acid spill. He was rushed to St. Luke's Hospital, but they didn't have a bed long enough for his tall frame, so they rigged two beds together, end-to-end to accommodate him.

Dad became a schoolteacher. Besides carrying a full-time teaching load, he was director of the athletic department, coached basketball, worked part-time for a laboratory, scouted basketball talent and filmed high school and college football games. In the summer, he also did carpentry work and projects for the school.

Dad's schedule was so hectic there wasn't much time when he wasn't working. He took his vacation after summer school ended and we occasionally got away for a long weekend.

My Dad, Jay Yeanish, in Aunt Emma's portrait 1932

Dad usually made dinner on Saturday nights and his specialty was Clam Stew. He loved any kind of clams. It didn't matter if they were raw, cooked, in soups, stuffed or fried.

Dad used a big, heavy steel gadget (which I've never seen anywhere else) to open the cherrystone clams. It was about 10" long, had a square handle and a blunt, slightly pointed blade. He chopped the clam meat, then added the broth to milk with butter and heated it until it was hot—never boiled or the tender clams would turn to rubber. Hard oyster crackers, preferably the O.T.C.® Oyster Crackers brand, were crumbled into each connoisseur's bowl.

Mom and Dad always looked forward to their Spring Tonic. Tender dandelion greens were picked before they even flowered. The taproot was cut with the greens, then carefully removed after they got home.

After the dandelion leaves were gently washed and dried, they were served with a warm bacon dressing and boiled new red potatoes.

Dad's Clam Stew

12 large **cherrystone clams** *opened, chopped, juices reserved*
1 quart **whole milk or half and half**
Dash **celery salt**
Dash **Lea & Perrins® Worcestershire sauce**
Dash of **hot pepper sauce**
Several tablespoons of **soft sweet butter**
Chopped fresh **parsley**

Lots of oyster crackers *(We always used the hard OTC® brand)*

Carefully open the clams.
Chop the meat.
Heat the milk with the seasonings.
Add the clams and all their juices.
Continue heating until soup is hot, **but never boiling.**
When bubbles form around the edge of the pan
or when you see it has scalded,
remove it from the heat.
Pour into bowls, top with butter and chopped parsley.
Add as many oyster crackers to the stew as you like.

CHEF SAYS

Here's an easier way to open clams: *Wash the clams, then freeze them overnight.*

The next day, take them out of the freezer and let them thaw.

As they defrost the clams shells will open and all of the natural juices will still be there, plus the shells will be easier to separate.

The clams can be chopped by hand or in a food processor.

Cranberry Orange Vinaigrette

We often made this salad dressing at Thanksgiving.

1 **small peeled shallot**
½ cup **whole cranberries**
3 Tbs **orange juice concentrate**
1 Tbs **Dijon-style mustard**
¼ cup **red wine vinegar**
Freshly ground pepper to taste
1 cup **canola or light salad oil**

In blender add shallot, cranberries, orange juice concentrate, mustard, vinegar and pepper.
Puree until smooth.
Remove blender top and slowly add oil while running on low speed until emulsified.

A Culinary Journey with Chef Steve Yeanish

Grammy

Mom was born the day before my Dad. Her parents were of English and German decent. They had three other children, two boys and a girl. Sadly my grandfather died of pneumonia at a fairly young age, so our dear Grammy, as we called her, was the only grandparent that Ruth Ann, Jayne or I ever really knew.

If you were to blindfold me today, I could still maneuver my way around her old house on West Laurel Street in Bethlehem. Visits to her house were always a treat, as it was still a beautiful city then. We drove through the Saucon Valley, up the winding road on one side of the mountain and down the other side. Then we crossed the Hill-to-Hill Bridge, with the old Bethlehem Steel plant still running in its prime. After we drove through the old downtown shopping district and passed Moravian College, we turned into her street.

Our arrival always felt like Christmas. As soon as the car was parked, we threw open the doors and ran to Grammy, who was usually waiting at the door for us. After lots of hugs, we settled in. She always gave us A-Treat® ginger ale, (in returnable glass quart bottles which used to be sold by the dozen in a wooden crate). To this day that first sip of ginger ale still brings back a memory of her. Grammy didn't have much, but she lived comfortably and shared generously with all her children and grandchildren.

Years ago, Mom used to go to the Globe Movie Theatre on Saturday afternoons, when the matinee cost was just a nickel and they gave glass dishes to the movie attendees. Grammy had a set of those ruby-red Depression glass cups and saucers. Their square shape made them unique and we kids thought we were quite special when we were allowed to drink hot tea in those teacups. We really coveted them, but as years went by, many were broken. I recently found some and gave them to my sisters for Christmas.

At Grammy's we went on picnics in a beautiful wooded park called Illick's Mill. There was a large stream with a waterfall, where we loved to wade in the water, feed the ducks and swans, and enjoy a picnic lunch. New-improved paper plates, which were coated and waterproof, had just come out back then. Grammy got a real kick out of being able to wash and re-use those paper plates. She was another Great Depression survivor.

Grammy's house was near a large retail florist called Sawyer and Johnson, which had several large greenhouses, where they grew flowers, attached to the shop. During one of our many walks round the neighborhood, we kids discovered that broken or slightly wilted flowers were being dumped behind their greenhouse. Most were still in good condition, but not good enough to sell. We thought it was so cool to bring them home for Mom and Grammy and they always made a delighted fuss over them.

Grammy's Oven-Fried Chicken

Oven-Fried Chicken and Oven-Fried Potatoes are recipes Grammy brought back from Alaska.

After my Uncle Earl graduated from college, he was sent to Alaska to work as a missionary. Mom's sister Aunt Margie, and their infant son, Earl Jr. went with him.

Grammy joined them in Alaska for a time to help with the baby. Since she was quite a good cook, Grammy also worked in the kitchen of a hotel while living there.

Aunt Margie was happily married to Uncle Earl and pregnant with their second child when a trolley car struck the car she was driving. Tragically, she died. I can't imagine the pain our families went through.

Preheat oven to 375 degrees

One whole **fryer chicken 3-4 pounds** *cut into pieces.*

Place chicken pieces in a heavy **Zip-lock® plastic bag** with:
1 cup **buttermilk**
Let it sit in refrigerator for at least ½ hour to 2 hours, max.

Put these ingredients into a large, clean plastic bag:
2 cups **all purpose flour**
1 Tbs **salt**
1 tsp **black pepper**
1 tsp **garlic powder**

Shake until mixed well.
Add chicken pieces 2 or 3 at a time.
Shake until well coated.
Place chicken pieces in heavy baking dish coated with a generous coating of salad or canola oil.
Bake 25 minutes, then carefully turn pieces over.
Bake 25 minutes longer, until brown and juices run clear when stuck with fork.
Drain on paper towels and serve.
Serves 4 people

Grammy made a simple dish I fondly remember called Pasty *(PASS-tee)*. This simple savory turnover is known as Cornish Pasty. English copper miners in Cornwall took them down into the mines. Their clever wives filled one end of the pasty with a savory meat and potato filling and the other with jam or preserves. The savory part was the meal and the sweet part was dessert. As a kid I thought they were the height of ingenuity. Now, I realize many cultures make a version of this dish, such as empiñadas, a knish or a strudel.

Grammy's short crust pastry was made with lard, or beef suet and filled with meat and potatoes. The meat was always chuck or shank beef that was slowly cooked with onions until fork tender.

The meat was then cut up, mixed with cooked, diced potatoes, onions and parsley, then placed on a round of pastry, which was folded to make a half moon shape. Then the dough was crimped together and baked until golden brown. They were served hot or at room temperature.

A Culinary Journey by Chef Steven Yeanish

Cornish Pasty

There are many pasty recipes. Most use whatever meat is available. Mom and Grammy usually used cooked shank beef, or even ground beef. Here is a combination version.

CHEF SAYS
How to Cook Shank Beef on the Bone:
Put these ingredients into a large pot: 3 large cross-cut beef shanks, onion, celery, carrots, bay leaf and garlic. Cover with water. Simmer 2-3 hours until tender.

Preheat oven to 350 degrees
Yield: Each Pasty can be cut to make 3-4 portions

Make or purchase enough pastry for three 9 inch crusts
(Can be made with lard or beef suet or combined with shortening)

2-2½ pounds **lean or cooked beef** *(all fat and gristle trimmed)*
3 **medium Idaho potatoes** *peeled, sliced thinly*
1 large **onion** *peeled, sliced thinly*
1 **rutabaga or turnip** *peeled, sliced thinly*
Beef gravy *optional*
1 **egg** *beaten*

Roll out the three pieces of pastry into 9" circles, then set aside.

Cut or chop lean meat or shred cooked beef shank meat into bite-sized pieces.
In large bowl, combine sliced potato, onion and rutabaga or turnip.
Season mixture with salt and pepper.

Place each pastry round on a lightly floured surface.
Place vegetable mixture on one half of each pastry round, leaving a 1" border.
Top the vegetable mixture with the meat.
Top this mixture with 1 rounded tablespoon of gravy.
(If you're using boiled shanks, reduce and thicken the cooking stock to make gravy).

Brush lower edge of each pastry with beaten egg.
Bring top half of pastry over the meat and vegetables and press crust edges together.
Crimp with finger and thumb to seal the edges.
Place on a large baking sheet.
Brush the surface of the pasty with more beaten egg.
Using the tip of a knife, cut 1 or 2 vents in the center of the Pasty so steam can escape.
Bake for 30 minutes in 350 degree oven, until browned and center is bubbly.

The Oley Valley Inn

Oven-Fried Alaska Potatoes

Preheat oven to 400 degrees

Melt 1 stick of **butter** in a microwave or over low heat.
Add ½ cup **salad or canola oil.**
Pour into heavy baking pan.
Cut 8 **Idaho potatoes** in half, lengthwise, then cut again into 4 quarters, making 8 wedges out of each potato.

Place potatoes in the pan with oil and butter.
Season generously with salt and black pepper.
Toss potato wedges in oil and butter to coat them with a thin layer.
Bake 30 minutes, then carefully turn potatoes so they brown evenly.

Bake an additional 30 minutes until potatoes are nicely browned on both sides and soft in the center.
Drain off any extra fat.
Serve hot while still crisp.

The nostalgic smell of an apple pie baking is one of those sensory experiences that many of us remember fondly. For me, the only other aromas that compare are the smell of chopped onions being added to rendered bacon, and veal or chicken stock simmering.

Grammy's apple tarts were the best. To this day I give her credit for the recipe I have used for the last 30 years. Her pastry was always very flaky. It was usually made with lard, and never rolled too thickly. Grammy would mix flour, sugar and cinnamon then sprinkle a thin layer of this on her rolled-out crust. Peeled and cored apple halves were then placed cut-side down, as closely as possible. More cinnamon sugar was sprinkled over the top, and then a very generous spotting of butter was the final touch.

The tart was baked until the pastry was golden, the apples tender and the juices were bubbling. We ate it warm, with vanilla ice cream, whipped cream or even as a meal with a bowl of warm milk.

One of the last meals we had together as a family in Grammy's dining room was when I was about seven years old. It was Easter. Grammy made a yellow cake frosted with white icing for dessert. She decorated the top with a coconut nest tinted green and inside the nest was a little cluster of jellybean eggs. I thought this cake was the most incredible thing I had ever seen! After Grammy was diagnosed with terminal cancer, she began to eat less and less. Mom made a special meat broth, which Grammy relished as one of the few foods she could still enjoy. Grammy may have died young, but my siblings all remember her fondly.

A Culinary Journey by Chef Steven Yeanish

Fresh Apple Tart

(This is my version of Grammy's recipe, which I've been using for thirty years.)

Preheat oven to 350 degrees

12" tart pan, with removable bottom

The Shortcrust Pastry:

Place all these ingredients
in a food processor:
2 cups **all-purpose flour**
2 **egg yolks**
6 ounces **very cold sweet butter**
cut into small pieces
¼ cup **granulated sugar**
¼ cup **cold water, apple juice or cider**
½ tsp **salt**

Process all ingredients in short pulses.
Mixture will become meal-like.
Pour mixture into a large plastic bag.
Squeeze pastry in the bag into a ball.
If the mixture is too dry, add a tiny bit of
water to bring it together.

Shape dough into a flat round disc.

Refrigerate 1 hour.

Roll chilled dough into a 14-inch circle.

Fold dough in half.
Place in center of pie tin.
Unfold, and fit crust into pan edges.
Going around the edge of the surface,
evenly spread dough to form a ridge
around the top of the pan to keep juices
from overflowing as it bakes.

The Apple Filling:

Combine:

1½ cups **granulated sugar**
½ cup **all-purpose flour**
2 Tbs **ground cinnamon**
½ tsp **salt**
8 large or 10 medium apples
*(I prefer Red Rome, Golden Delicious,
Jonagold or Cortland.
Mom and Grammy used McIntosh Red.)*

Peel, core and slice apples.
Toss them in the sugar/flour/cinnamon mix.
Mound into pastry lined pan.
Add sugar mixture to top of apples.

Place tart pan on a baking sheet to
catch any drippings.
Dot surface with 4-6 tablespoons of
soft butter.

Bake 1 hour, or until apples are tender,
or you see juices bubbling at the edges.
Rotate pan periodically while baking
to brown evenly.

Serve warm with vanilla or cinnamon
ice cream or drizzle warm caramel on top
as we do here at the Oley Valley Inn.

The Oley Valley Inn

Grammy in Alaska

Grammy with Baby Jayne

After my Mom passed away, we asked Dad for some of Grammy's things and he graciously said we could take whatever we wanted. I described several of Grammy's china pieces in perfect detail and my sisters Ruth Ann and Jayne got them for me from Mom's china closet. They also surprised me with several other treasures, including a very old box which Grammy brought back from Alaska after visiting Aunt Margie and Uncle Earl in the 1940s. Inside the box are knives and forks, sized for hors d'oeuvres and cheeses, with handles of carved ivory. The six napkin rings are carved with walrus heads and halibut and there was also a set of six walrus head buttons carved in ivory.

I asked Dad for two old photos. He gave me one of Grammy in a fur parka, standing in front of the hotel where she worked before it burned to the ground. The other photo is of an Eskimo family. I needed a place to show these treasures, so one of my customers created a beautiful burled wood shadow box to display the two photos and carved pieces. Then an engraved plaque was added with Grammy's name and the dates of her visit to Alaska. This is one of my most treasured possessions. It hangs in the Inn today.

Cousin Earl Shay Jr recently visited me and I was amazed when he recognized the Eskimo girl in the photograph! Earl used to walk to school with her and the other American kids teased her because she was an Eskimo, but my cousin defended her saying, "She's not an Eskimo, she's my friend!" Many years later, my Uncle Earl visited Alaska and found the girl in the photo, who had grown up, and she told Uncle Earl how she described that incident in a school paper. My new treasure had even more sentimental value.

A Culinary Journey by Chef Steven Yeanish

Mom

This photo of my parents was taken while they were dating.
Their pose says it all. They adored each other.
You can tell they were very much in love. They were married for nearly sixty years.

Mom and her sister Margie went on a double date and met their future husbands. Mom met Dad and Aunt Margie met her future husband, Earl Shay, who was studying theology at Moravian College in Bethlehem. My parents had planned a large wedding, but with World War II looming, they eloped in Elkton, Maryland instead. Then Dad joined the Army to serve his country.

After the war, my parents bought a two-story stucco house with a big front porch on Centennial Street in Schwenksville, a quaint, working-class town.

Planned Parenthood wasn't around back then…and they didn't have television either! Every time Mom got pregnant, Dad just smiled. Mom said one of our new neighbors thought we were an Italian family because we had seven kids.

Dad began his teaching career in Whitpain Township. With seven kids to feed on a modest schoolteacher's salary, I often wonder how they made ends meet.

Mind you, we never went without anything. There was always a hot meal at dinnertime, which was when we all sat down together to eat as a family. We sure as heck had to eat whatever we served ourselves! Salads were part of almost every meal, and I learned to appreciate all kinds of greens and vegetables because Mom bought whatever was seasonal and reasonably priced. We usually had some kind of fruit for dessert, and occasionally something baked.

After making a hot breakfast for everyone, Mom always packed our school lunches. It was amazing to watch as she made seven or eight sandwiches at a time, speedily dealing out bread and meat like playing cards. She'd then wrap 'em, bag 'em, add a piece of fruit, and a home-baked goodie, or chips and pretzels on a good day.

We walked briskly home from school and most days the aroma of good home-cooking enveloped us as soon as we opened the door. Mom was always either baking, roasting or stewing something.

Mom's Basic Red Sauce

Beef, pork, chicken or sausage was often used.
Sometimes it was made with just ground beef.
Almost any leftovers can be added to the sauce.

1 pound **ground chuck or lean ground beef**
2 Tbs **olive oil**
3 cups **onions** *chopped*
1 **clove garlic** *chopped*
1 quart of **whole, canned tomatoes** *chopped in a blender or pushed through a food mill*
OR one 32 ounce **can of crushed all purpose tomatoes**
one 12 ounce can **tomato paste**
1 large can **Campbell's® tomato soup**
1 Tbs **salt**
2 Tbs **sugar**
½ tsp **oregano**
¼ tsp **thyme**
½ tsp **basil**
⅛ tsp **black pepper**

Heat olive oil in a large, heavy-bottomed pot.
Add ground beef, breaking it up as it cooks until it has browned.
Add onions and garlic.
Cook briefly.
Add remaining ingredients.
Stir, heat to simmer, then allow sauce to cook slowly for 3 hours.

Spaghetti dinner was a weekly rite. Mom cooked three pounds of pasta for nine people and there were never any leftovers! She always made her sauce from scratch using whatever was on hand, so it never tasted the same way twice. It was cooked slowly for a long time and she often added beef, pork, or meat leftovers from another meal.

Mom loved a strong, sharp Locatelli cheese. Dad hated any cheese as strong as Parmesan, let alone Locatelli. He preferred a mild Cheddar cheese, yes, even on spaghetti. Forgive him, please!

We compared notes on food with other kids in the neighborhood after dinner, or at playtime. Some of our neighbors ate TV dinners every night. Their sectioned aluminum trays held a main course, vegetable and potato. Some even included dessert. In the 1950s these dinners were brand new. We were fascinated by them and a bit jealous, feeling deprived because we had to eat home-cooked meals prepared from scratch every night. Our envy didn't last long, though! Once we had the chance to taste a TV dinner, we rapidly, and happily, returned Mom to her culinary pedestal.

A Culinary Journey with Chef Steve Yeanish

Mom's Garden

Steve helping in the Yeanish family garden.

We had a large garden and everyone, even the youngest kids, helped tend, weed and pick crops when they were ready. Every inch was used, then re-planted again. We ate what was ripe and the rest was either frozen or canned by Mom, usually with Dad helping into the wee hours of the morning.

Mom and Dad wasted nothing. They had a compost heap and kitchen scraps went there instead of the trash. Their garden soil could grow anything. In the spring we loved to watch the robins flock to feast on the exposed earthworms in the freshly-tilled earth.

Several rhubarb plants provided a bountiful surplus to go with the strawberries and there were two double rows of red raspberry bushes. Mom grew rows of tomatoes, peppers, onions, corn, peas, green and wax beans, lima beans, peas, beets, radishes, lettuce, cabbage, broccoli, cucumbers, zucchini, kohlrabi, parsley and several varieties of mint, which we used to make iced tea every night.

Mom loved her flowers, so there were roses, daffodils, gladioli, hollyhocks and zinnias.

White grape vines, three sour cherry trees, a golden delicious apple tree, two Macintosh apple trees, a pear tree and a few peach and apricot trees also grew in the arbor. Dad decided unsprayed fruit trees had too low a yield, so he and my brother, Ray, built a tree sprayer.

Apples were abundant. As soon as they ripened, we gathered them to eat as snacks. Mom made apple sauce and apple tarts. We usually had crumb or streusel-topped pies, rarely double-crusted. Applesauce was often made with several varieties of apple and never sweetened much. Cinnamon Heart candies were often added to make applesauce pink, and any extra apple sauce was usually canned or frozen.

Mom, Jayne and I took "the drops," which were picked up off the ground, or over-ripe fruit from the end of the season to a local cider press. The machinery seemed old, even back then. There were huge wooden boxes full of apples everywhere and enormous piles of discarded apple pieces, which were swarmed by yellow jackets. We watched in amazement as the apples were pressed between huge slabs of wood until the juice trickled down into a trough. The cider was good in the days before pasteurization or the fear of salmonella.

Every June, we had a bumper crop of sour cherries, but Mom insisted on not picking them until they turned almost blood-red. Now I know why. Not only were they less tart, but they were juicier and had a more pronounced flavor. Picking cherries was a lot more fun than picking raspberries. It was shady and best of all, we got to climb up ladders to pick bucket after bucket of fruit. We had cherry pie, cherry cobbler, cherry everything. My favorite was Mom's cherry preserves. I still get a craving for a peanut butter and cherry preserves sandwich.

Strawberry Lemonade

A nice alternative to plain lemonade! I often make this for large events. I have a 5-gallon jug with a faucet, and the lemonade looks beautiful in it. I have found that freezing some of the lemonade in containers that are just large enough to fit into the jug helps to keep the lemonade cold without diluting it.

6 **lemons** *zest removed using a vegetable peeler, juiced, seeds removed*
2 cups **granulated sugar**
2 cups **water**
Two 16 ounce packages frozen or fresh **strawberries**
1 quart **store-bought lemonade** *(Country Time® Lemonade Mix is a good brand)*
Lemon slices *for garnish*
Sliced strawberries *for garnish*
Fresh mint sprigs *for garnish*
Cold water or lemon-lime soft drink

Remove just the zest from lemons *(the yellow part only)*
Juice lemons.
Remove seeds.

To make Simple Syrup:
Place sugar and water in a saucepan with lemon zest.
Heat just to simmering.
Remove from heat and cool.
Strain Simple Syrup.
Discard lemon zest.

Purée strawberries in blender.
Place lemon juice in a non-reactive jug.
Add Simple Syrup, strawberry purée, and lemonade mix.
Mix thoroughly.
Add cold water or lemon-lime soft drink to desired taste.

Fill pitcher or glasses ⅔ full of ice.
Garnish glasses or pitcher with lemon slices, strawberry slices and fresh mint.

A Culinary Journey with Chef Steve Yeanish

Mom specialized in making jams and preserves. If dead-ripe fruit was abundant and she had sugar and Sure-Gel® (her thickener of choice), then she made preserves. Always concerned with getting the biggest bang for her buck, Mom rarely made jellies or seedless preserves because the yield was lower. Her raspberry jelly was always good, unless the season was dry; then the result was flavorful, but had lots and lots of seeds. Around the Fourth of July we often picked wild black raspberries near our Bungalow in Lenhartsville. They used to grow everywhere until the state sprayed the roadsides with herbicides. We came home with scrapes, cuts and sunburn, but that jelly was worth it all.

After I opened the Oley Valley Inn, I mentioned to Mom that I'd like to try using her quince jelly as a glaze on our Roast Duckling. Much to my surprise, when she and Dad arrived on their next visit, she proudly handed me a jar saying, "Here's your quince jelly, Stevie!"

Strawberry Muffins

Mom had a real knack for finding a good recipe. She handed me this one when they drove up to help renovate the Inn. These muffins freeze very well.

Preheat oven to 350 degrees
Place paper liners in 3 muffin tins (makes about 36 muffins)

Sift together dry ingredients:
3 cups **all-purpose flour**
1 tsp **baking soda**
2 cups **granulated sugar**

Whisk together until combined:
4 large **eggs**
1⅓ cups **canola oil**
4 tsp **lemon zest**
3 cups **strawberries,** *hulled, cut in half, sliced in small pieces*
¾ cup **toasted sliced almonds**

Gently stir egg and oil mixture into sifted dry ingredients, add strawberries and almonds, combine until just mixed.
Scoop into paper-lined muffin tins, filling no more than ⅔ full.
Sprinkle top with cinnamon sugar and additional almonds.

Bake in 350-degree oven about 20–25 minutes,
or until a wooden pick inserted in the center comes out clean.
Remove from tins when partially cooled.

The Oley Valley Inn

The Queen of Shoppers

What Mom and Dad didn't grow in the garden or on trees in our yard, they found at farms, orchards and farmer's markets in the area. Mom traveled throughout the county looking for the best buys she could find. During the summer months, Zern's Farmer's Market, or the Gilbertsville Sale were the best produce outlets. They were not typical farmer's markets. They had something for everyone, from local produce to clothing and vacuum cleaners (or sweepers as we called them). On Wednesdays the food section of the local paper listed all the local supermarket specials. Mom's shopping mission was all planned in detail before Saturday morning when Ruth Ann, Jayne and I set off with Mom in her trusty Catalina station wagon.

Kemp's Market, a small independent local market that specialized in cutting their own meats, was a favorite. Mom said they were the best, and took good advantage of their specials.

As lunchtime approached on our shopping quest, Mom would buy a loaf of bread, some cold cuts, a jug of milk and potato chips. She would find a quiet, shady place to park the Catalina and we had a roadside picnic. She always had a jar of mustard in the glove compartment, along with a paring knife, and her ever-trusty dishcloth.

She would make us each a sandwich, and we would pass around the jug of milk and chips. We thought this was the greatest. This was before Micky D's changed the palates of the youth of the world.

Damaged and dented cans were often prime picking for bargains. As long as there were no visible signs of leakage or bulging ends on the can, it was fair game. After all, the label even said, *Reduced For Quick Sale*.

Returning home Saturday afternoon was never fun. We all had to lug it into the house and listen to Dad complain, "I don't know where the hell we're going to put all this stuff!" We always found room, and we never went hungry. Mom was a firm believer in, "to the victor go the spoils." If there was a bargain or a sale on something, she would buy all of it if she could. Once, beef tongues were on sale and Mom took every one they had. (Even in the 1960s, tongue was not a real hot commodity, but we liked it, especially when we didn't know we were eating it.)

We went through a lot of bread, and day-old bread was a staple. Mom had several haunts for this: the reduced section of the local supermarkets, or the retail store where the bread was returned after the expiration date. My brother John always marveled, "Good *fresh* bread!" when there was an occasional fresh one.

One thing I did learn from Mom—if I see something now and I know it is a one-time opportunity, grab it, because it won't be there tomorrow. You snooze, you lose!

Dad was just as thrifty as Mom. He could repair anything. If there was a way to pop-rivet it back together, he would. Nothing was beyond repair. Absolutely nothing. Once, Mom's favorite rubber girdle *almost* wound up in the trashcan. She stuck her finger through the girdle while pulling it on one morning. It was ordinary wear and tear, but she was devastated. It was like losing her best friend. Dad rescued it from the trash and worked his magic.

The next day, Mom had her favorite corset back, ready to wear complete with a black tire patch. He could have done a commercial for Pep Boys with that job saying: *"Our blowout patches can fix anything!"*

Mom made incredible soups. She would go to the local poultry vendor at the old Farmer's Market in Pottstown and buy 10 or 15 pounds of turkey backs and necks for 15 cents a pound. First, Mom would simmer them with onions, celery, parsley and garlic to make a rich broth, and then she'd add all the meat that was pulled off the bones.

Mom got ingenious making *three meals for two dollars!* Turkey Noodle Soup, Turkey Pot Pie, and crisp, brown Turkey Croquettes, which were my favorite.

Mom made at least 189 wholesome meals a week, from scratch and that's not counting snacks!

Turkey Noodle Soup

1 large **onion** *chopped*
4 **ribs celery** *washed, trimmed, diced*
4 **carrots** *trimmed, peeled, diced*
2 Tbs **turkey or chicken fat OR** *(substitute butter or margarine)*
1 **clove garlic** *chopped*
3 quarts **turkey or chicken broth** *fat removed*
1 pound **noodles** *your choice*
Cooked, diced meat *for garnish*
(or leftover, frozen meat from another meal)
Chopped parsley, *preferably flat-leafed*

In large pot, heat the turkey or chicken fat.
Add diced onion, celery, carrot and garlic.
Gently sauté or sweat the vegetables briefly.
Add turkey or chicken broth.
Simmer soup 20 minutes.
Add noodles and cook directly in broth.
Taste broth, and season with salt and pepper, as needed.
Add meat garnish and several spoons of freshly chopped parsley.

Turkey Croquettes

Mom also made these using chicken, ham, clams, shrimp or fish.
As I look at her recipe now, I realize these are actually fritters.
Sometimes she'd even add mashed potatoes.
I do admit to love eating these with ketchup!

1 cup **chopped cooked cold meat**
1 **medium onion,** *peeled and chopped*
2 **ribs celery,** *washed, trimmed, diced*
1 Tbs **salad oil**
1/8 tsp **black pepper**
1/2 tsp **salt**
1 cup **all purpose flour**
1 **egg**
2 tsp **baking powder**
1/2 cup **milk**
1 Tbs **chopped parsley,** *preferably flat-leaf*

Sauté onion and celery in oil briefly.
Cool to room temperature.

Beat egg in mixing bowl.
Stir in milk, flour, baking powder, salt and pepper.
Mix to smooth batter.
Fold in the meat, onions, celery and parsley.
Stir until combined.

Dip spoon in hot oil then carefully drop teaspoonfuls of batter into hot oil.
Fry in 350 degree hot oil.
Turn croquettes over to brown on both sides evenly.
Drain on absorbent paper.
Serve with cream sauce or gravy.

Turkey Pot Pie

This is a traditional Pennsylvania German soup, (not a pie) made with broth, dumpling-like egg noodles, celery, onions and turkey chunks.

Pot Pie Dough:

3 cups **all purpose flour**
4 **eggs**
2 Tbs **turkey or chicken fat**
1 tsp **salt**
Place ingredients in mixer.
Using paddle or dough hook, combine just until dough becomes smooth.
Wrap dough in plastic wrap and let dough rest at least thirty minutes.

Prepare these vegetables:

1 **large onion** *peeled and diced*
4 **ribs celery** *washed, trimmed, sliced*
3 **carrots** *trimmed, peeled, sliced (These are optional. Not all Pennsylvania Dutch add carrots.)*
6 **medium potatoes** *peeled, cut in half, then in ⅜ inch slices*
3 quarts **turkey or chicken stock**
Meat for garnish *(from stock or leftovers)*
3 Tbs **chopped fresh parsley** *preferably flat-leaf*

Place broth into a large pot.
Add onions, celery, carrots and potatoes.
Bring to a boil.
As you are heating the broth, roll the pot pie dough out on a floured surface.
Roll to the thickness of a quarter, and cut into 1" squares.
(Some cooks make them larger, but I think they should fit on your spoon.
I always use my pasta machine to roll this dough out.)
Add the pasta squares and the vegetables to the boiling broth.
Both will cook at the same time.
Taste broth and season to taste with salt and pepper.
Add cooked meat for garnish.
Add 3 Tbs chopped fresh parsley to finish.

The Oley Valley Inn

Mom's Apple Fritters

2 cups **all purpose flour**
3 tsp **baking powder**
½ cup **granulated sugar**
1 tsp **salt**
2 **eggs**
1 cup **milk**
1 tsp **vanilla extract**
2 Tbs **melted butter**
4 **large baking apples** *peeled, quartered, cored, sliced thinly*

Put all the ingredients (except the apples) in a bowl and beat until mixed.
Fold in sliced apples.
Stir until combined.
Heat oil to 375 degrees.
Dip a teaspoon in hot fat to warm it,
then **carefully** drop a teaspoon of batter into the hot fat,
being careful not to splash yourself.
Turn once to brown on both sides, then remove with a slotted spoon.
Drain on absorbent paper.
Dust with powdered sugar or cinnamon sugar.
Serve hot.

Charming Chickens

When I was growing up we had a flock of chickens in our backyard at home. When Mom needed eggs, we loved to go into the hen house and get them for her; then we'd run back with pockets full, clutching the rest in our hands. Sometimes, between dropping them or falling on them, the eggs didn't make it all the way back to Mom's kitchen.

We had a temperamental rooster named Henry, who would chase us kids. We were scared to death of him! The older he got, the nastier he became. One day, Dad finally had enough. Henry was going to be dinner. We all knew what we were eating, but we didn't care. Henry turned out to be just as nasty stewed as he had been in the yard. He was as tough as an old boot.

There is a great photo of the smaller kids playing in our oversized sandbox one winter. Henry is strutting in the background with his harem of hens surrounding him.

Occasionally, when we were little, Jayne and I would swipe some eggs and go to play in the crawl space under our front porch, which was probably about three feet high. There were some old crocks under there, garden soil and old plants that had died. We enjoyed many an afternoon of 'cooking', as we called it. For hours on end, we'd make mud pies using the eggs, old kitchen utensils, and crocks of dirt. Mom didn't mind. We were content and staying out of trouble.

Eventually our flock had to go. Dad said it cost too much to feed the chickens compared to the number of eggs we were getting, so we hauled them off to the butcher, then returned to pick them up neatly dressed, wrapped and frozen.

Mom soon found a new farm for eggs. This was a large production facility with white Leghorn chickens, which was run by a Mennonite family. Mom got to know the owner's mother, who could quickly fill a carton with the eggs (pointed end down to keep the yolk centered in the egg) while holding three eggs in each hand. That amazed me.

One year when I was about twelve, Katie, the owner's mother, mentioned they were getting a new flock of chickens, because the old birds were not laying. She said the old hens would be sold for 50 cents each. Of course, Mom being thrifty ordered 30 for the freezer. When she arrived at the farm to pick them up, the chickens were not freezer-ready, if you catch my drift. Dad was not pleased when she arrived home with several wooden crates full of these squawking bargains!

Fortunately my new sister-in-law Jeanette was born and raised on a farm. She called her mother Alma and they organized everything. The axe was sharpened. A large enamel canning pot was filled with boiling water. Wash tubs were filled with cold water. By the time everything was ready all the onlookers had disappeared and I was the only kid left, so I was put to work.

I pulled a bird out of the crate and held its legs so the neck would stick out. Then I draped the neck over an old stump while Dad did the honors with the ax. One lop and it was over. By the way, a chicken really can flop around with its head cut off. I was doing pretty well until one got away from me and took off into the neighbor's yard with me in pursuit. Dad was getting more exasperated by the minute until I finally cornered the escapee. Next

Mom scalded the dead birds in the canning boiler to loosen their feathers. Have you ever smelled hot, wet chicken feathers? It is not an aroma you'll ever forget. Jeanette and her mother were stationed at the newspaper-covered picnic table where they patiently pulled out all the feathers.

Then the Ax Man and I moved on to the evisceration detail. First we cut off the *Pope's nose* (the gland at the base of the tail), then the body cavity was opened, organs removed and the feet and neck cut off. I was fascinated to find two or three unlaid eggs inside the body cavity in some degree of development. Some even had hard shells. Alma told me the liver had to be carefully separated from the gizzard without breaking open the emerald-green gall bladder because the bile is very bitter. Finally the bird was plunged into a cold water bath to lower the body temperature. After all this fun we had to clean up the mess.

Every fall, Mom would buy about five hundred pounds of potatoes from farmers. They were stored in an old cistern beside our house, which was once used to store rainwater. It was dark, musty and stayed a constant cool temperature, even in the summer. There was a wooden ladder that reached to the bottom, where the potatoes were transferred from bags to bushel baskets and stored. My little sister Jayne and I had to climb down there in warm weather to remove the sprouts from the potatoes. It was a job we did reluctantly, but quickly. We were scared to death of all the spiders down there!

In the early years, we had milk delivered to our door. Back then our milkman Barney would even bring it into the kitchen and put it in the refrigerator. We had one full bathroom, which was on the first floor. One morning after all the big kids had gone off to school, Mom took a nice leisurely bath, then dried off and headed to get dressed only to be greeted by Barney with his morning delivery. She was mortified!

Steve's chicks

A Culinary Journey with Chef Steve Yeanish

Citrus Cooler

2 cups **sugar**
3 cups **water**
3 **lemons**
2 **limes**
2 cups **ginger ale**

Squeeze juice from the lemons and limes.
Place their peels in a pan with sugar.
Mash well with a potato masher to extract zest from fruit.
Add water.
Cook gently for 10 minutes.
Strain, then cool.
Add the lemon and lime juice, and then the ginger ale.
Serve with lots of ice.

We enjoyed spending an afternoon at a state park with a picnic lunch or dinner, or I should say, feast. One autumn afternoon the leaves were starting to fall, so Mom made a roast beef dinner and we went to Hopewell State Park. We sat at two picnic tables by the lake and dined on roast beef, gravy, salad and vegetables. Dad had a Coleman butane camp stove with two burners, so Mom fried potatoes and there was probably even cake for dessert. Mom made a lemon-lime and orange drink and took it to picnics in a Tupperware bucket with black handles. It was so thirst quenching that I just loved it!

Snowy Cream Frosting

This is the recipe that launched my baking career

Yield: enough frosting to fill and cover a 9 or 10 inch cake

2 **egg whites** *beaten until stiff*
2 cups **confectioners sugar**
2 Tbs **milk**
2 Tbs **flour**
¼ tsp **salt**
½ cup **soft butter**
1 cup **vegetable shortening**
2 more cups **confectioners sugar**
2 tsp **pure vanilla extract**

In the mixer bowl:
Slowly add 2 cups of confectioners sugar to
the stiffly beaten egg whites, while mixing on low speed.
Then add milk, flour, salt, butter, and vegetable shortening.
Turn mixer to high speed and whip until fluffy.

Return mixer to low speed, then gradually
add 2 more cups of confectioners sugar.
Add vanilla extract.
Whip again on high speed until frosting becomes light and fluffy.

Chef Gorey made Steve's Good Luck cake when he left Brookside C.C. for CIA

Young Steve with one of his first "professional" cakes. It takes hours of practice to decorate a wedding cake.

By the time I was in high school I was becoming quite a baker. Cakes and pies were my specialty. There were plenty of eager tasters available and they weren't that critical so long as it was available and reasonably tasty. My creations weren't all Pillsbury® Bake-Off® winners, but I soon learned to follow recipes exactly.

I experimented with the finishing touches. I could hardly wait to frost the cake before it cooled. My sister gave me a recipe for a frosting. I mastered it quickly and began using it as my own. It tasted good, had enough body for decorating, and wasn't too sweet.

A Culinary Journey with Chef Steve Yeanish

We kids loved to "help" Mom while she baked. Mom never made just enough of anything. Recipes were usually doubled or tripled. If she made cookies, there would be enough for days. Her cookies had a little bit of everything in them, so if you didn't like raisins, or nuts or dates or whatever, you were just out of luck. There was no such thing as a fussy eater. Even at dinner, it was take-it-or-leave-it.

Pies were also mass-produced. We always waited for the best part of pie making—the left over pie crust. We gathered all the dough trimmings and rolled it out to fit whatever pan was available. Then we spread "a penny-thick" of sugar over the bottom, added flour and milk, then the top was sprinkled with cinnamon, dotted with butter and baked in the oven until the crust was golden and the center was bubbly. We called our confection Slop Pie. It was heavenly eaten warm with a glass of cold milk.

Once while working in a professional kitchen (just for a giggle), I made some and shared it with the staff. Everyone loved it and told stories of how their family made something similar. Some called it *Schlop Kuche* (Pennsylvania Dutch), Milk Pie or even Slappy Pie. Whatever the name, the pie tastes just as good.

The kitchen fascinated my little sister, Jayne and me. On snow days we'd cut vegetables up with dull knives, then we'd go outside and get snow to melt in old metal cups on the cast iron radiators in the dining room. We would push the table to the side of the room and cover it with old sheets to make a fort. After the snow melted on the radiator, we'd add our vegetables, salt and pepper and make soup, which warmed, but never cooked.

Mom's Funny Paper Chocolate Cake

There was a chocolate cake recipe Mom made that was in the comic section of the Sunday newspaper. We called it the Funny Paper Chocolate Cake. I think I could make this cake in my sleep. It became my specialty.

Grease and dust with cocoa powder: two 9" pans or one 9 x 13" pan

Preheat oven to 350 degrees

2 cups **flour**
2 cups **granulated sugar**
1 cup **cocoa powder**
2 tsp **baking soda**
1 tsp **baking powder**
¼ tsp **salt**
2 **eggs**
¾ cup **salad or canola oil**
1 cup **milk**
1 cup **hot black coffee**

Sift the dry ingredients together.
Mix the liquid ingredients together.
Add the dry ingredients to liquid mixture.
Mix on slow speed until all of the dry ingredients have been incorporated into the mixture.
Mix on high-speed 2 minutes.

Bake in two greased, cocoa dusted 9" pans or one 9 x 13" pan at 350 degrees until a wooden pick inserted in the center comes out clean, about 25-30 minutes.

Award Winning Oley Valley Inn Chocolate Cake

This cake won the Hershey's Best Chocolate Cake Award at the Oley Valley Community Fair in the 1990s. I have often seen many variations of this recipe, so I've made mine even more moist and rich. I still use this recipe today as a base for chocolate desserts.

Preheat oven to 350 degrees

Sift these together:
2 cups **flour**
1 cup **granulated sugar**
1 cup **cocoa powder**
¼ tsp **salt**
1 tsp **baking soda**
2 tsp **baking powder**

Combine:
3 eggs *lightly beaten*
¾ cup **vegetable oil**
⅔ cup **hot coffee**
⅔ cup **milk**
⅔ cup **Hershey's chocolate syrup**
1 cup **light brown sugar**

Mix liquid ingredients until combined.
Add sifted ingredients.
Mix 2 minutes on high speed.
Divide batter into two 10" cake pans that have been greased and dusted with cocoa powder.

Bake at 350 degrees for 25-30 minutes,
or until a wooden pick inserted in the center comes out clean.
Invert cake onto a cooling rack.
Invert again so the bottom of the cake is on the cooling rack as it cools.

A Culinary Journey with Chef Steve Yeanish

Mary Lou's Cheesecake

My eldest sister Mary Lou was a home economics major in high school. She was an incredible homemaker and many evenings she would prepare dinner for us. (This was still the June Cleaver-Mom-at-home era back then). As the younger children arrived, she took a more active roll and became Mom's right-hand helper. I often wonder if she realizes the important role she played in our family, especially during those early years. For as long as I can remember Mary Lou has made a most unusual cheesecake. It's light as a feather, creamy and oh, so rich! She tops it with blueberry or cherry filling. It is nothing like a New York-style cheesecake.

10" Springform pan

Have all ingredients at room temperature.

1 pound **creamed cottage cheese** *(forced through a sieve)*
Two 8 ounce **blocks cream cheese**
1⅓ cups **granulated sugar**
4 **large eggs**
Juice of one **lemon**
¼ tsp **vanilla**
3 Tbs **cornstarch**
3 Tbs **flour**
¼ cup **melted butter**
One 16 ounce **container sour cream**

Cream cottage cheese with cream cheese and sugar.
Add eggs one at a time, scraping bowl after each addition.
Add lemon juice, vanilla, cornstarch, flour and butter.
Beat well.
Fold sour cream into batter.
Pour into greased 10" springform pan.
Set pan in a cool oven,
THEN heat oven to 325 degrees.
Set timer for 1 hour.
Do NOT open the oven door.
Turn oven off after hour is up, BUT leave cheesecake in oven at least 2 more hours.
Top with fresh strawberries, blueberries or canned cherry filling.

Lemon Chiffon Meringue Pie

One **10" pie crust,** *pre-baked until golden brown See page 88 for Pie Crust recipe.*

The Filling:

5 **egg yolks**
¼ cup **fresh lemon juice**
¼ cup **water**
2 Tbs **cornstarch**
1 tsp **grated lemon rind**
½ cup **sugar**
5 **egg whites**
½ cup **sugar**
½ tsp **cream of tartar**

Beat egg yolks in the top of a double boiler until they are lemon-colored.
(The bottom of the double boiler should have simmering water in it.)
Dissolve cornstarch in ¼ cup water.
Add lemon juice and the water with the cornstarch dissolved in it to the egg yolks.
Stir in lemon rind and ½ cup sugar.
Continue beating and cook until thickened.
Remove from heat.

In a spotlessly clean bowl:
Whip egg whites with cream of tartar.
Continue beating until soft peaks form.
Add the other ½ cup sugar in a steady stream.
Beat until meringue is stiff and glossy.
Take ⅓ of meringue and gently fold it into the cooked lemon mixture.
Pour into piecrust.
Top with remaining meringue, and spread out to sides so that meringue touches the crust.
Bake pie at 350 degrees for 20 minutes until browned.
Cool to room temperature and serve.

Cut with a hot, wet knife.

Blueberry Streusel Coffee Cake

Preheat oven to 350 degrees
Grease and flour 9-inch square pan

1 cup **fresh blueberries**
2 Tbs **all purpose flour**
½ cup **butter or margarine** *softened*
2 cups **all purpose flour**
2 tsp **baking powder**
¼ tsp **salt**
1 cup **sugar**
¾ cup **milk**
1 **egg**

Combine blueberries and 2 tablespoons flour, toss gently.
Set aside.

Combine butter and the next 5 ingredients in a large bowl.
Beat using the medium speed of an electric mixer for 2 minutes.
Add egg.
Beat one minute.
Fold in blueberries.
Spread batter evenly into a greased and floured 9-inch square pan.
Sprinkle with Streusel Topping. *Recipe follows.*

To make the Streusel Topping:
½ cup **sugar**
⅓ cup **all purpose flour**
½ tsp **ground cinnamon**
¼ cup **butter or margarine** *softened*

Mix the sugar, flour and ground cinnamon.
Cut in butter until mixture resembles coarse meal.

Bake at 350 degrees for 50 minutes.

The Oley Valley Inn

My Sisters' Sour Cream Pound Cake

My three sisters are all incredible bakers. There is some debate over which one of them discovered this recipe. This is my version. I think the flavor of this cake improves after it has been allowed to sit for a day. This cake is delicious plain, with fruit, or iced.

Preheat oven to 325 degrees
10" tube pan *greased and floured*

6 ounces (¾ cup) **sweet butter** *softened*
2¼ cups **granulated sugar**
½ tsp **salt**
1 tsp **vanilla extract**
¼ tsp **lemon extract** *(You can also substitute 1 tsp of grated lemon zest)*
4 **large eggs** *room temperature*
2¼ cups **cake flour**
⅛ tsp **baking soda**
¾ cup **sour cream** *at room temperature*

Cream softened butter with sugar in mixer until light and fluffy.
Add salt, vanilla and lemon flavor.
Add eggs one at a time, mixing well after each addition.
Scrape bowl after each addition.
Sift flour and baking soda together.
Add flour alternately with sour cream, mixing each until combined.

DO NOT OVER MIX AT THIS POINT
(For best results, don't over mix this batter after the eggs and flavorings are added).

Remove from mixer, hand stir to be sure batter is thoroughly mixed.
Pour batter into tube pan, then tap pan sharply on a table to release the air pockets.
Bake in middle of the oven for approximately 1 hour.

Cake is done when toothpick inserted in center comes out clean.
Invert onto cake rack, and remove pan.
Turn cake over again onto another rack so the cake cools on the bottom side.
(I always cool cakes on bottom side. This prevents them from sticking to the rack.)
After cake has cooled, it can be wrapped in clear plastic wrap or frosted.

A Culinary Journey with Chef Steve Yeanish

Fresh Strawberry Pie

Remember the Strawberry Pie that was served in the Patio Restaurant of Hess's Department Store in Allentown by waitresses wearing white uniforms with a diagonal red, blue and green logo? It's flaky crust was filled high with whole, fresh berries and covered with a very sticky, sweet strawberry glaze topped with mounds of whipped cream. My sisters, who are very talented cooks, shared this recipe with me. I think this will bring back happy memories. Yes, it does use Jell-O®.

Yield: one 10 inch pie

The Crust:

2 cups **all purpose flour**
6 ounces **very cold unsalted butter** *cut into very small pieces*
¼ cup **granulated sugar**
2 **egg yolks**
1 tsp **grated lemon zest**
¼ cup **orange juice**

Put all of the above ingredients into a food processor bowl.
Pulse several times until mixture looks like coarse meal.
Pour mixture into a large plastic bag.
Knead the bag of dough until it comes together.
If mixture is too dry or crumbly, add a bit more orange juice.
Shape dough into a flat, round disk.
Refrigerate at least 1 hour or overnight.

Lightly flour a work surface.
Roll dough into a ¼ inch thick circle, measured to fit a 10-inch pie tin or a Pyrex® pie dish.
Brush off excess flour.
Fold dough gently then place in pie dish.
Unfold and shape into bottom of pan.
Trim dough, and crimp edge, if desired.
Poke holes in dough in bottom of pie pan using a fork.
Cover surface with foil.
Refrigerate again, for ½ hour to prevent shrinkage.
Fill bottom of foil-covered pan with pie weights or beans.
Bake 10-12 minutes @ 350 degrees.
Remove pie weights from bottom of pan, then remove foil.
Bake an additional 5-7 minutes until lightly browned.
Cool baked crust to room temperature.
Recipe continues on the next page.

The Oley Valley Inn

Hess's was destination shopping at its finest. There was always something new and exciting going on. They often had celebrity appearances or fashion shows during lunch. Attractive models strolled through the restaurant and described what they were wearing, what collection it was from, and where to find it in the store. Hess's, as it was known, had a Patio Restaurant, which wasn't on a patio; it was in the store basement. The menu was huge in both size and scope, and the food was actually very good and ahead of its time—they had a list of sandwiches, salads, entrées and an Asian section. Children's dishes were brought to the table on a little miniature stove. Portions were enormous and two people could easily share a sandwich or salad, and dessert. I have a friend that still talks about their Chicken and Lobster Egg Rolls. I particularly liked their Lump Crab Salad Sandwich.

The Strawberry Pie Filling:

3 or 4 **pints of strawberries** *washed, hulls and white "shoulders" removed*
Starting at the center of the crust, arrange berries with the pointed side up all over the bottom of the pan. This is like creating a puzzle, so place the next a layer of berries with the pointed sides down. Fill in the gaps with large and small berries to avoid large holes. Place the final layer with the pointed side up, starting from the center and work towards the outside, finishing with an even row around the outside edge.

The Strawberry Glaze:

In heavy-bottomed saucepan, stir together:
1 cup **granulated sugar**
¼ cup **cornstarch**
¼ cup **strawberry flavored Jell-O®**
1 cup **cold water**

Thoroughly mix the dry ingredients.
Stir a cup of cold water into the saucepan.
Place saucepan on stove over medium heat.
Stir constantly until mixture comes to a complete boil and turns clear.
Remove from heat.
Allow to cool to room temperature.
Slowly pour glaze mixture over the strawberries in the pie pan working from the center to the outside of the pie.
The glaze holds the pie together, so if there is any extra, go back and fill in the gaps.
Chill thoroughly at least 2 to 3 hours before serving.
Garnish with fresh whipped cream and mint leaves, or vanilla ice cream.

Stella

Our neighbors, Frank and Stella, were a wonderful couple. They owned a beautiful old house with a slate roof, a large brick barn with a pump house and a summer kitchen.

Stella passionately loved to cook and bake. She was outstanding, and ranks among the first of my mentors, having cooked in a hotel in her younger days. One of her most memorable delights was Fastnachts, the Pennsylvania Dutch doughnut confection, which she always shared with us.

Fastnachts are prepared for Shrove Tuesday, the day before Ash Wednesday. Their appearance marks the beginning of Lent.

Stella's were pure heaven. They were light as a feather, and lightly glazed with sugar. You could taste a hint of potato in the crisp, fatty richness.

When Frank and Stella had their 50th Wedding Anniversary, I was thrilled to be asked to make their cake. In Mom's kitchen, I made a very special five-tier cake for 150 people. I received a heart-felt thank-you note from Stella, which I still have today. She even enclosed a 20-dollar bill, even though the cake had already been paid for!

Stella continued cooking for her family until she was in her early eighties. We had many conversations about food and cooking. She was fascinated that I wanted to become a professional chef and study at the Culinary Institute of America.

Fastnacht Doughnut Glaze

Doughnuts should be dipped into this glaze directly after frying, while still hot, then cooled on wire racks.

2 envelopes (or 2 Tbs) **plain gelatin**
1 Tbs **cold water**
¾ cup **cold water**
5 pounds **confectioners sugar**
1 tsp **vanilla extract**

Add gelatin to 1 Tbs water and allow gelatin to soften.
Bring ¾ cup water to a rolling boil.
Remove from heat and stir in gelatin.
Gradually add sugar and stir until dissolved.
While mixture is still warm, dip hot doughnuts into glaze.

The Oley Valley Inn

Stella's Fastnachts

Traditional Pennsylvannia Dutch Fastnachts are rectangular potato doughnuts eaten to celebrate Shrove Tuesday, the day before the start of Lent. They have a small slit cut in the center. They can be glazed, sugared or eaten plain. They are often served with Mrs. Schlorer's Turkey Syrup® or Golden Barrel Table Syrup® poured on top.

2 cups **plain mashed potatoes**
2 cups **scalded milk**
2 **yeast cakes OR**
2 **envelopes OR 2 Tbs instant dry yeast**
3 **eggs** *lightly beaten*
1¾ cup **granulated sugar**
1 cup **soft butter**
8-9 cups **all-purpose flour**

Combine potatoes and milk in a mixer.
Add remaining ingredients and mix well to make dough.
If dough seems too soft, add more flour.
Place dough in a large bowl.
Cover bowl with a towel or plastic wrap, and place in a warm spot free of drafts.

Let dough rise until it doubles.
Punch dough down, then place dough on a floured surface.
Roll dough out to about ½ inch thickness.
Use a cutter or knife to cut into rectangles.
Place rectangles on lightly-floured trays with enough space to allow them to rise again.
Cover with towel.
Fastnachts are traditionally fried in lard, but you can use oil.
Heat about two inches of lard or oil to 375 degrees in a deep skillet or Dutch Oven (There should be enough fat to "float" the Fastnacht and room to turn them over.)
Slide donuts into hot fat tilting them away from you.
Avoid splashing hot oil.
Fry on one side until brown.
Turn over with slotted spoon.
When browned on all sides, remove from pan and place on absorbent paper.
Dip into Glaze. *(See recipe on previous page)*

A Culinary Journey with Chef Steve Yeanish

Sand Tarts

Stella's cookies were wonderful. We kids appreciated the way she shared her recipes with Mom!

Preheat oven to 325 degrees

3 **eggs** *beaten until lemon colored*
1 pound **butter**
1 pound **confectioners or granulated sugar**
1 Tbs **vanilla extract**
1½ **all purpose flour**
¼ tsp **baking powder**

Beat eggs.
Cream butter and sugar together until light.
Add beaten eggs.
Add vanilla.
Gradually add flour and baking powder.
Roll dough into a cylinder.
Chill thoroughly.
Cut dough cylinder into thin slices.
Place slices on greased cookie sheets.

Bake 325 degree oven 8-12 minutes, rotating racks after 6 minutes.

My First Job

My professional cooking career started when I was 16 years old. I earned $1.40 an hour at the Collegeville Inn, which was one of two restaurants located on opposite sides of the Perkiomen Creek in Collegeville, Pennsylvania. There was always tremendous rivalry between the two restaurants and they both featured smorgasbords. The Collegeville Inn was larger and more popular. The Perkiomen Bridge Hotel, parts of which dated back to 1701, was smaller, and more charming. For the most part, their rivalry was intense.

I was determined to get a job, so I filled out an application at the Perkiomen Bridge Hotel, then I immediately went over to the Collegeville Inn and applied there. I was interviewed briefly, then hired on the spot by the Head Chef. I couldn't have been prouder when he asked me to report to work later that week. Of course, I had no idea what I'd been hired to do and I hadn't even seen the kitchen yet!

The Collegeville Inn resembled a Swiss chalet and its vaulted-ceiling lobby was large enough to accommodate long lines of people waiting for tables. The restaurant attracted bus loads of folks, who were serious eaters, determined to get their money's worth. The dining room held a massive buffet, or smorgasbord, with several stations for appetizers, salads, main courses and desserts. Four clocks showed the time in America, Germany, Sweden and China, the four countries abundantly represented in the smorgasbord cuisines.

Downstairs from the restaurant was a banquet facility that fed hundreds at a time. The basement also housed the largest walk-in freezer I had ever seen and two modern, open kitchens, one upstairs, one downstairs, that featured many cooking stations.

On my first day, after a 30 minute training session in the art of deep-frying, I became the new fry cook. There were two deep fryers. The one big enough to sit in was used to fry sheet-pans full of Chinese egg rolls, pre-breaded frog legs, scallops, shrimp and chicken pieces in vegetable shortening.

When those buses of hungry diners unloaded, we really moved fast. Sometimes it was quite an effort to fry enough food to refill those massive hot buffets in the dining room. I had to make sure that one pan of every item was always frying, or waiting under the heat lamp, so it was not unusual to have three or four different things cooking at the same time.

The second fryer was reserved for frying apple fritters in rendered lard. They were made continuously and were actually quite good. Apple fritters required a bit more attention, as they had to be flipped over until each side was golden brown.

I quickly learned these three important lessons of apple fritter frying:

One:
Dip the spoon in hot lard before dipping it into cool batter.
Two:
If you drop the batter into the hot fat from the spoon at too great a height, the 375 degree lard will splash up and burn your arms and hands.
Three:
If you don't let the fryer basket drain thoroughly, the hot dripping oil will drip and burn your arms.

A Culinary Journey with Chef Steve Yeanish

After several hours of fast-paced frying came the hour-long cleanup. At the end of the evening, the fryers were turned off, then a large machine on wheels, which looked like a vacuum cleaner, was plugged in. Inside the larger fryer was a cold zone where the sediment, or loose bread crumbs collected. This residue was cleaned out and thrown away. Then, a hose was attached to the bottom of the fryer and hot fat was filtered into a holding tank. After the inside of the kettle was scrubbed, rinsed, and drained, the hot fat was pumped back into the clean fryer.

By the end of the evening my hair, body and clothes reeked of fried fish and my shoes were caked with grease. We were never given a break or time to eat during our shift, so you had to sprint to the rest room while the egg rolls browned or munch while you worked. In my entire life I never ate so many apple fritters or fried scallops, which were tasty and easy to pop into your mouth.

During the second week of my deep frying career, I was offered another job at the far more exclusive Perkiomen Bridge Hotel directly across the Perkiomen Creek. Though the wages were the same ($1.40 an hour), the job promised to be a step up, though it didn't involve much cooking. I was responsible for refilling all salads and appetizer dishes on the smorgasbord. They also promised to teach me to cook during summer vacation when school was out.

The decision was easy, but I had to do the right thing and give my customary two-week's notice at the Collegeville Inn. I politely gave the chef my notice. He listened for a minute, then got very agitated and demanded to know where I was going to work. The answer didn't please him. "Get the %#@^ out of here, if that's where you're going!" he barked as the veins popped out of his temples.

Working in a professional kitchen is not a place for the faint of heart. To the spectator, it will seem like chaotic bedlam during peak hours.

First of all, it can be very noisy. People are shouting, the staff is running and multi-tasking. Food is flying off the stations as servers grab plates, then return to the kitchen with trays full of dirty dishes and glassware.

On more than one occasion, a first-time employee has been scared to death when they were thrown into their first round of service. Sometimes they run out the door without ever looking back, or even calling to explain why they're not coming in again. It happens more often than you'd expect, especially with naïve innocents who cook at home, or as a hobby. It is a big shock to be suddenly blasted with the full force of real life in a professional kitchen.

The language of a busy kitchen is generally not for the saintly either. Most chefs call a spade a spade. Actually, most of them call it a #%*& shovel. Conversations can be quite colorful, too.

You have to remember, most of the kitchen employees spend more time with their co-workers than they do with their significant others, so you *really* get to know them. Conversations cover any topic, ranging from politics and sports to sex and religion, especially when people from every culture and walk of life are working together.

The Perkiomen Bridge Hotel

The historic Perkiomen Bridge Hotel was a beautiful, old, white two-story building with a panoramic view of the creek and bridge. Their famous smorgasbord was in the center of a large dining room, which easily seated 100 diners. Several smaller dining rooms and a bar were located on the first floor and there were guest rooms for long-term tenants and staff upstairs. The restaurant served the smorgasbord and an à la carte menu offering steamed lobster tails with drawn butter, shrimp cocktail and tiny Swedish meatballs, which were very good. The salad side was always the same, but the hot foods changed according to whatever the owner found interesting and the chef prepared.

Sam, the Italian owner, could find a bargain anywhere. His buffet cost more per person than the competition's, but it was worth it, especially if you devoured the lobster tails. Sam's sister, Rose was the cashier and hostess. Her son, who was the pride of the family, was studying Hotel and Restaurant Management at Cornell University. He knew I wanted to become a chef, and convinced me to apply to the Culinary Institute of America in Hyde Park, New York. The Culinary Institute of America, or CIA as it is known, became my goal from that point on.

Chef Zach ran a tight kitchen. He was a tall, slender black man with a short gray beard, who always wore whites and a tall, tapered chef's hat. One of his specialties was Snapper Soup which, in the Philadelphia area, is made from fresh-water snapping turtle cooked with herbs, spices and vegetables. The hotel was on the bank of Perkiomen Creek, which occasionally flooded, so there were plenty of turtles available for soup. Snapping turtles can grow quite large. (I once saw one with a shell the size of a large watermelon.) They have a long tail and legs, sharp claws and a large round head with a blunt beak. After the turtle was killed and dressed the chef put it into a pot with onions, celery, and other spices, then covered it with water and the biggest handful of bay leaves I have ever seen a chef use at one time in my entire 36 years of working in professional kitchens. After the turtle meat was cooked until tender, it was removed from the pot and cooled. Then I had to remove hundreds of tiny bones from the meat, which had an earthy, fishy odor. The worst part of it all was working with that gelatinous sticky mess. That's one job you want to start and finish without interruption! Zach finished his soup with more bay leaves and lots of sherry wine.

Sam once got a deal on canned blueberry, cherry, apple and lemon pie fillings, then told me to bake up as many pies as I could. I used one of Mom's recipes for pie crust and made several batches of both double-crusted and open-faced with streusel crumbs. The lemon filling was used for lemon meringue pies. This was a big accomplishment, which took most of the day and my pies turned out fairly well. Sam was pleased. The only trouble was that they were baked on Monday. Mom often quoted an old proverb, "Pies don't sleep well overnight," meaning if you want a good piece of pie, eat it the day you bake it. By Friday when the smorgasbord started, the pies were a few days old. I watched in horror as a waitress used an eight-section pie cutter and the entire meringue topping came off at once. If only she had used a hot, wet knife!

A Culinary Journey with Chef Steve Yeanish

Brookside Country Club

The start of Steve's fifteen year assocition with the Brookfield Country Club in Pottstown, Pennsylvania: Young Steve, Mr. William Partridge, who was Brookside Country Club Manager, Chef de Cuisine Patrick Gorey

After a year at the Perkiomen Bridge Hotel, I knew it was time to move on. I checked the local paper and found a classified ad for a salad and sandwich person at the Brookside Country Cub in nearby Pottstown, so I called about the job, and they set up an interview.

The club manager, William Partridge, was a big jovial man, who stood over six feet tall. He was a retired Army officer who had run many officer's clubs during his time in the service. Over the years I found him to be a gentle giant of a man, who rarely raised his voice. After a brief interview, he took me to meet the chef.

We walked through the clubhouse ballroom into a large, open kitchen. I was introduced to Chef Patrick Gorey and he asked about my experience. I explained about my cooking duties at the Perkiomen Bridge Hotel; then he asked me if I knew how to roast a duck. I quickly admitted that the chef actually cooked the duck and I only finished it. Then I mentioned that I was also baking cakes and desserts and I had even purchased my own large capacity mixer. The job was explained, and I was hired. Brookside Country Club! I really had it made now, so I gave my notice to Sam at the Perkiomen Bridge Hotel.

My fifteen year association with the Brookside Country Club started right after my graduation from high school. My schedule was always Tuesday to Sunday. The crew there was fun to work with, especially when they were in a good mood, and I learned a lot about life from them. We all worked doubles, which is usually lunch from 10 to 2, followed by the dinner shift from 5 to 9 or 10 o'clock.

The Clubhouse was originally an old army barracks that had been added onto many times over the years. It sprawled on top of a hill overlooking Pottstown and was surrounded by a prestigious 18-hole golf course.

Soon after I reported for work on that first morning, Chef Gorey arrived. Patrick Gorey was quite a character. He had apprenticed as a chef in his native Ireland, then worked at many fine hotels all over Europe until he reached his final position, Chef de Cuisine. Pat, as I was told to call him, was probably in his mid-thirties when I first met him. He was small, but mighty. Pat wasn't

The Oley Valley Inn

Bleu Cheese Dressing

This is based on the recipe Chef Patrick Gorey taught me at Brookside Country Club. This dressing tastes better after it has been allowed to sit for a day or so to allow the flavor to develop. It can be made with any bleu-veined cheese or a cheese combination of your choice. Gorgonzola is my favorite. This may seem like a rather large amount for home use, but the quantities can be cut in half. It can be kept for a few weeks in the refrigerator if it is stored in airtight containers.

afraid of anyone, and he never backed down. His huge kitchen was tidy and immaculate, and he always wore black and white checked pants and a starched double-breasted chef's coat.

Pat was known for his onion soup, Bleu cheese dressing, (which I still make to this day) steaks and prime rib. This was back in the 1970s, when beef was still king.

The quality of beef was incredible back then. Beef production was not what it is today, and we used prime grade beef, which was flavorful and tender. Others may argue, but I ate enough of that rib to be the snob I am today.

By the way, that beef was *always* roasted on the bone, and the fat cap was left on to bard the roast as it cooked. The National Association of Meat Purveyors, the organization that defines the market, called this a "109 rib." He served two sizes of filet mignon, and two different sizes of New York Strip steak. We roasted two whole ribs of beef every Saturday and sometimes on Sunday as well.

Yield: about one quart

¼ cup **red wine vinegar**
4 ounces **crumbled bleu cheese**

Combine vinegar and bleu cheese in heavy bottomed saucepan.
Heat over medium heat until cheese has just melted. **Do not boil**.
Cool to room temperature.

In large mixing bowl, add:
Vinegar and cheese mixture
2 cups **dairy sour cream**
3 cups **good quality mayonnaise**
1 Tbs **Lea & Perrins® Worcestershire Sauce**
Dash of **white pepper**
3 dashes **hot pepper sauce**
12 ounces **crumbled bleu cheese**

Mix all ingredients together.
Store in airtight containers.
Refrigerate until used.

A Culinary Journey with Chef Steve Yeanish

Welsh Rarebit

*This dish is classic Country Club cuisine.
Some Brookside members requested this dish several times a week.*

Serves four
Grease 4 individual casserole or ramekin dishes

1 Tbs **butter** *melted*
1 rounded Tbs **flour**
1 cup **dark English ale or beer**
1 Tbs **Lea and Perrins® Worcestershire Sauce**
Dash of **hot pepper sauce or cayenne pepper**
½ tsp **ground dry mustard**
1 pound **grated sharp chedddar cheese**
Toast points
Tomato slices
Crisp bacon

Melt butter in a heavy saucepan.
Add flour, stirring over medium heat until lightly browned.
Add ale or beer and cook until thickened.
Add Worcestershire sauce, hot sauce or pepper and mustard.
While stirring, add grated cheese a little bit at a time.
Continue until all the cheese has been added.
Heat until bubbly.
Pour into individual casserole dishes.
Place tomato slices around the edge of dish.
Garnish with toast points and criss-cross crisply cooked bacon on top.

Chicken and Oyster Bisque with Shiitake Mushrooms

This is based on a soup Patrick Gorey taught me to make.
I like to add shiitake mushroom or sometimes I add blanched asparagus tips instead.

Yield: About 4 quarts (Any extra freezes well.)

2 **whole chicken breasts** *with skin and bone*
(Or if you are in a hurry use the meat of one deli-roasted chicken, that's been cooled and diced.)
One 48 ounce **can chicken broth OR** *6 cups* **home-made chicken broth**
1 **medium onion** *peeled and sliced*
3 **ribs celery** *sliced*
Several **parsley stems**
2 **bay leaves**
1 tsp **thyme leaves**
salt and white pepper
4 Tbs **melted butter**
8 ounces **shiitake mushrooms**, *stems removed, caps sliced thinly*
1 cup **dry vermouth**
24 **shucked oysters** *with their natural juice, cut into pieces about 1 inch square*
Roux or slurry to thicken
1 quart **half and half or light cream**
Fresh chives, *snipped*
Hot sauce, *if desired*

Place the breasts of chicken in a soup pot and cover with the chicken broth.
Add the onion, celery, parsley stems, bay leaves and thyme.
Simmer gently 45 minutes or until chicken is tender.
Remove cooked breasts from pot, and cool to room temperature.
When cool enough to handle, remove skin and then discard the bones.
Cut meat into ½ inch dice for soup garnish.
Skim any excess fat from broth. Remove bay leaves.
Season stock to taste with salt and white pepper.
(A chicken bouillon cube can also be used to boost the flavor, if necessary.)
With a hand-held purée wand, carefully pulse until the vegetables are completely
blended into the soup.
(This can also be done in a blender in small batches. Be sure the blender lid is securely attached and use
a kitchen towel to cover the top of the lid to prevent hot liquid from splattering.)
In a large skillet, briefly sauté shiitake mushrooms in butter.
Add vermouth to mushrooms and stir to de-glaze the pan and reduce by one half.
Add the cooked chicken, oysters and their juices to the soup and heat gently.

Brookside Crew

Dennis, the chain-smoking assistant chef, was as skinny as a rail and moved through the kitchen with incredible speed. At lunchtime, when the pace was the quickest, he flew like a whirlwind. He had nicknames for everyone, especially the waitresses.

Pauline, also known as Schultzie, was funny, quick and sassy. One time, a particularly rude club member complained that there was a fly in his soup. She bent down, looked right into the bowl and said, "We've been looking for that little guy all morning long!" The man was speechless.

Vera had beautiful olive skin and an incredible head of thick, black hair. We worked together for ten more years and we stay in touch to this day.

Thelma was one of the sweetest women I've ever met and she treated me like a son. She had waves of long, flowing red hair, so I called her Rusty Brown. She was a hard worker, never complained, and stayed until the job was done. She also had a great sense of humor. One year in honor of St. Patrick's Day, she dyed her underwear emerald green. It was quite a sight under her white polyester uniform.

Thelma always loved a chance to dress up. Every summer the club held a Hawaiian Luau. As *Blue Hawaii* played, Thelma appeared dancing the hula in a blue bra covered with shimmering blue flowers, and a very short skirt made out of party streamers.

Thelma and Grace, the housekeeper, often warned me about using foul language, but I didn't listen. One morning they grabbed me from behind and Thelma literally washed my mouth out with soap.

When I was 18 years old, Pat, Dennis and I went to the Restaurant Tradeshow in New York City. There were four or five floors of exhibitors presenting food products, equipment, beverages, services and cleaning supplies. The main attraction for us was the Salon of Culinary Arts. This prestigious show had its own judges. It was incredible to see the talent of the world's finest chefs and pastry chefs on display. It was truly awe-inspiring. I remember chefs from that show who are renowned today.

Cold meat and fish platters were arranged and accompanied by intricate tallow sculptures, made from a blend of animal fats and paraffin or beeswax. Decorated cakes and and hundreds of sugar sculptures were displayed. I spent hours studying it all.

Steve made this Rabbit Butter sculpture with Rabbit Pâté en Croute for a culinary competition.

The Oley Valley Inn

Chicken Française

You can use chicken breast, veal cutlets or turkey cutlets, one per serving. Pound them until they are thin.

Preheat oven to 250 degrees

To Make the Batter:
    Place all these ingredients in a blender:
    6 **large eggs**
    1½ cups **milk**
    2 **medium cloves garlic** *peeled, sliced thinly*
    1 large or 2 small **peeled shallots** *peeled, sliced thinly*
    2 Tbs **flat leaf parsley** *chopped*
    Purée mixture until batter is smooth.

Mix the seasoned flour:
    1 tsp **kosher salt**
    ¼ tsp **ground black or white pepper**
    2 cups **all purpose flour**

Dredge the cutlets in the seasoned flour.
Dip floured cutlets into the batter until they are thoroughly coated.
Let excess batter drip off.

In a sauté pan over medium-high heat, add clarified butter or an oil and butter mixture. Add cutlets and brown lightly on one side, then turn and brown lightly on the other side. Place cooked cutlets on a baking tray in a low 250 degree oven to keep them warm while you're cooking the other pieces.

To Make the Lemon-Herb Butter Sauce:
Drain sauté pan of cooking fat and add **a few Tbs butter.**
Melt butter over medium heat.
Add **juice of 1 lemon.**
Add a few **Tbs chopped flat leaf parsley or chives.**
capers *are optional*

Arrange cutlets on a platter, then pour foaming Lemon-Herb Butter over the top.
Serve hot, with lemon wedges.

Chef Pat Gorey

Pat was a talented ice sculptor. Back before the days of Japanese chisels and chain saws, he worked with ice picks and a 6-prong rasp. It wasn't long before he started teaching me this art.

During the 1970s many lavish parties were held at Brookside. There was still a lot of old money about back then and our members enjoyed entertaining grandly. The club excelled at really sensational parties. On one particular occasion, a huge retirement party was being planned and the gentleman's wife requested an ice carving for the hors'd oeuvres buffet. She wanted a heart-shaped sculpture, with an opening in the top to hold a huge arrangement of flowers. Pat gave me this opportunity to shine.

Conway's Icehouse was nearby and the owner let us work in the icehouse, which was kept at 26 degrees. If you dressed warmly, it wasn't too bad. Pat got me started, then left and I worked for hours chipping the ice in one direction, getting every angle just right, and smoothing the corners. I thought I did a really good job. The day before the party, we took the pickup truck to move my ice sculpture into the walk-in freezer at the club. As we moved the sculpture, I heard a loud crack and it split into two pieces. I thought my masterpiece was ruined, but Pat came to the rescue by carving out a depression in the base, then fitting the heart piece into it. He was my hero that day!

On the evening of the gala, the flowers were arranged and the sculpture was put in place, then backlit with red light. The party was well under way when Pat ran into the kitchen shouting, "Oh my God, Stevie, the ice carving just crashed on top of a guest!" He was a good actor and I was taken in, until I realized he was just joking.

Ice sculptures for galas at Brookside

The Oley Valley Inn

Every year, the club held an annual Holiday Buffet, which was attended by hundreds of people. This was a chance for the chef to showcase his talent, so Pat always included ice carvings and other impressive creations. One year he made an exact replica of the Brookside Clubhouse out of gum paste, or pastillage, which was the highlight of the buffet. This was quite an endeavor, featuring an elaborate snow scene and the entire building was lit from the inside. Even lobster shells were transformed into people in various poses.

The first year, Pat let me do two or three ice carvings. They were very amateurish, but showed some potential, and I was hooked. That Christmas I did three ice carvings, a central dolphin with its tail in the air, holding fresh flowers flanked by two other dolphins. Pat said, "That's Stevie's buffet!" and I proudly carved the Roast Sirloin Strip of Beef that was featured on the buffet.

Pat was like a parent to me and I was always learning something. He was constantly reminding me to "Stand up straight!" or "Don't stand with your hands in your pockets," and "Make long slices with the knife, don't saw at it!"

A young bride was marrying an English gentleman and she wanted a traditional English-style dark fruitcake loaded with raisins, currants, Muscat raisins and citron. The three-tiered cake was dense, rich and took forever to bake. The layers were then wrapped in brandy-soaked cloth and stored.

When it was time to assemble the cake, the layers were spread with apricot preserves, coated with rolled gum paste, then decorated with royal icing, which is white and gets rock-hard as it dries. It was quite an experience, and the new bride was very pleased as well. Pat kindly gave me credit for it, even though he did most of the work.

Holiday buffet at Brookside

Steve working on the buffet

A Culinary Journey with Chef Steve Yeanish

Culinary Institute of America

The Culinary Institute of America (CIA) was the first culinary college devoted to teaching culinary, baking and pastry arts. They literally wrote the book (*The Professional Chef*) and created the curriculum for a culinary education. CIA is now considered to be "the world's premier culinary college" and their degree is considered to be "a prized passport to the world of food professionals." They had more than one hundred teaching professional chefs from all over the world on staff. They taught everything in sequence starting with kitchen skills to food preparation, food service and cuisines.

I was determined to study there, so I picked up an application and the rest is history. They had just moved their campus to Hyde Park, New York and I wanted to see it, so Mom and I travelled up on a cold winter Monday. When we got there, I was totally blown away. The impressive main campus had once been a Jesuit monastery. As we walked through those huge halls, I smelled veal stock cooking for the first time. Then came the aroma of fresh bread from the bake shops.

I gave the office photos of some of my projects and cakes to file with my application and drove home in a happy daydream. Weeks passed with anxiety mounting until finally, in April the envelope arrived. I was accepted to start in the summer of 1973.

One morning Pat noticed I was preoccupied and asked me what was up. I told him I was worried about getting all my tuition money together. I had no idea what he was up to. Then a few weeks later, he and the club manager, Mr. Partridge, handed me a letter. The Scottish Rite Cathedral, (our local Masonic organization) was giving me a $500 scholarship! I was ecstatic, and my parents were very grateful too.

Suddenly, it was time for me to say goodbye. By then, the people at Brookside were like a family to me. Pat told me to be at the Club one Monday evening before I left. Mom, Dad and I drove to the Club in my blue Tempest convertible. The entire staff was there for my going away party. Pat had prepared a hot and cold buffet, then he presented me with a beautiful traditional Génoise cake filled with preserves, and coated with pale green marzipan. A marzipan figure of a chef perched on top of the cake, which was inscribed, "Good Luck, Stevie!" Mom and Dad were really proud of me, my new friends, and their gracious send off.

While I was at Brookside, I had worked my way up through the kitchen ranks by doing whatever needed to be done—peeling, chopping, stocking the storeroom—and I learned as much as I could. Soon I was working on the line with Pat and Dennis and also running the pantry. By the time I left, I could grill steaks and also handle the weekend lunch crowd of golfers coming in for burgers or club sandwiches.

I learned a lot that year. Pat took me under his wing and corrected my mistakes. The knife skills he taught me have been used throughout my career. He taught me to work neatly and finish one job before starting another. I learned to keep the ingredients of a sandwich on the bread. He taught me that nothing should ever touch the rim of the plate. I learned the basics of how to cut steaks and how to carve prime rib.

Pat encouraged my creativity and taught me how to carve ice and work with tallow. He opened my eyes to the world of a professional chef and encouraged me to become more. He reinforced the respect I learned at home and hopefully carry through life. If, perhaps, I never said it outright before, then I'll say it now, "Thank you, Chef Patrick Gorey!"

The Oley Valley Inn

Oley Valley Onion Soup

I have been making this soup for almost thirty years. We use Demi-Glace instead of beef stock and bouillon cubes. Rich brown gravy from roast pork or beef is also a good substitute. (Use about 2 cups) The soup can also be finished with brandy or applejack, to your own taste.

Yields about 4 quarts or 10 average portions

4 large **Spanish onions (or 4 pounds small onions)**
peeled, cut in half point-to-point, cut in half again at center, then slice ¼ to ½ inch thick
3 Tbs **melted butter or salad oil**
2 **cloves garlic** *peeled, finely chopped*
2 cups **dry white or red wine** *(we use either one)*
2 whole **large bay leaves**
½ tsp **dried thyme leaves**
1 tsp **dried oregano**
½ tsp **ground black pepper**
6 cups **chicken stock OR** *substitute* one 49 ounce can chicken broth, *like College Inn®*
4 cups **beef stock OR** *substitute* two 19 ounce cans beef broth, *like College Inn®*
1-2 **beef bouillon cubes (such as Knorr®)**
one 15 oz can **tomato sauce**
½ cup **brandy or applejack** *(optional)*

Heat a large 6-8 quart Dutch oven or other large, thick-bottomed pot.
Add butter or oil, and sliced onions. Set heat at medium and cook until onions are soft and evenly browned. **The onions must be cooked slowly and stirred frequently to get the sweet, caramelized flavor in the finished soup. This should take 10 to 15 minutes. If the onions get too brown, or burn slightly, take the pot off the heat.**
Add garlic, stir briefly. Deglaze pan with wine, stirring to dissolve any bits of residue in the bottom of the pot. Add bay leaves, thyme, oregano, black pepper, chicken and beef stock, 1-2 bouillon cubes and tomato sauce. Bring soup to boil. Lower heat to simmer slowly, and **cook 30 minutes**. Season to taste with additional salt and pepper, as needed. Add brandy or apple jack. To serve, top with croutons and sprinkle with grated Parmesan cheese.

Chef Says
To bake cheese in the soup:
We prefer using Swiss cheese, such as Finlandia, or Jarlsberg. Some restaurants use Gruyere, but it is very sharp for most tastes. You can use a blend of cheese if you like, just grate it over the croutons. Mozzarella and Provolone are not good choices because when melted they get very stringy and become difficult to eat.

Fill soup crocks or oven-proof bowls with hot soup, to about ½ inch from the top of the bowl. Top each with croutons. Place sliced Swiss, Gruyere or Emmenthal cheese on top of croutons. Put soup bowls on sheet tray to catch any spills or cook-overs. Place in 450 degree oven or under a broiler until cheese is bubbly and brown. Place bowl on saucer, then serve.

Studying at the Culinary Institute of America

Full of nervous excitement, I started my professional culinary education on a clear, warm day in 1973. This was well before the days of celebrity chefs like Emeril, Rachel and Bobby. We weren't dreaming of becoming the next media star; we just wanted a serious culinary education.

My room on the fourth floor had an incredible view of boats sailing up and down the Hudson River, and the hike to the top floor kept me in good shape. There were communal bathrooms and our no-frill rooms had a sink, bunk beds and two desks.

There were 75 students and we lived in our white uniforms that the school provided. We each had ten sets of uniforms and were assigned one day a week to send five dirty sets to the laundry and get five clean uniforms back. We also had white aprons and clean sidetowels, which we guarded with our lives.

All students were given a large stack of textbooks on topics such as table service, *garde manger* (cold food preparation and decoration), baking, and many other subjects, but the book, *The Professional Chef* (or *Pro Chef* as we called it), which was published by the CIA was our Bible.

We were each given a greatly-coveted and closely-guarded knife set. Our first official set of knives and tools contained a butcher's steel, French knife, carving knife, boning knife, utility knife, paring knife, carving fork, vegetable peeler, Parisian scoop (melon baller) and a metal spatula, which were all rolled up in a blue Naugahyde® case. Sounds impressive, but they were just average by today's standards. We were taught to sharpen them on an oilstone, but not many students could do that well, and if you didn't know what you were doing, the edge was easily ruined.

First semester our theory classes were six hours long, then a quick lunch break, followed by five hours of hands-on work in the kitchen. If you were absent a day, then you missed a major part of the class, so attendance was mandatory. After intense lectures, followed by work in hot kitchens every night, I was so tired I frequently fell into a dead sleep in my stuffy little room. I studied hard and fortunately could remember a recipe just by reading it quickly. Our classmates produced the food we ate and we were served by students from the Table Service class. A part of this class was theory, learning about fine table service, wines and mixology—and the other part was hands-on when we served as waiters. The entire school ate lunch and dinner together, and the cuisine depended on Chef de Jour and his whims or favorite touches.

I drove home most weekends and worked at Brookside because I needed the money and they were glad to have my help. One cold Monday, Chef Gorey drove the Brookside gang up to visit me on campus and they had a full day of touring the school. It was a memorable visit that I still remember fondly.

In free time, the students, who came from all over, talked about food or restaurants and gossiped about upcoming classes and teachers.

Hyde Park is beautiful, and the summers were especially fun. We'd often stop for beer at Shop-Rite, then go to the drive-in theater in my Tempest, with the top down, if it was hot enough. If we had a long dinner break, we'd eat, then take a walk down to the Hudson or sit on a large veranda high above the river and watch the rowers of the Marist College crew team practice on the river. I'd go back to those days in a heartbeat!

Some of our instructors were incredible chefs. Others were great teachers. It was rare to find a great chef, who was also an incredible teacher. Anyone not used to a military-type discipline should think twice about the CIA. The chef is always in charge of the kitchen. "Yes Chef, your way is the correct way." Even though you were taught an entirely different way the week before, you had to learn to be flexible. And, you'd better learn how to take criticism.

In the real world, there are dozens of recipes featuring many different techniques for a single dish. Not too much is original anymore. Every house has their own style, or way of doing things. Some work better than others, but it all comes down to business. One of the first things they taught us at CIA is that food establishments are *businesses* and the primary goal of any business is to *first make a profit*. A fortunate few may be lucky to work as a private chef with an unlimited budget, but in the end, food and labor expenses are the greatest cost of any operation.

CIA Memories

One of my favorite teachers was **Chef Fritz Sonnenschmidt**, the author of *The Soul of a Chef*, a book I highly recommend. I honestly believe he's one of the most knowledgeable and talented chefs in the world. He can cook, teach *and* inspire. I feel sorry for anyone who hasn't had the privilege of being in one of his classes. Worldly and gracious, he always addressed students courteously saying, "Hello Chef," or "How are you Chef?" Fritz was one of the authors of the CIA's *Garde Manger* textbook, and he taught that class and illustrated it with tales from his own experience. Fritz, a round jolly German, was also our instructor of International Cuisine. Most of our training until then had been classical French, but he

Master Chef Fritz Sonnenschmidt & Steve

expanded our repertoire to include German, Spanish, Italian, Greek, Scandinavian, Middle Eastern, Jewish and Oriental cuisines.

Fritz made the most incredible patés and terrines, which were works of art, and he taught us about caviar and foie gras. He told us charcoal, used to color inexpensive caviar, will turn teeth black!

Fritz and **Chef Anthony Seta**, another favorite teacher, loved to needle each other. Fritz bet he could make a classic brown veal stock using ketchup. Chef Seta took the bet. Working side by side to make the stock, Fritz used ketchup and Seta used tomatoes—and Fritz won the bet.

Chef Anthony Seta was another inspiration for me. He was a purist, and his style was clean and classic. I learned a lot from him. He was a short Italian, who wore the tallest starched chef hat I'd ever seen. Many years after graduation I returned to the CIA for a refresher course and, much to my delight, Fritz and Tony were teaching the class. I will never forget that wonderful week of learning and sharing while working one-on-one with my two heroes.

Chef Cleefeld was our Pantry instructor, who taught us about the fun of breakfast cookery at 4 a.m. One dark winter morning after I moved off campus, I accidently locked my car keys in my apartment, so I started walking over icy, snowy roads to get to class on time. I finally hailed a passing cab and had just enough money to pay the fare. I got to class, but he marked me tardy.

Most of us were still half-asleep at that hour, but we loved to pull pranks on each other. I took an egg, pierced the ends with a pin, carefully blew out the contents, dropped it in a sleepy chef's coat pocket, then smashed it. Fortunately, he was a good sport.

Chef Steven Beno was another great chef, who taught Garde Manger II, our final class. I really enjoyed his class. He was one of the best—and quickest—ice sculptors I have ever seen. He dazzled us with his skill, then taught us his technique using saws and large chisels. We also learned the classic chaud-froid and aspic work that was popular in the 1970s.

Chef Beno and I got along well. He encouraged my work on the final project for our Grand Buffet, which was the biggest part of our grade. We had to make aspic plates with a design made of artificial truffels that we sliced thinly, then cut into shapes that were layered on a glass aspic-covered plate. The aspic was made of crystal-clear reduced veal stock, flavored with Madeira or sherry, which solidified after it was chilled. The tiny pieces of truffelette were dipped in room-temperature aspic, then placed on the plate in a pattern. Chef Beno let me use two pieces for my final showpiece. One was a whole ham decorated in chaud-froid, a Béchamel, or cream sauce, mixed with gelatin or aspic to coat the surface. My "ham" was actually a fake, made of instant mashed potatoes and gelatin shaped on a lamb bone, then decorated with a foil frill. The aspic sheet portrait of a Greek soldier in a tunic was transferred to the top of the ham. I made columns of Grecian ruins out of butter, then set them on the tray with sliced ham roulades filled with mousse.

Chef James Heywood was also a Garde Manger instructor. He married a classmate of mine. I saw him and Fritz Sonnenschmidt recently at a CIA reunion. He looks much the same and is now the king of barbeque.

Chef Eric Saucey was a dry-witted Swiss-trained chef, who inspired me. He was our instructor for Classical Cuisine, and he taught as well as he cooked. I got one of my highest scores from him. We often talked about shortcuts, and as classically trained as he was, he knew there were times when a quick substitution had to be used. He sagely advised, "So long as it tastes good, who really cares?"

My friend Betsy and I found a set of old napkins printed with: *"Lest your kissing be spoiled, make sure your onions are fully boiled."* We thought Chef Saucey would love this, so we dropped one in his briefcase. During our morning lecture, he waved the napkin in the air and asked if anyone could explain the motto. One student patiently explained that cooked onions loose their pungency. That wasn't nearly as cute as our quote.

Chef Eddie Bradley, a Navy veteran, was my first bakeshop instructor. He was a tall guy who had run several commercial bakeries, and he had big, strong, arms from handling all that dough. I couldn't wait to get started in his class, as I always loved baking and wanted it to be the focus of my education. Our day started with making both hard and soft roll doughs. The routine was: scale, knead, proof, shape, bench proof, cut dough, shape, egg wash, proof and then bake. Shaping was the fun part. Once the dough was cut, we divided into teams. When we scaled the dough into balls for bench proofing, Edie showed us the proper technique. "You place your hands on either side of the dough and you gently massage and caress it into a ball, just like you were caressing a beautiful woman's breast," he would tell us.

The Oley Valley Inn

Stracciatella Italian Egg Drop Soup

There used to be a very small, quaint Italian restaurant not far from the CIA campus. Their food was excellent and very reasonably priced, especially for students on a budget. They made the best Stracciatella (Italian Egg Drop Soup) I have ever tasted. I make this soup occasionally, and always remember the good times Betsy, the gang and I had when we took a well-earned break on weeknights.

Yield: about 3 quarts

1 Tbs **olive oil or chicken fat**
1 **medium onion** *peeled, diced fine*
3 **ribs celery** *trimmed, washed, diced fine*
2 **cloves garlic** *peeled, chopped fine*
2 large (48 ounce) cans **chicken broth OR** 3 quarts **home-made chicken stock**
1 cup **egg pastina**
(You can usually find pastina in the pasta or baby food section of the grocery store.
Or you can substitute one cup of instant couscous)
6 **large eggs** *lightly beaten*
12 ounce **fresh baby spinach leaves** (*A chiffonade-bunch of leaves cut in a julienne or coarse cut*)
Freshly ground nutmeg *to taste*
Grated Parmesan cheese *to taste*

In a heavy soup pot, sauté diced onion and celery in oil or chicken fat.
Add garlic and cook briefly, but don't let it get brown.

Add chicken broth or stock.
Simmer soup for about 15 minutes, or until vegetables are soft.
Season broth with kosher salt and white pepper to taste.
Bouillon cubes or chicken soup base can be added to fortify the flavor.

Add pastina or couscous and simmer 5 more minutes.
Turn heat source off.
Stir soup briskly to make a whirlpool,
then pour beaten eggs in a thin, steady, stream into the center of the whirlpool in the pot.
Return soup to simmer.
Add chopped spinach leaves.
Season soup to taste with nutmeg.
Top each serving with a generous spoon of grated cheese, then serve.

The large dough ball was then put in a press and cut into one or two-ounce pieces. We'd then shape the dough into the shape of the day. Hard roll dough was always shaped like a mini loaf of bread, then lined up on sheet pans covered with parchment paper liners.

Eddie would bark, "Make five rows of six, end to end. Write your name in pencil on your rows!" Then, as we placed our finished rolls on the tray, Eddie would march up and down inspecting our work. "Yeanish, we're not making *dog biscuits*!" he'd growl. I struggled, and eventually got it right.

Then we worked on soft roll dough. Roll the dough out into a cigar shape. Let it relax. Go back and shape them: knot rolls, double knots, and one Eddie called the "Tokyo Twist." Then we had to learn to round the dough: cup the dough under a closed hand; then in a rotating motion, smooth it into a round ball with the bottom pulled tightly.

The dough waiting to be baked was kept in proofing boxes at a moist 100 degrees. They were next to a large oven called the windmill, which had rotating racks. This oven had six revolving trays, which held one full sheet pan on each tray. Every tray swung independently and was always level as it rotated.

One person was selected to be the daily oven person, which was a cool job. There was no room for error. You had to open a small door and stop the oven as the tray approached. If the tray was not put in the oven correctly, the contents of the pan dropped all over the bottom of the oven. You were in trouble if this happened while there were 20 or 30 pans of rolls ready and waiting to bake in the oven.

Someone ordered a decorated cake and Chef Eddie knew I was already pretty good, so he asked me to decorate it. I proudly presented it for his approval and all he could say was, "For Christ's sake, Yeanish, why did you do it in purple?" In my own defense, it was lavender, but I got a good grade from him in the end.

Chef Walter Schryer and **Chef Albert Kumin** were both pastry chefs while I was at CIA. We had morning classes taught by Shryer and we made petites fours, cookies and pastries for the Escoffier Room, the fine student-run French restaurant. Pecan Diamonds were a staple, too. We learned pulled and blown sugar, gum paste or pastillage, nougat, marzipan and chocolate work. This class was over way too soon for me.

My final project was a tiered wedding cake decorated with marzipan roses and coated in pastillage and ornate white royal icing. I was disappointed I didn't get to do pulled sugar since I was already experienced with cakes. Chef Kumin went on to become the pastry chef at the Carter White House and also the Four Seasons restaurant.

Chef Peter Van Erp ran the AM kitchen in the Escoffier Room. In those days, the students who graduated then stayed on to work as a Chef's Assistant were called fellowships. They worked at all the stations in the kitchen. There was a large brick arch filled with glass so the kitchen was visible to the customers. Chef Van Erp screamed orders to his kitchen staff and heaven help you if you screwed up! We spent our days chopping shallots, garlic and parsley, but we *did* get to play waiter in the dining room.

Chef Wayne Almquist had the most distinctive voice. He enjoyed many things in life and one was good food. He was our instructor for the coffee shop part of the dining room service. This used to be held in an old red and stainless steel diner, where they served a simple sandwich menu with light fare and beer and wine.

One summer evening before graduation, we had a boring theory class and a 45-minute dinner break. It was a very warm day, so we

Pork and Sauerkraut with Kielbasa

A ham shank can be added in the start of the cooking stage. Bratwurst, knockwurst or frankfurters can be used in place of kielbasa during the final half-hour of cooking.

Preheat oven to 350 degrees
Yield: 6-8 servings

One 3-4 pounds **Pork loin roast (with bones)** or 1 **pork Boston butt**
Kosher salt and cracked black pepper
½ pound **country-sliced slab bacon** *cut into small dice*
1 cup **dry white wine**
2 cans **Silver Floss® sauerkraut** OR one 2 pound bag **barrel-cured sauerkraut**
1 **large onion** *peeled, cut in half, sliced thin from end to end*
1 **large apple** *peeled, cut in half, cored, sliced thinly*
1 Tbs **caraway seeds**
1 **bay leaf**
2 Tbs **brown sugar**
½ tsp **ground black pepper**
About 1 cup **apple juice or cider**
4 pieces **smoked kielbasa sausage**

Season pork roast generously with salt and pepper.
In a large Dutch oven or frying pan, fry diced bacon until crisp, then remove from pan.
Remove all but 1 Tbs of bacon fat.
Over medium high heat, brown pork roast on all sides, then remove from pan.
Add white wine, deglaze browned bits of meat in the pan, then remove pan from heat.
If you prefer a milder sauerkraut flavor, you may rinse kraut under running water.
(I DO NOT! I find when the onion, apple and sugar are added, the flavors will marry beautifully.)

Add sauerkraut, onion, apple, caraway seeds, bay leaf, brown sugar, pepper, reserved crisp bacon and apple juice or cider.
Stir mixture well.
Place the meat in the center of the pot, so it is almost completely covered by the sauerkraut mixture.
Cover pot tightly with a lid or use clear plastic wrap, then cover with foil.
Place in 325-degree oven for 2½ hours.
Open pot and add links of kielbasa, then cover with sauerkraut.
Bake an additional 30 minutes.
Serve with mashed potatoes and applesauce.
German rye bread and apple butter rounds out the meal.

quickly headed for the coffee shop and had a couple of cold brews in frosty mugs that went down easily. We returned to class far too happy and were reprimanded for drinking on the job. My "Goody Two Shoes" image was totally tarnished. I recently saw Chef Almquist at the CIA. He was as jovial and fun as ever —and he still enjoys good food.

On that same trip I saw my classmate **Chef Joe Mure,** who was teaching Pantry. We talked for a while and got caught up comparing notes. It was strange to see him older and rounder (just like me), but he hadn't changed a bit. It was great to see him interact with his students as he guided them like a pro. Unfortunately, that was the last time I saw him. He died of a massive heart attack while teaching in that classroom. Our current Oley Valley Inn Chef Luigi, a CIA graduate, also had him as an instructor and loved him almost as much as I did. Heaven will never be a hungry place with Chef Joe up there.

Graduation was always a big event at the CIA. Our commencement was held in one of the large agricultural exhibit halls at the Duchess County Fairgrounds in nearby Rheinbeck. My entire family, all thirteen of us, gathered for the event. We stayed at a nearby campsite overlooking the Hudson River. It was a cool October evening and we sat around an open fire with pizza and beer. My friend Betsy was there as well. The evening passed quickly and my sisters and I still reminisce about that memorable time.

The legendary Executive Chef of the Waldorf Astoria in New York City, Arno Schmidt, was our guest speaker. His inspiring speech let us know our culinary education was only just beginning—the Real World comes next. And so it did.

The students and faculty prepared a grand reception for the family and guests of the 200 graduates that day. The buffets overflowed with food, rolls and pastries. Many of the students' showpieces decorated the buffets, including my wedding cake from Advanced Pastry class.

My family was so proud of me that day. Dad was glowing. He could not get over the size of the school and he was impressed by the level of discipline there, which was almost military. He admired the fact that everyone wore the same uniform, everyone was called Chef, and everyone at CIA had similar goals and expectations.

It was finally over. I graduated with honors in the top 10 percent of my class and I was very pleased.

The foods we made and ate at the CIA still stand out in my mind. There were really good soups…really bad curries…butter-laden Danish pastry that melted in your mouth…Paella…Linzer Torte…Pecan Diamonds from the Escoffier Room…glorious pâtés, gallantines and terrines…consommé…croissants…gravlax…artichokes…avocados…real petits fours with frangipane…calves' liver…lamb…Hollandaise Sauce…truffles…foie gras…Roast Duckling…Roast Chicken…prosciutto…Dover sole…*real* demi-glace…Napoleons…Palmiers…Goulash…Spätzle…enough already!

**The Wedding Cake
My final project for Advanced Pastry Class**

The Oley Valley Inn

Linzer Torte

Preheat oven to 325 degrees
Yield: one 12 inch tart pan with a removable bottom
A smaller pan such as a Springform pan can be substituted, but the tart will be thicker and need a longer time in the oven.

1 pound **sweet unsalted butter** *softened*
1½ cup **granulated sugar**
2 tsp **pure vanilla extract**
½ tsp **pure almond extract**
1 **large egg** *at room temperature*
1½ cup **ground almonds, hazelnuts or combination of both**
(see Chef Says)
2 tsp **ground cinnamon**
4½ cups **all-purpose flour**
Two 8 ounce jars **red raspberry preserves**

Chef Says
How to Toast Nuts:

If you are grinding your own nuts, toast them briefly in a 325 degree oven until a toasted nut fragrance permeates the oven. Rub hazelnuts between towels to remove the skins.

In a mixer, lightly cream butter and sugar together.
Add egg, vanilla and almond extract, then mix briefly to incorporate egg.
Scrape down bowl with a rubber spatula.
Add half of the flour and cinnamon, then mix briefly.
Add chopped nuts, then mix briefly.
Add remaining flour, then mix briefly.
Scrape down sides of bowl, mix again to be sure mixture has combined evenly.
Divide dough into two balls, one slightly larger than the other.
Place both balls of dough between waxed paper or parchment and flatten into round disks.
Refrigerate dough for at least ½ hour.
Take the larger circle and roll it out to fit the base of a **12 inch removable bottom tart pan**.
Spread jam over the dough to within one inch of the sides.
Roll out remaining circle until it is the size of the base, then cut it into 1½ inch strips.
Make a lattice top by placing the 1½ inch strips at regular intervals first in one direction, then place the strips in the opposite direction.
Trim dough to the edge of the pan.
Leftover dough can be rolled into small marble-size balls, then flattened and pressed into the edges to fill in any gaps.

Bake in 325 degree oven for 1 hour, until golden brown and bubbly.
Cool on wire rack.
Remove side of pan from base while it is still slightly warm.

Beef Braised in Beer and Onions

I like to serve this with Poppyseed Spätzle with Brown Butter. See recipe on the next page.

Yield: 6-8 servings
This can be cooked several different ways:
If using a Crock-pot®: cover and cook for 6-7 hours on the high setting.
If using a Dutch oven: cover with a tight lid, then place in a 350 degree oven for 2½-3 hours, or until the beef is fork-tender.
If using the top of stove: cover and simmer slowly, for 2-3 hours, or until beef is fork-tender.

3 pounds **beef** *cubed for stew*
Kosher salt and freshly ground black pepper
3 Tbs **all purpose flour**
3 Tbs **oil**
6 large **Spanish onions (about 3-4 pounds)** *peeled, halved and sliced with grain of the onion*
6 **cloves garlic** *peeled and sliced*
3 Tbs **sweet Hungarian paprika**
one 12 ounce bottle of **dark beer or lager**
1 Tbs **caraway seeds**
¼ cup **Lea & Perrins® Worcestershire sauce**
½ cup **tomato ketchup**
Salt and pepper
Grated zest of 2 lemons
Roux or slurry *if needed*
Sour cream to garnish

Season beef cubes well with salt and pepper.
On a tray, spread out the seasoned cubes of beef in one layer, then dust them with flour.
Heat oil in a heavy skillet.
Make sure the pan does not burn, or the burned taste will be picked up by the meat.
Brown each side of the beef cubes in at least four batches. As each batch browns, remove it from the pan and put it into a Crock-pot® or Dutch oven to keep warm.
Add more oil to the pan, if necessary, while continuing to brown the batches of beef.
When the last batch of beef is in the skillet, add the sliced onions and garlic or more oil, if necessary.
Over medium heat, stir occasionally with a wooden spoon until onions have caramelized.
Add paprika and caraway seeds.
Pour the beer or lager into the pan and stir to de-glaze the pan.
Add the onion and beer mixture to the browned beef cubes.
Add Worcestershire sauce and ketchup.
Serve with mashed potatoes, buttered Spätzle or soft polenta.

The Oley Valley Inn

Poppyseed Spätzle with Brown Butter

Spätzle are little German dumplings.

Yield: 6 servings as a side dish

4 **large eggs** *lightly beaten*
¾ cup **milk**
1½ cup, plus 2 Tbs **all purpose flour**
½ tsp **grated nutmeg**
½ tsp **salt**
1 Tbs **poppyseeds**
4 quarts **boiling, salted water**
4 Tbs **butter** *for browning*
A large bowl half full of **ice water**

Combine eggs, flour, milk, nutmeg, salt and poppy seeds in large bowl.
Beat with the paddle of a mixer or by hand with a wooden spoon.
Batter will be thick, so mix only until it has combined.
Put a large-hole disk into a food mill, or spätzle mill.
Spray the disk with shortening or Pam® pan primer.
Place half the batter into the mill and force it through.
Scrape all the dough off the mill.

Add the dough shapes to boiling, salted water.
As soon as the spätzle rise to the surface of the boiling water,
remove them with a slotted spoon,
then place them in a bowl of ice water to stop the cooking.

Repeat until all the batter has been cooked.
Pour the spätzle in the cold water into a colander to drain.

Lightly brown butter in a skillet.
Add spätzle just as the butter starts to brown.
Sauté spätzle briefly to heat through until lightly crisp.
Season to taste with salt and pepper, then serve.

Roast Duckling Oley Valley Inn

Roast duckling was on our original menu. It has become a beloved favorite of many diners. The method we use to cook our duckling has evolved over the years. I started learning the classic French Canard a l'Orange (Duck with Orange) at the CIA. At Brookside Country Club, I developed my own recipe, which has stood the test of time for the past 20 years.

Preheat oven to 350 degrees
Yield: 2 large or 4 medium portions

One 5 pound **duckling**
Kosher salt and pepper
½ **orange** sliced thinly (with the skin on)
½ **apple** sliced thinly (with the skin on)
1 **small onion** (sliced thinly)
Make a Mirepoix of vegetables for the roasting pan:
1 **medium onion** peeled, sliced thick
2 **medium carrots** remove ends and slice thick
3 **ribs celery** washed, trimmed and sliced thick
5-6 **parsley stems**

Place mirepoix vegetables in a roasting pan that is just large enough to accommodate the duckling. *(The pan should be deep enough to keep fat from spattering the oven.)*
Remove duckling from the packaging and rinse thoroughly inside and out.
Pat dry with paper towels.
If there is a neck and organ package, place the neck in the roasting pan with the giblets and heart. Discard the liver, or reserve it for another use. *(At the Inn we make Duck Liver Pâté.)*
Place the duckling on a cutting board.
Cut excess skin off of neck area leaving about a 1" flap of skin. (This shrinks during roasting and keeps the breast meat basted).
Cut off the wing tips and the thin 2-boned wing section and place them in the roasting pan.
Season cavity generously with salt and pepper.
Fill the cavity with the sliced apple, onion and orange.
Tie drumsticks together using butcher's twine. They should overlap and close the cavity.
Place duckling in the roasting pan on top of the mirepoix and duck trimmings.
Roast for approximately 3½ hours until the skin is very crisp.
Basting is not necessary, as the fat under the skin does an excellent job on its own.
Remove the duck from the pan and place it on a wire rack in a baking dish for glazing.
The duckling can be held for up to 1 hour and glazed just before serving.
To make the glaze:
Combine in a blender: ¼ cup orange marmalade, 2 Tbs orange juice concentrate and 2 Tbs brandy and pulse until the mixture is smooth.
Baste duckling with the glaze. Broil until it is golden. Watch it carefully as it burns easily.

Osso Bucco with Gremolata

This braised boneless veal dish is made with readily available veal cubes, instead of veal center cut shanks. It tastes nearly the same, as well. This can be cooked in a Crock-Pot® or Dutch oven.

Yield: 6-8 servings
3 pounds **veal cubes for stew**, *trimmed of all fat and silver-skin*
Kosher salt and fresh ground black pepper
3 Tbs **flour for dusting**
3 Tbs **olive oil**
1 large **onion** *peeled, halved and sliced*
3 **whole carrots** *ends removed, peeled, sliced*
4 **ribs celery** *trimmed, washed sliced*
4 **cloves garlic** *peeled, sliced thin*
2 **bay leaves**
1 Tbs **fresh rosemary leaves**
2 cup **dry white wine**
one 24 ounce can **crushed all-purpose tomatoes**
Several **parsley stems**
4 cups **veal or strong low-salt beef broth**

To Make the Gremolata:

½ cup **flat Italian parsley leaves**
Zest from 2 lemons *(yellow part only)*
2 **garlic cloves** *peeled, finely diced*
6-8 **anchovy fillets** *finely chopped*
Combine ingredients and mix well.

Place trimmed veal cubes on a tray and season generously with salt and pepper.
Stir cubes to distribute seasoning to all sides of the cubes.
Sprinkle cubes with flour to lightly coat all sides.
Heat olive oil in heavy Dutch oven or skillet.

Brown the veal cubes in 3 or 4 batches, until veal has browned on all sides.
As the meat browns, remove it from the pot and place it in a separate dish or Crock-Pot® (if you're using that method).
After the veal has browned, add more oil if necessary, then add onions, carrots and celery.
Cook briefly on medium heat.
Add garlic, bay leaves and rosemary.
Add white wine.
Stir to deglaze any of the bits remaining from browning the veal.
Add tomatoes, parsley stems and veal stock.
Bring to a simmer.
Add the stock to the veal in Crock-Pot® or add the browned veal to the simmering liquid.
Cover Crock-Pot®, cook on high for six hours or until veal is fork tender.
OR put covered Dutch oven into 325 degree oven for two hours.
OR simmer over a low flame on top of the stove for about 2 hours or until fork tender.
Lift the tender veal from the cooking liquid.
Remove and discard bay leaves. Serve with the Gremolata on top or on the side.

A Culinary Journey with Chef Steve Yeanish

Roasted Rack of Lamb

This dish has been a staple at the Oley Valley Inn since our opening. American lamb is delicate so it's worth spending the extra money on it. Australian lamb is also good. New Zealand lamb is readily available, but it has a much stronger flavor. I love to serve a White Bean Ragoût with Garlic and Tomatoes with this lamb dish as well.
Tomato helps to cut the richness of the lamb.

Preheat oven to 400 degrees
Yield: Two 4 rib portions

One domestic or Australian lamb rib roast, *chime bone removed*
Kosher salt and cracked fresh ground pepper
2 Tbs **coarse-ground Dijon mustard**
2 Tbs **smooth Dijon mustard**
2 **cloves garlic** *peeled, finely chopped*
1 cup **breadcrumbs** *made from cubes of stale bread*
1 Tbs **melted butter**
1 tsp **fresh rosemary leaves** *chopped*
1 tsp **fresh thyme leaves** *chopped*
1 tsp **fresh marjoram leaves** *chopped*
1 tsp **flat leaf parsley** *chopped*
½ cup **veal demi-glace or strong beef stock** *(low salt)*
1 **shallot** *chopped*
¼ cup **Madeira wine**

Remove fat-cap layer from the bottom of the loin where the chime bone was removed.
Peel back the fat cap toward the tips of the rib bones.
Remove any fat between the rib bones, cutting down almost ½ inch to the loin of the lamb.
If your butcher has not already done this, French, or scrape the ends of the bones clean.
Rub the entire surface with kosher salt and freshly ground pepper.
Heat a skillet large enough to accommodate the entire rack.
Add 1 Tbs olive oil.
Add lamb loin, flesh-side down and sear.
When this is golden, stand the rib to brown the bottom.
Place the rack in a sauté pan in the oven.
For medium rare, roast approximately 12-15 minutes.
Check temperature with instant-read hand held thermometer.
Remove from oven when internal temperature reaches 140 degrees.
Place lamb in small baking pan. *Recipe continues on the following page.*

The Oley Valley Inn

Roasted Rack of Lamb
(continued)

Drain any fat from the sauté pan.
Chop breadcrumbs in food processor.
Add melted butter and herbs, then pulse to mix.
Combine both mustards with garlic.
Spread an even coat of mustard over entire browned surface of the lamb.
Sprinkle seasoned breadcrumbs over the mustard.
Return lamb to oven for an additional 5-7 minutes until crumbs are golden brown.
Remove from oven.
Cover lamb lightly with a foil tent and allow it to rest in a warm part of the stove.

The Rack of Lamb Sauce:
Add chopped shallot and any pan drippings to the sauté pan and sauté briefly.
Add demi-glace and Madeira wine and reduce until sauce thickens.
Carve lamb into 8 individual chops.
Place a mound of mashed potatoes or polenta on the center of a platter.
Arrange the chops around the center with bones overlapping.
Pour reduced sauce around the edge of lamb chops, then serve.

Asiago Polenta

Yield: 4 servings

4 cups **boiling water**
1 tsp **salt**
1 cup **cornmeal** (preferably Goya®)
½ cup **grated Asiago cheese** *mounded*
1 Tbs **chopped herbs** *(parsley, chives, etc.)*
Freshly ground black pepper to taste

Chef Says
A Polenta Alternative:
Spread cooked, seasoned polenta on a lightly oiled cookie sheet.
Spray surface of polenta with Pam® pan primer.
Cover with plastic wrap.
Refrigerate until cold.
Cut polenta into any shape, then carefully grill or sauté until golden.
Serve as a side dish, or as a base for a dish.

Set up a double boiler with one inch of boiling water in the bottom.
Pour 4 cups of boiling water into the top section of the double boiler.
Add the salt.
Gradually sprinkle the cornmeal over the surface of the water.
Whisk continuously to avoid lumps.
Cover and cook one hour until soft and smooth.
Stir in grated cheese and herbs.
Serve immediately.

Milos Country House Restaurant

John Milos owned a very popular restaurant called Milos Country House. After I graduated from the CIA, Brookside Chef Pat Gorey mentioned John wanted to speak with me. I arrived at the restaurant and John interviewed me for the job of Sauté Chef working on the line for lunch and dinner. I accepted with all the enthusiasm of a twenty year old and started immediately.

Milos Country House Restaurant was in an old building that used to be called Green Gables, and it was rumored to have had quite a colorful past. John, who was something of a celebrity, turned the place into a state-of-the-art restaurant. His wife, Jean, ran the front of the house.

The restaurant had two dining rooms. The largest featured long banquettes, subdued lighting and red and black table cloths. The other dining room was gold, and together they sat about 140 people.

This was the 1970s, so portions were large and the menu was quite extensive, featuring prime steaks, fresh seafood, chicken, their famous Roast Duckling and several veal dishes. A lobster tank offered Maine lobsters ranging in size from 1¼ pounds to 5 pounds. Many dishes such as Crêpes Suzette and Cherries Jubilee were flambéed tableside.

John knew his wines and the wine list was amazing for its time. It featured 400 bins from all over Europe.

The restaurant often served more than 300 covers on a Saturday night and around 100 at lunchtime, so the pace was intense. It was certainly equipped to handle these numbers. The kitchen was state-of-the-art and the line was impressive. They also cleverly put a time clock on the pickup line. (This was in the days before computerized ordering systems.) The time was stamped on the order to track it when it was placed. Order forms were printed with the entire menu, so a server only had to write the quantity in front of any item. They were way ahead of their time!

I learned the job quickly and actually grew to like it, but compliments were rarely heard. The work was really intense and the owners ran a tight ship. I worked a split shift there. After working lunch, I prepped a bit and took a break. At dinner, I sautéed dishes like veal, Beef Stroganoff or Lobster Newburg. I also finished their famous signature dishes, Roast Duckling and Chicken Michelle *(boneless half chicken, the leg stuffed with crab and wild rice and the breast with a traditional bread stuffing, then roasted)*. I also steamed Maine lobsters and lobster tails. We served thin, crisp onion rings on top of all the steaks. The onions were sliced thinly, covered in milk then dredged in flour and fried until crisp.

The restaurant often held private parties. On one occasion, a stuffed suckling pig was ordered. When I arrived at work that morning, the chefs were stuffing the piglet. They really packed in the stuffing and sewed up the belly cavity with butcher's twine. Then the pig was put into the deck oven to roast. After hours of careful tending, John stuck his nose into the oven just as the pig exploded, shooting stuffing all over the oven floor.

I worked at Milos for 18 months. Then out of the clear blue, Pat Gorey called and said "Congratulations Stevie, you're the new chef at Brookside!" Pat had resigned, and had strongly recommend to the Club House Committee that they hire me as his replacement.

The Oley Valley Inn

Potatoes Milos

These potatoes make a really nice brunch or side dish with eggs or omelets. Our potato cakes are flipped in the air with one swift, confident motion.

Yield: one 10 inch "cake" or 8 servings

6 **large Idaho potatoes** *peeled, sliced paper-thin*
1 **medium onion** *peeled, halved, sliced thinly*
½ cup **crisp bacon bits**
2 **Tbs cornstarch**
Kosher salt and freshly ground black pepper *to taste*
¼ cup **oil or bacon fat** *(or a combination of both)*

Rinse sliced potatoes in water.
Drain on paper or kitchen towels until dry.
Place potatoes in a large mixing bowl.
Sprinkle sliced onions and bacon bits over potatoes.
Dust surface with cornstarch.
Season with salt and pepper.

Toss mixture to evenly coat the potatoes with the seasoning.
Stir in onion and bacon.
Heat oil in a 10-inch, non-stick or cast iron skillet.
Pan must be hot, but not smoking.
Add the potato mixture.
Spread it evenly over the entire surface of the pan.
(This will more than fill the pan.)

Lower the heat to the point where the pan is still sizzling, but NOT smoking.
Cover the pan with an aluminum pie pan to trap the steam.

Cook for approximately 10-15 minutes.
Uncover pan.
Use a large spatula to invert the entire "cake" so the brown side is on top.
Continue cooking uncovered for about 15 more minutes.
Both surfaces should be brown and crisp and the center should be cooked through.
Invert potatoes onto a cutting board and cut into 8 wedges.
Serve hot.

Brookside Country Club Chef de Cuisine

Brookside Chef de Cuisine Steve

In April of 1976, at the ripe old age of 22, I started working as Chef de Cuisine at Brookside Country Club. Of course, I already knew the place like the back of my hand, but not from this position. So Chef Pat Gorey worked with me for a week, guiding me through the purchasing routines, and I became familiar with all the purveyors.

Warren, a 40-something year old retired Navy mess cook, was assistant chef. There were a lot of changes ahead for both of us. This was the 1970s and these were still the serious meat (prime rib and steaks) and potatoes days of Country Club Cuisine. Baked potatoes were still wrapped in foil and covered with sour cream. Frozen and canned vegetables were staples. Anything and everything was readily available prepared and pre-packaged by Sexton, Melani or Kraft. The first time I made real creamed spinach, a club member asked if it was Mrs. Stouffer's® Creamed Spinach and Vera, our waitress quickly replied, "No, it's Mr. Yeanish's!"

When I started as chef, not many vegetables were made-to-order. Take green beans, for example. They were dropped in a stock pot, covered with water and salted, then baking soda was added to retain the bright green color. After that they were boiled until tender, drained and cooled. When a customer ordered the beans they were re-heated in boiling water and buttered. Get the picture? Bright green, flavorless mush.

It was a hard sell by a still-wet-behind-the-ears chef, but eventually the beans were steamed as needed and sautéed to order.

As the 1970s rolled into the 1980s, I was gradually able to work more interesting dishes into the menu. We were still under the influence of classical French cooking. Years later, one of the members said to me, "When we found you, we found a diamond in the rough!" I made lots of mistakes, but fortunately learned from them.

Anyone who has ever worked in a private club has probably heard the comment, "Our dues pay your wages!" Fortunately, I got on well with most of the club members. There were only a few times when members were losing at a card game or after a bad round of golf that they snapped at the kitchen or wait staff.

Many members would eat lunch at the club almost every day, then return for dinner several evenings a week. I couldn't, for the life of me, understand why they never got tired of eating the same old things, over and over again. I could recognize the members by what they ordered or their special requests. Some were quite odd, so they were memorable. It's not every day someone orders a grilled cheese on burned rye bread with thinly sliced, peeled tomato!

Cooking at home was not always a top priority for some of the members, or their spouses, so we often had down-home comfort foods as lunch specials, which were well-received. Meatloaf and Braised Brisket always sold out. I really got a kick out of the waitress returning to the kitchen to ask if the mashed potatoes were made from scratch or instant, so I finally said, "Tell them if they can't taste the difference, then they don't deserve to know!"

My Sous Chef during the 1970s was Dennis, a wonderful guy, who is still a good friend. He was an eager chef and had worked in several area restaurants. We always had a stock pot simmering and we made incredible soups. You name it, we made it. We only ever disagreed on one thing—fresh clams versus canned clams in the chowder. I like fresh and Dennis preferred them canned and chopped. The debate went on. Both efforts were good, so I eventually started using canned or even frozen clams, but I still use finely-chopped fresh clams right at the end to finish the soup.

One of our favorite members became terminally ill with cancer and his beautiful wife cared for him. We gladly made soups for her to feed him, as they were one of the few things he could still eat. She picked up our soup whenever she had a chance. We were glad to comfort this kind man and help his devoted wife with his care.

There was a group of ladies who met on Saturdays for lunch and always sat at the Mid, a coveted round table at the end of the grillroom. The same women seemed to have complicated, special request orders every week: "The bacon can't be too crisp, because it hurts my mouth. Can we see the chicken salad before we order it? We want to make sure it has big chunks, and not a lot of mayonnaise. I want a sardine and onion sandwich. Center-cut onion please. Is it real turkey breast or the fake stuff? Chop my Chef's Salad fine, no ham, 3 shrimp and 1 tablespoon of fat free

Chef Steve at Brookside

dressing tossed through it. Have what's-her-name in the kitchen make my usual, and tell her to not burn the toast this time, etc."

The last straw was when a couple of women insisted that the corned beef they ordered was actually ham. They all fell silent when I calmly appeared at their table, speaking clearly and firmly, "Ladies, you insist on corned beef being *very lean*, so we use closely-trimmed corned beef rounds *not* corned beef brisket, which is much too fatty! I assure you that I *do not, nor* have I *ever* substituted ham for corned beef! Thank you and enjoy your lunch." They were speechless as I walked away from their table.

There was a certain gentleman who frequently dined at the club. He had very specific tastes, and only liked things prepared his way. One thing he was very definite about was his baked potato. He insisted it had to be small. The only problem was the potatoes we bought were 100-count Idahos, which means every potato was big and about the same size.

"For the tenth time, I only have one size potato!" I snapped, then I thought of a quick solution. I cut the potato in thirds, jammed the two ends together, made a new slit, then fluffed it open and the customer was happy. Lesson learned: "Dwell on the solution, not the problem."

In Brookside's formal dining room, the décor was plain and utilitarian. Walls and linens were white. They had simple black leather chairs. The room really needed help, so I asked for some bud vases and the manager agreed to order cut flowers. When dining in other fine restaurants, I was disappointed to see how casual dining had become, so I really wanted to improve the dining experience at the club.

Steve relaxing

The cuisine at the club really evolved rapidly in those days. We started with the typical steak house fare of the time and gradually developed a more gourmet menu. I had learned Continental cuisine at the CIA with a major influence of French cooking and classical technique, but the tide was changing and new trends were on the horizon.

Pioneering French chef Michel Guérard created Cuisine Minceur, which shunned fat, heavy creams and favored healthy, lighter preparations. Cauliflower purées, and yogurt were substituted in sauces; butter was never used.

Creole chefs gave us Gumbo made with okra and a slow-cooked dark roux and Jambalaya. Paul Prudhomme, the new star Cajun chef of New Orleans, gave us Blackened Redfish and Shrimp Étouffée. Blackened Catfish and Blackened Steaks soon followed.

We started to see Southwest food influences around this time. The jalapeño pepper arrived, then the habanero, pablano, Scotch bonnet and many others were becoming commonplace.

Foods from all over were gaining popularity. Diners realized Mexican food was far more than Taco Bell®. Caribbean food was catching on, too. Customers were looking for new flavors and dishes influenced by hot trends. Purveyors were beginning to market mini Empanadas, Spring Rolls, Jerked Chicken, Jalepeño Poppers and Buffalo Wings. The restaurant scene was taking on a far more casual outlook. The theme restaurant franchises were bursting out all over.

Vietnamese and Thai cuisine distinguished themselves from the old traditional regional Chinese restaurants by using unfamiliar items with distinctive flavors, combinations and preparations. Other ethnic foods emerged as well. Italian restaurants went beyond Spaghetti and Meatballs or Breaded Veal Parmesan. Northern Italian restaurants were achieving the same sophisticated status as fine French restaurants.

Then along came Fusion Cuisine, where clever chefs mixed foods, flavors and techniques of different cuisines. What nerve! This must have really raised the feathers of purists, who knew only one way to prepare anything.

I was always somewhat involved in the dining room operations because there were seven different club managers during my time at Brookside. If the manager was away, I often had to book banquets, etc.

I started doing Caesar Salad and Steak Diane tableside for diners when time allowed. We usually had two or three dining rooms, and frequently there was a banquet in the ballroom *and* only three of us were working on the line. So sometimes it was quite a disruption if I had to finish or carve a dish tableside.

Now was the time to step up to the plate and break out to new taste adventures. I'll admit it was really scary at first, even though I had a solid education in ingredients and cooking methods. New trends were out there and customers were curious. It was up to the individual chef to learn about these new foods. You couldn't just read about it; you had to go out and taste it. Newspapers were flooded with reviews and articles on these new establishments. And the best part was, they weren't only in large cities or ethnic neighborhoods anymore. They were moving out to the suburbs.

Years later, while I was visiting the Napa Valley, I looked up my CIA classmate, Mark Derkhising. I asked him about some of the hot shot chefs, who were opening new eateries and getting a lot of media attention. His response was, "Don't be envious. Many have limited talent and specialize in one style of food. They're a flash in the pan, because when the tide or trend changes, they are stuck with their limited abilities."

He continued to say, "We're both very fortunate to have our CIA background. We know food and we know how to use the appropriate cooking technique for the product we are using. We can try any unfamiliar food, spice or herb and create new dishes using the fundamentals we learned in school." I walked away with renewed confidence that day.

Frankly, that's the basis of all good cooking, when you get down to it. Many cuisines prepare similar dishes, like Empanadas, my Grammy's Cornish Pasties, Knishes, Strudels and so on. Cooking became a lot more challenging and fun. If we could get our customers to try it and they liked it, we were set. For the most part, customers were receptive.

You can't change an entire menu overnight, but if you do it gradually, it will work. I've learned you can never give up on the old standards, which will be around forever. They helped me to round out my menu, so there was something for everyone. We had many conservative customers who weren't interested in my new fancy soup, but enjoyed a classic Oxtail with Barley Soup. As James Beard once said, "Even a hot dog can be a wonderful experience, especially a really good quality one on a nice roll with your favorite condiments and the perfect setting."

A fellow chef, Pierre Rausch, once said to me, "If you don't continue to offer your guests new and interesting dishes, they will eventually get bored with *your* restaurant and go somewhere else to find them."

I thought about his comment and realized he was right. If you don't change, *your* customer will leave you and your competition will become their new favorite place to spend their money. I had lived in my comfort zone long enough. Now, my great new challenge was to travel outside of it.

A Culinary Journey with Chef Steve Yeanish

Celebration Cakes

When I started working as chef, the ovens and ranges at Brookside were more than thirty years old. The thermostats were shot and the ovens baked unevenly at two temperatures, hot or hotter. One time I pulled a cake out of the oven and the bottom was burned black, but the center was raw. Talk about frustrating!

I showed the charred cakes to a very active Brookside board member and he understood my frustration, but parts for the ovens were no longer available. Thankfully, the Board approved purchasing new equipment, and soon a double convection oven, vertical broiler, six-burner flat top ranges and griddles arrived.

Top Photo: Detail of top layer of the cake
Middle Photo: The rest of the cake

Some of Steve's cakes that were made for weddings, birthdays and other gala celebrations at Brookside Country Club.

The Oley Valley Inn

The Safari Party

One of my favorite club members entertained often, graciously and with flair. She had the best parties! A memorable one was her husband's birthday celebration. He was a Leo, so the lion theme was carried throughout the party, starting with the invitations.

My friend Jan arranged ferns and palm trees everywhere. Lush greens and tropical foliage flanked the entrance. Jan created incredible tiered centerpieces with palm tree risers that held votive candles and sprays of exotic orchids.

There were exotic stuffed animals and a large trunk full of pith helmets for the guests. All kinds of great foods were arranged at stations in a large tent set up next to the ballroom.

The hostess gave clever names to the party food. Ribs were called Monkey Bones. Chickens cooked on a spit were called Parched Parrot. White Gazpacho became Missionary Stew.

I carved an elephant out of two blocks of ice. The staff wore khaki trousers, Banana Republic® tee shirts and pith helmets. As the guests arrived, jungle noises played in the background. That was one fun party!

Steve, wearing a pith helmet, prepares Roast Chicken, also known as Parched Parrot.

Chef Steve had to use a fan to keep the smoke from the barbeque out of the ballroom.

A Culinary Journey with Chef Steve Yeanish

For the Safari Party I created a three-dimensional lion for a member's birthday cake. It was magnificent. I started with a three-foot oblong mirror and cakes were stacked vertically to create the contour of the body, which I carved, then covered with frosting in shades of tan and brown. I was asked by the hostess to dramatically present the cake at the appropriate time. On the afternoon of the party, I had a brainstorm and collected a five foot long leopard print scarf, black spray-on hair dye (which washes out), a gold hoop bracelet and a pair of black queen-size pantyhose. Then I burned as many corks as I could find and soon I was all set.

Everyone was excited about the evening, which got off to an exciting start when one of the centerpieces caught fire. I quickly lifted it off the table and extinguished the flames with a pitcher of water. The party was a big success and it was soon time for the cake.

My friend Beth was one of the waitresses back then. She had agreed to help me get ready for the dramatic presentation of the birthday cake. Secretly Beth and I disappeared into the men's employee locker room. I stripped down to my black briefs and struggled into the pantyhose. All I can say is, God bless you women—what you go through to look gorgeous! I am 6' 2" and weighed about 185 pounds back then. Beth and I nearly killed ourselves laughing as I got into those queen-size pantyhose! Beth helped me to blacken my torso with burned cork, while I did my chest and face. Then I tied the leopard skin around my midsection like a loincloth. With my face blackened, and my blond hair sprayed jet-black and standing on end, I split the bracelet and made it into a nose ring.

Steve arranging gala celebrations

I got into position with the birthday cake on a draped mobile cart. On cue, just as the sound of *Happy Birthday* filled the air, I strolled into the party. Once they finally recognized me, everyone howled with laughter, especially the surprised hostess. She was beside herself with delight. Although everyone thought it was planned, she knew it was my final addition to the party. The cake was cut and served under the tent while I flambéed Bananas Foster in true safari fashion. Another staff member had rented a gorilla suit. We had so much fun that night!

The Oley Valley Inn

Steve dressed as the Pancake Lady

There were many parties and black tie affairs which lasted late into the night. At most of these affairs, we served breakfast around 12:30 or 1:00 in the morning. This was kind of a drag. After a long day of getting ready and a night of working, we were already tired. We prepped everything ahead of time so we only had to cook bacon, sausage, hash-browned potatoes and scramble eggs. This was an easy job.

One year, the party was pretty low-key, so I decided to liven it up a bit. I borrowed an old, matronly-looking long dress, which was huge, with a big gray and white gathered skirt. I sprayed my hair black, tied it up with red and black rags, then blackened my face and arms with burned cork. Bright red lipstick and lots of gold bracelets came next. Then I padded "my boobs" to the hilt with more rags.

An electric griddle was set up on the buffet. Just as breakfast was about to be served, the Pancake Lady made her way into the dining room and proceeded to make pancakes. Everyone was already pretty merry by this point, but the room grew quiet as the members noticed this unfamiliar guest. As I started making my flap-jacks, I hollered over to the crowd, "Don't y'all be bashful, Shugga, I got flap-jacks for all of you!" They finally realized it was me and everyone had a really good laugh.

A Culinary Journey with Chef Steve Yeanish

Culinary Competitions

My Cocoa Painting on Pastillage won a Blue Ribbon for Best in Show

I was becoming more and more comfortable with my job at Brookside. My confidence was growing and I was baking a lot of cakes, too. The International Foodservice Executives of America was sponsoring the Culinary Salon at the Armory in Philadelphia. Mr. Partridge, the club manager, gave me his blessing, then I sent in my registration and started planning my display. I was intimidated at first, but determined. The show coincided with the 60th Anniversary of Brookside, so I used that as my theme and entered individual pieces in several categories.

My centerpiece was a four-tiered 60th Anniversary Cake decorated in shades of chocolate. Then I created a cocoa painting of the clubhouse exterior on a flat, oval pastillage platter. I used melted cocoa butter dissolved in different amounts of cocoa powder to make lighter and darker tones, and framed it with marzipan rolled and coiled into a crescent of roses in different stages of bloom. The entire marzipan border was then carefully browned with a blowtorch to give it an antique effect. It was displayed in front of the anniversary cake on a pastillage plate stand. Then, I sculpted two 14 inch tall cherubs in tallow. There were two other 12 inch decorated cakes, one trimmed in yellow and white, the other in chocolate.

The judges awarded my cocoa painting a Blue Ribbon for Best Piece in Show and Second Place and Honorable Mention for two of my cakes. The club was very proud of my achievement. I got the bug to do more!

The Delaware Valley Chef's Association sponsored the next salon at the Adams Mark Hotel in Philadelphia. I was eager and entered an edible centerpiece and four individual cold food displays in the Mini Buffet category. I also entered two decorated individual cakes, a tiered cake and a marzipan sculpture. I had my work cut out for me, so I began planning my entries and created many sculptures ahead of time.

The Edible Centerpiece was a butter sculpture of a dramatic fish poised with its tail in the air and a large open mouth. I stored it in the walk-in cooler until showtime, then made two other small butter pieces as garnishes for my cold trays.

The Cold Food Displays:

Duckling Galantine
The duck is de-boned and the meat left intact with the skin in one large piece. This is then spread with a rich ground-meat mixture, called forcemeat, with garnishes. Then it is rolled and tied with butcher's twine in cheesecloth and poached very slowly in stock until cooked. It is usually served as an appetizer after being chilled and sliced.

Whole Poached Salmon
This was presented cold, standing vertically on its belly with the shin partially removed to expose the flesh decorated with piped cream cheese and bits of colored aspic. (Clear, or in this case colored with various puréed vegetables, reduced gelatinous stock flavored with wine.) Carved vegetable "flowers" and aspic croutons (uniform shaped cubes of aspic cut and used as garnish) surrounded the fish.

Chaudfroid Ham
This was the third piece I presented. It was a fake ham, similar to the one I made for my Senior Garde-Manger Project at the CIA. It was decorated with wild mushrooms that were actually carved out of raw vegetables made to resemble a cluster of mushrooms growing in the wild. Complete with a shiny foil frill, it was surrounded by thin slices of ham rolled into roses in various stages of bloom. The tray was finished with radishes carved as mushrooms.

Roasted Capon
My final piece was a cooked breast that was de-boned and sliced. The breast cavity was then refilled with mashed potatoes, using gelatin to firm them. The breast area was covered in white chaud-froid, and decorated with a geometric pattern of colored aspic cut from thin sheets. The entire piece was glazed with clear aspic. Then the sliced meat was fanned out in front of the capon in a mirror image of the bird, and it gracefully wound around the sides back to the thigh area of the legs. Foil frills covered the exposed tips of the legs.

My Individual Cakes were both 14 inch rounds. One was my favorite, shades of chocolate with frosted chocolate roses. The other cake was iced with pale yellow sides and a white surface. I had just mastered the art of color striping using a dual-colored pastry bag. *(Two colors of icing are used in different chambers of the bag, so the piped frosting comes out in a stripe or variegated tones.)*

I copied real pansies and piped perfect, detailed replicas in shades of blue, yellow, purple and lavender. The crescent of pansies on the surface of the cake was accented with white and green lilies of the valley. It looked magnificent!

The tiered cake I presented was all white with three tiers and sugar columns *(every exposed surface must be edible)*. It was decorated in ornately piped white frosting and trimmed in pastel spring flowers.

A Culinary Journey with Chef Steve Yeanish

My final piece was one of my favorites. I had made it for one of the Holiday Buffets at Brookside. There were five individual pieces sculpted in marzipan *(a mixture of finely ground-blanched almonds and sugar, kind of like edible clay)*. There was a lamp post adorned with a wreath, holly and red ribbon. A young girl stood with a songbook open on top of her head in front of three whimsical Victorian Christmas carolers poised in song. They were about 12 inches tall. The first, a jolly looking character with rosy cheeks, glasses, a top hat and long coat bore an uncanny resemblance to the club manager, Mr. Partridge. The middle, red-headed character with her hands in a muff looked a lot like Thelma. The last figure was a tall, thin blond fellow who resembled me, or so I was told.

This was an ambitious project, and I worked many nights until the early hours of the morning. On the night before the show, I slept at the club on the floor of the boardroom. I had borrowed a station wagon to take my work to the show and started loading it around 3 a.m. with linens, skirting, floral pieces and decorations. All of my pieces had to be arranged on trays or mirrors at the show, so packing was very important.

I picked up Thelma and Margo, and we arrived at the Adams Mark at about dawn. Judging was at eight that morning, so we carried everything in and I set it up. By the time we finished, we were exhausted. It felt like we had run a marathon, so we found a place for breakfast, and killed time until we could return to the salon at noon.

I won a Second Place prize for the Mini-Buffet. My Duckling Galantine was awarded Best Duckling Piece in the show with a special prize sponsored by Maple Leaf Ducklings. The individual cakes, tiered cake and marzipan Victorian carolers were all awarded First Place Blue Ribbons.

It was my shining moment. All that hard work had paid off! Several club members even traveled to the city to see the show and it was shown on a local news broadcast. Unfortunately, my Victorian carolers were stolen.

The Delaware Valley Chef's Association sponsored another show at the Holiday Inn in King of Prussia. This was being judged by the American Culinary Federation (ACF), which had both established guidelines and a new set of criteria for scoring culinary competitions. We would have to follow the same rules as the Culinary Olympics held in Frankfurt Germany where the *really* big chefs competed. All work was scored with a point system and ribbons were awarded for the total amount of points scored, not a first for the best work, etc. If no one scored a first place, then it wasn't given.

My piece was done in tallow. It featured a bird with its nest of young on a tree branch. I created a base covered in tallow, then a nest of tallow pieces rolled and shaped like twigs. The nest held three young birds and the mother bird was positioned over them. It was a balancing act trying to get the large bird far enough away from the nest to look real, but close enough to keep it in balance. It became very frustrating. On the buffet was a spring flower arrangement of forsythia and yellow roses. This swept up behind the piece and set it off beautifully.

My Cold Tray presentation was Pâté of Rabbit en Croute

The pâté is baked in a special hinged pan lined with a short pastry. A portion remained whole, and the slices were presented in an overlapping display, with the contents of each slice and the placement of the garnishes baked into the pâté. A silver hâtelet, a decorative skewer topped with a running rabbit, held a colorful *array of vegetables. This was inserted into the uncut block of pâté and the tray was decorated with a butter sculpture of a rabbit.*

My Fish Tray presentation was Poached Salmon Fillets

Identical pieces of center-cut salmon were placed end to end on my salmon board—a wooden cutting board, which featured a brass fishhead and tail. (I purchased this board at Hess Brothers in Allentown.) Each fillet was garnished with a slice of lemon and a sprig of dill, then coated with aspic. The mirror that held the salmon was surrounded by bundles of steamed asparagus tied with leeks, and mushroom caps intricately carved with three intertwined fishes.

My final piece was a Roast Baron of Beef a very well-trimmed and roasted strip loin. *The trick was to get the roast cooked just enough so it retained a nice red color. A portion remained whole on the tray, and the slices were presented in a row impaled on a hâtelet decorated with the head of a horned steer. This was surrounded by an array of vegetables and accompanied by artichoke bottoms filled with tiny peas. A butter sculpture of a farm girl carrying a bucket of vegetables completed the tray.*

For the pastry pieces, I did my favorite chocolate on chocolate cake, and a hexagonally-shaped cake in yellow carefully covered with a white lattice all around and above the cake. *This was greuling and precision was critical, as any imperfection showed. Small, dark yellow and orange roses finished the piece. I also entered a small round cocoa painting on pastillage of a stone bridge and a stream in a European village. This was my best work and the three pieces were scored together as one piece.*

I knew going into this show many of the rules and trends had changed. Chaud-froid pieces were now passé and a lighter, cleaner look was in. There was some incredible work at this show. The judges were tough. My CIA teacher, Chef Fritz Sonnenschmidt, was one of them. The Mini-Buffet received a Third Place. One of the judges was available to review your entries and show where points were lost.

My last mistake was the most significant—my garnishes did not equal the number of portions on my trays. I would have done this if I had known, but I had been so concerned about the flow of the display, and covering empty space with an eye-appealing presentation. I heard many favorable comments from fellow chefs and guests. They said how clean my work was, and how well the presentation was pulled together.

Several years later, the Berks-Lehigh Chef's Association held a show at the Abraham Lincoln Hotel in Reading. It was a small show, but was being judged by American Culinary Federations standards.

I had sculpted a really great Buddha out of tallow. It had nice clean lines, an expressive face and a big belly. My father made two shadow boxes and I purchased enough green fabric for a top cloth and trim to hand-pleat a ribbon of green around the exposed area of both risers. The table was skirted in a wild, sheer, floral fabric leftover from a club luau. The tropical centerpiece had lots of variegated foliage and orchids. It really was a great look.

One tray was a Smoked Pork Chop on a round of fresh pineapple and decorated with a fan of snow peas. A carved vegetable palm tree graced the tray and a pig (carved out of a yam) was sleeping lazily under it. They liked the Buddha, and I received an Honorable Mention.

Teaching Teens

Seeking a change of pace after a few years, I left Brookside with a bit of fanfare. I'd always wanted to teach and thought of it as something to do when I got tired of working in the kitchen. I enjoyed demonstrating techniques, so I replied to an ad for a trade school baking instructor. The interview went well, and I was hired as a full time substitute teacher because the bakeshop teacher was on medical leave. The last part of the interview should have raised a red flag, but because of my naiveté, it went right over my head. The Shop, as it was called, was expected to turn the bakery products the students made into cash on a regular basis.

The teachers at the school were all strictly union, but I couldn't join. The pay was $12 an hour, but first I had to get a teaching certificate, and take the Pennsylvania Occupational Competency Test at a technical school where the baking exam was given. It was pass or fail, and the test was very intense because you had to produce a lot of product in a very short time. In four hours I had to produce: bread dough shaped into bread loaves and rolls, sweet yeast dough for both individual and large breakfast cakes, a decorated cake, pies and cookies. Fortunately, I planned well and used my time wisely, so I was able to finish baking everything required. Then the examiner congratulated me. I had passed, and was certified to teach baking in Pennsylvania.

On my first day, I felt like Daniel thrown to the lions. My name was the first thing students had to learn, so *"Yeanish rhymes with Danish"* became a sing-song for some kids. The culinary program featured morning and afternoon sessions that were divided into three different sections. Students rotated through sections during each marking period.

The other teachers were very competent and taught students about all aspects of a professional kitchen. Each student was responsible for learning basic competencies, and they were tested by doing projects. Gradually, they progressed through, and mastered each skill on the list. The students also cooked and served lunch to both the faculty and the general public. The school had a small dining room with about six tables, where students waited on tables, and the modest tips went toward expenses.

The bakeshop was very well-equipped with three sizes of mixers, a wind-mill oven, refrigeration units, proof box and maple-topped baker's tables. There were dough presses, ingredient bins and a small storeroom behind the locker room where students changed into their whites. A classroom connected the locker room to the actual bakeshop area.

Every day started in the classroom with theory, which was the biggest challenge of all. Most of the students seemed to be there just to get out of regular high school classes. Don't get me wrong, there were some serious culinary students, but many kids were classified as EMRs, or Educationally Mentally Retarded and they were learning to be utility workers or dishwashers.

I quickly learned the biggest obstacle most kids had was a lack of basic math or measurements. Straightforward recipes written in weight were one thing, but if the kids had to convert weights to tablespoons or cups, they were hopeless. Dough and batters were often ruined because no one measured accurately. Or they couldn't be bothered to make the correct measurements and necessary mathematical conversions. My frustration level got higher and higher.

For weeks at a time, we'd work on these concepts every day covering basics such as:

The Oley Valley Inn

3 teaspoons = 1 tablespoon
16 tablespoons = 1 cup
2 cups = one pint
2 pints = one quart
4 quarts = 1 gallon
16 ounces = one pound
And one cup of flour does not *weigh as much as one cup of sugar.*

Then, we would go into the bakeshop, and have to produce products to sell in the cafeteria. All the kids ever wanted to make was chocolate chip cookies. They'd double the amount of chocolate chips in the recipe, then cookies would magically disappear while cooling until there was nothing left to sell in the cafeteria.

The last straw was when one of my students stuck his hand into a running mixer. He had been mixing cookie dough when he dropped a teaspoon into the bowl of a 30-quart floor-model Hobart mixer. That's one powerful mixer! The flat paddle caught him squarely on the back of his hand, which swelled beyond belief.

Fortunately, I was nearby and got him to the school nurse immediately. He was in pain, but as high as a kite. I soon found out the teacher was *always* responsible for *whatever* happened, so I decided it wasn't worth the risk. Fortunately, Brookside welcomed me back with open arms.

Some Common Cooking Terms:

Demi-Glace

A reduced stock, made by slowly cooking veal and/or beef stock and red wine or Madeira until it is reduced by half.
The result is a thick glaze that coats a spoon. This intense mixture is used as a base for many other sauces.

Mirepoix

A mixture of diced carrots, onions, celery and sometimes herbs sautéed in butter. Mirepoix is used to season sauces, soups and stews, or as a bed on which to braise food, usually meats or fish.

Roux

A mixture of flour and fat slowly cooked over low heat. It is then used to thicken mixtures such as soups and sauces. There are three classic roux—white, blond and brown. The color and the flavor of each is determined by the length of time the mixture is cooked.

Slurry

A thin paste of water and flour or cornstarch that is stirred into hot soups, stews and sauces, and used as a thickener. After the slurry is added, the mixture should be stirred and cooked for several minutes in order for the flour to lose its raw taste and achieve its full thickening power.

to Sweat

A technique by which ingredients, particularly vegetables, are cooked in a small amount of fat over low heat. With this method, the ingredients soften without browning, thus extracting their flavors.

Water Bath

To place a container (pan, bowl, soufflé dish, etc.) of food in a large, shallow pan of warm water, which surrounds the food with gentle heat. This technique is designed to cook delicate dishes such as custard, sauces and savory mousses without breaking or curdling them.

A Culinary Journey with Chef Steve Yeanish

Pie Crust

Makes one 9 or 10 inch single crust

1⅓ cups **all purpose flour**
½ tsp **salt**
½ cup **vegetable shortening OR** ¼ cup **shortening** and 3 Tbs **lard**
3-4 Tbs **ice water OR** 3-4 Tbs **fruit juice**

Combine flour and salt in a mixing bowl.
Add shortening.
Using pastry blender or knife cut the shortening into small bits, about the size of peas.
You can also "rub" this mixture together with your hands.
Be careful not to over-mix at this point.
Add the liquid, just 3 tablespoons at first.
Continue mixing just until the dough comes together into a ball.
Add additional liquid gradually only as needed.
Shape the dough into a round, flat disc.
Roll out dough on a floured surface into the size needed for a crust.
It is best to chill the dough in the refrigerator for half an hour.

CHEF SAYS
Variations can also be added to enhance the flavor of the piecrust you are baking:
Different spices such as cinnamon or nutmeg,
Grated fruit zest,
Herbs such as parsley, chives, thyme

Chef Steve's Buffet and Ice Sculpture
L. The buffet with the Lobster People

R. Detail showing the Lobster People

The Oley Valley Inn

Short Crust or Pâte Sucrée

This is a sweet dough used for tart shells.

Makes one 10-12 inch pastry circle

2 cups **all purpose flour**
½ tsp **salt**
¼ cup **sugar** *(omit this if you are making a savory or quiche crust)*
12 Tbs (6 ounces) **frozen or very cold sweet butter** *cut into very small pieces*
¼ cup **ice water or fruit juice**
2 **egg yolks**

Combine all ingredients in the bowl of a food processor.
Use pulse motions *(turning machine on and off)* until the mixture looks like fine meal.
Note: mixture should *not* come together into a ball.
Put dough into a large plastic bag.
Squeeze the mixture until it comes together.
Shape it into a round, flat disc.
Wrap dough.
Chill it for at least 30 minutes in refrigerator.
Roll dough out on floured surface.

Chef Steve's Neptune Buffet
Neptune is sculpted in tallow

Detail from buffet showing pastry fishes

A Culinary Journey with Chef Steve Yeanish

Cookie or Graham Cracker Crust

This is suitable for a cheesecake. I sometimes add chopped nuts or other spices to flavor the crust.

Makes one 9 or 10 inch crust

1½ cups **graham cracker crumbs**
(or you can substitute any kind of cookie to make crumbs in your food processor)
⅓ cup **granulated sugar**
⅓ cup **melted butter**

Rub the ingredients together with your hands, or mix in the food processor.
A simple way to test if there is enough butter is to squeeze the dough in your hand.
If it holds its shape like wet sand, it is fine.
If its crumbly or dry, the crust won't hold together when baked, so add more butter.
If it is too wet, the crust will be very difficult to cut when baked, so add more crumbs.

Mr. Partridge, "Mr. P"

My good friend Mr. Partridge, the Club Manager of Brookside, left the club in the late 1970s. Still distinguished and dapper for his age, he managed a club in the Philadelphia suburbs and I still saw him occasionally.

Mr. P. and his wife, Sally, loved to go antiquing at estate auctions. Once they both bid on an old apple peeler, which was razor-sharp and in excellent condition. Later they had a good laugh when they found out they had accidentally bid against each other without realizing it.

When they found out I collected old kitchen tools, they gave me the apple peeler, much to my surprise! I've used it happily for many years. It was even patented on my birthday. It works better than the newer models, as it cuts less of the flesh off when it peels.

Another time, Mr. P. came into the kitchen of the club and gave me an old, beautifully-finished hinged box. He said, "I saw this and thought of you. I know you'll appreciate it."

Inside was an old maple rolling pin with ball bearings. In the bottom of the box was a cloth sleeve for the pin, and a perfectly hemmed and neatly folded canvas pastry cloth. The box was obviously hand-made to fit the pie maker's tools and was at least 75 years old. I was deeply grateful. These pie maker's tools are now on permanent display in the Garden Room of the Inn.

My parents and I spent a great afternoon with Mr. P and unfortunately he died shortly after our visit. I lost a great friend that day.

At his funeral service I shared my condolences with his family and told them, "Mr Partridge has touched more lives than you will ever know. It was an honor to have known this wonderful man, who helped me, and so many others over the years."

Moravian Sugar Cake

The Moravians originally came from Bohemia in the Czech Republic and settled in Pennsylvania.

Preheat oven to 350 degrees
Makes seven cakes

In a large bowl mix:
2 cups **granulated sugar**
2 tsp **salt**
2 cups **hot mashed potatoes**

Then add:
4 **eggs**, *beaten*
3 sticks **melted margarine**
3 packages **active dry yeast** dissolved in 2 cups **warm potato water** (105-110°F) *(reserved from cooked potatoes)*
8 cups **sifted all purpose flour** *(if necessary, add 1½ heaping tablespoons more flour)*
Cover and let the dough rise to the top of the lid.
Punch down dough and spread it into 7 greased and floured 8-inch pans.
Let dough rise again until it is not sticky to the touch.
Sprinkle the top with brown sugar and cinnamon.
Make holes in the top and fill them with melted butter or margarine.
Bake at 350° degrees for 20–25 minutes, checking frequently.

Many hours of preparation go into a well-planned event.

A Culinary Journey with Chef Steve Yeanish

Advice to a Young Chef

You can't please everyone, no matter how hard you try. This is just an impossible task. People have so many different expectations.

This is true whether you're discussing food, clothing, art or anything in between. Some people eat to live, others live to eat. Fast food eaten at 35 m.p.h. may be considered good food. There are many folks who just eat for sustenance. I know there are people who are content to eat the same things for lunch or dinner every day. I also know there are young toddlers who eat baby food for so long their parents find it impossible to transition them to real food. I suppose that has to do with the convenience of it, but I can't remember us ever eating jars of baby food when we were kids. We ate table food as soon as we were able.

For me, it is unbearable to sit at a table and hear a kid scream, "I don't like that!" Chances are they never even tasted it before and it's just unfamiliar to them. Parenting isn't easy, I realize, but neither is running a restaurant with 20 employees, and feeding at least 100 people the meal of their dreams within a four-hour time frame.

I grew up eating food that was not only nutritious, but tasty and varied. The nine of us rarely, if ever, ate out, and when I was a kid fast food was only just beginning to come on the scene. We tasted our first McDonald's® burgers and fries back when the burgers cost about 25 cents each.

I always taste all the new convenience and pre-packaged foods at trade shows. You name it, and chances are it is available frozen, canned or ready to just microwave and serve. Some of it is very good, but it's never, ever, as good as what can be made from scratch. They make some good clam chowder, but I make great clam chowder—all the time.

I try to explain to my new, and especially the young, employees the difference between good and great. Let's compare cheeseburgers. You could stop at Burger King® and get a cheeseburger with melted cheese on the patty, a thin slice of tomato, some onion, a piece of iceberg lettuce, and maybe some ketchup, mustard or mayo and a pickle on top. I would call that an okay-to-good burger.

Now the next day, we want a *great* cheeseburger. That's going to be a bit more involved, but hopefully it will be worth it. We go to a really good butcher or market and pickup some ground beef. If we're not sure, we ask the butcher which grind would be the best for burgers. He recommends a lean ground chuck because it has lots of flavor, and just enough fat to be juicy when it's cooked. We move on to the baker and choose a chewy, crusty, fresh-baked kaiser roll, or maybe an onion roll. Then we stop and pickup some cheese. I am not a big American cheese fan. You like cheddar? Did you ever try Muenster, or Swiss? Pick your favorite. We go on to the produce section for vine-ripened tomatoes and a sweet Vidalia® or a red onion. The bright green leaf lettuce is so fresh and crisp. The deli has barrel-cured pickles and some basil-flavored mayonnaise as well.

We head home and fire up the grill, but don't let it get too hot. Then we wash our hands and the produce; peel the onion; slice the tomato and onion; cut some pickle wedges; split the rolls in half; season the ground beef with some salt and freshly ground black pepper. Now, carefully pat the meat into a patty, not too thick, and don't overwork the meat. When it is just a little bit bigger than the size of the roll, we put it on the grill. Don't be poking at it! After it sears nicely on one side, turn it over, just once. If you like it pink, we'll put the cheese on now to melt. We could toast the roll a bit on the grill, if you like. Now put some of that basil mayonnaise on the roll, or ketchup and mustard, too, if you like. When the burgers are done, build your favorite. Mine would be topped with a nice slice or two of onion and tomato. I like a little cracked pepper and kosher salt too, and just enough lettuce to fit the roll, and a wedge of that pickle on the side. Grab an ice cold drink, go outside on a warm summer evening, then sit back and enjoy what I guarantee will be the best burger you have ever eaten.

If your new employee is salivating and smiling, they get the idea. If you have a smart-ass who asks why bother, then show 'em the door!

Cooking has achieved unprecedented popularity. There are serious home cooks of every age and gender, as well as prime-time television and celebrity chefs. Thousands of new cookbooks and periodicals cover all types of cuisines from Down-Home cooking to Haute Cuisine. There are many different recipes and techniques for the same dish. Uniquely created dishes that have been popularized nationally, or even to world renown, can be modified by anybody to suit their own taste and become "theirs." We will each try a dish and develop it adding our own twists, flavors, preparations or even ingredients. Cooking really comes down to a matter of personal taste, the availability of ingredients and the taste of the people we are preparing it for.

Foodies have been arguing for centuries about who knows the real recipe.

Auguste Escoffier, (1846-1935) a French chef and writer, is considered the first chef to record all the dishes of classic French gastronomy. He simplified Haute Cuisine and elevated the profession of chef. My mentor Chef Pat Gorey, the first real chef I trained under, gave me a copy of *Le Repertoire de La Cuisine A Guide to Fine Foods* by Lewis Saulnier as a gift. It is a basic reference of the cuisine of Escoffier with 6,000 dishes for hor-d'oeuvre, soups, eggs, and fish entrées, salads, pastas, vegetables and pastries. If you have never seen it, check it out. I can't tell you the countless ways to prepare sole that are presented. The book focuses on the ingredients, not the method. There are no recipes, just inspiration.

Restaurant reviewers can tear a restaurant apart claiming their version of a dish is totally wrong. Many restaurant reviewers are not educated food professionals, they just eat out a lot. They should make a fair evaluation of an establishment. Their comments can sometimes make or break a business. People read reviews ravenously and use them as a guide for where to go.

One of my favorite reviewers was Elaine Tait, the retired *Philadelphia Inquirer* critic, who was always honest and fair. I remember she said every time you walk into a new restaurant, you are entering someone's dream. That project was their vision, into which they may have invested their entire life savings. They live it and breathe it every day, but in the end, it is just a business like any other. Our bank expects us to make a profit, which is the primary goal of any business.

Chefs have to be allowed to create and interpret. If we all made the same version of every dish, this great culinary world wouldn't have evolved. Alternatively, some people love franchises primarily because the food always will be exactly the same in Miami, Florida or in Nome, Alaska.

Thank God there are still adventurous customers who want a variety of new and different dishes and will allow us brave souls a chance to show them something new, creatively interesting and delicious.

Catering 101

Catering opens many doors. I have catered events for guests numbering from 2 to 500, in every kind of setting you can imagine. Caterers are primarily responsible for the success, or failure, of any event. Fortunately, I'm proud to have a huge file of letters full of praise and thank you notes.

Caterers are also very hard workers. They plan, cook, transport, supervise, load and unload trucks, set up, clean up and do everything else in between. Their event days can easily be twelve or fourteen hours long. Some caterers have several events going at one time, God bless 'em! The prep day before the event is often a busier day than the actual event because most of the food is either made or prepped then.

I have attended many professional seminars on off-premise catering, but I've learned more from experience than from any class or book. If you have catered, or are thinking about catering, there are some things you will need to know. Are you licensed as a caterer? How about being insured?

At one of my first seminars, the instructor read to us an article from the newspaper about a big-ticket fundraiser at a museum. The caterer made a fantastic buffet, but ran out of food. Guests were serving themselves at that function, so there was no portion control. If they had trained servers placing adequate portions on each guest's plate, they would have had ample food. People were not happy. It was bad enough that it happened, but making it into the newspaper because they ran out of food was a real kiss of death in the food service world.

Many, many caterers operate out of their home kitchen or garage. If you are only doing parties on a Saturday or Sunday, you *may* get away with working without a license for a while, provided your customers never get sick and your competitors don't report you. Many of these same folk carry no insurance either. I choose to be licensed and insured. I do it all legally and correctly because my clients expect very high standards of professionalism. It's really just that simple. So here's my advice:

#1 Do Your Homework

Where is this event being held? Is it accessible to delivery vehicles? Is hot and cold running water available? Is there adequate electrical power for lights and cooking equipment? Is the lay of the land suitable for a tent? How much will the tent cost? Is there enough space for a field kitchen? Are there enough bathroom facilities for guests *and* staff? Is there parking available? What if it rains? What is the backup plan? Who is going to be at the party? Senior citizens don't like the food the younger generation craves. Teenage boys can eat as much food as you put out, while girls the same age will pick at food or play with it instead of eating. A Garden Club won't want prime rib grinders for their tea. Some nationalities are famous for consuming large amounts of food, so you'd better have enough available. Are there going to be vegetarians, Kosher, Hindu, Buddhist or any other ethnic group that restricts your menu? Last, but most importantly, *What is the budget?* As Mom said, "You can't drink champagne on a beer budget."

#2 Make Lists
Make list of everything. Shopping lists. Preparation lists. Staffing lists. Packing lists. Lists of other businesses you will be working with. *(Will they need power? Space under the tent or in the venue? Do they have to be fed? If they do, then who pays for it?)* Now read your lists and re-write them, or better yet, make a list of your lists and keep them all in a place where you can find them!

#3 Be Flexible
Plans can change up until moments before the start of an event. Somebody didn't show up. French lilacs aren't available this time of year. The strawberry crop was ruined by heavy rain in Florida last week. Ten more guests are coming. The weather turned cold or it's suddenly 45 degrees outside in May. The weather forecast is for two solid days of rain. The count dropped by 30% because of another event the same day. Or worst of all, you undercut yourself on the estimated cost of running the event.

#4 Learn to Improvise
Due to some unforeseen oversight, substitutions have to be made. The florist didn't send enough centerpieces. You have fifteen minutes to make another one from flowers pulled out of other arrangements. The tent is leaking. The circuit breaker keeps snapping. You forgot to pack something. The host/hostess assured you they had sufficient alcohol, napkins, mixers, glassware etc, but they counted wrong.

#5 Getting There
Can you drive a truck and back it into a tight spot? Do you know how to load the food so it doesn't shift and destroy 300 hand-made canapés on a sheet rack? Is it better to own a truck or rent one? Do you need a refer, a refrigerated truck?

#6 The Law
Do you know the current *Guidelines for Safe Food Handling* put out by the United States Department of Agriculture? It is a legal requirement that at least one person in every operation be certified, and continuously recertify every four years? Are *you* certified?

Searching for My Own Business

By the time I was thirty, I had worked with seven different managers during my years at Brookside. Club managers are a rare breed. The biggest problem they face is being the middleman between the staff, the membership and the board. If they fall out of favor, they don't stay for very long.

Fortunately, I was still passionate about my job. I had the freedom to do what I wanted and I worked with an outstanding crew. I was comfortable in my job, enjoying life, and working about fifty hours a week. Dennis, my Sous Chef, and I were a great team. We were able to take advantage of a flexible schedule that allowed both of us time off. Dennis, Charlie, Thelma and Theresa were real team players and we all worked very hard. The entire club staff was like a family. The club kitchen had been upgraded with new floors, wall and ceiling surfaces. There was a new compartment convection steamer and a steam jacketed kettle, which we constantly used for our soups and sauces. Even though everything was going well, I got the itch to establish my own kitchen.

I had saved some money and started looking for my own place. It was such a thrill to dream of the possibilities. I viewed all kinds of properties and made a million lists. I also got information on new restaurant operations from the U.S. Department of Agriculture. "New operations" are the key words here. When you start a restaurant from scratch, you have to go by the book. Their book. You have to follow their rules exactly. "Grandfathered," or pre-existing operations, are a whole other story.

I figured my kitchen was going to be the really big expense. Parking was another big issue, as well as zoning, septic, and water supply, the list went on and on.

In Pennsylvania at that time, no new liquor licenses were available. You had to buy an existing license from a business that had closed or been destroyed. Also, a license had to stay in the municipality where it was originally issued. It couldn't be transferred out of the municipality, so BYOB would have to be an option.

I wanted to be licensed, insured and do it all correctly and legally. Three different times my hopes and plans were dashed when the sale of a prospective property fell through. I created floor plans, table placements, menus, inventories, sales projections and had even standardized all my recipes on 3 x 5 cards.

Then, when I had just about given up hope in the spring of 1987, Phil, my favorite antique dealer, called to say the Inn at Oley was up for sale and the price was right. Just when I'd given up hope of ever owning my own business!

I was familiar with The Inn at Oley and mentioned it to my family, who encouraged me to look at the property.

The Inn at Oley was owned by John Kalbach, who had purchased it from Nelda Bosler. Nelda, a spitfire of a woman, had run the Oley Valley Hotel for many years. Everyone knew her. She wore her dark hair up in a bun on top of her head.

When Nelda Bosler owned the Oley Valley Hotel, it was a popular place for the community. She roasted her own hams and beef and was known for her piled-high sandwiches. She said to me, "The only way to make it in business is with home cookin', and you better give 'em plenty, too." She told me a state policeman once stopped in to pick up one of her famous ham sandwiches to take directly to Washington, D.C. for President John F. Kennedy.

The Oley Valley Hotel

The Oley Valley Hotel had three major building additions. The original part of the building is a solid, stone, three-story building with a Mansard-style roof. The first addition was a two-story red brick building that ran along the side of the driveway. It housed a new kitchen and three additional rooms on the second floor. Years later, this was expanded with another addition for the kitchen.

The original old Summer Kitchen, with a Sunshine brand wood-burning stove, was attached to the rear of the building. (In this part of Pennsylvania, in the days before air-conditioning, cooking was often done in a small building located near the main house, which was often called the Summer Kitchen.)

The second floor had two full bathrooms and a dozen rooms that were rented out. The third floor, or attic, had once held a full kitchen and a maze of small cubicles.

There was also an area in the attic where meats were hung to cure, suspended from the ceiling on chains and ropes.

John Kalbach purchased the hotel to convert it to a fine French restaurant, one of the first in Berks. He hired Chef Jean Maurice and made many changes. A new kitchen was added to the building. The red and white paint of Nelda's era was sand-blasted away. The woodwork was refinished, the wall surfaces were covered in a deep green, and the original tin ceiling was painted dark gold. The bar was moved from the outside wall to the inside wall, cutting it in two pieces to make an "L" shaped bar. The front pool table room became the waiting area. The other two rooms were set up as dining rooms. The restrooms were on the second floor, or all the way back at the rear of the building. Other rooms were used for office space, storage, owner's quarters and best of all, the entire kitchen was set up with brand new equipment.

My friend Phil, the antique dealer, supplied some of the furniture and paintings. The restaurant opened to great reviews. Patrons travelled from all over to sample the French fare at this quaint new Inn. The waiting room overflowed with customers waiting for tables. The Inn at Oley was an instant success.

Oley, Pennsylvania Cuisine

Oley is a beautiful farming community located in the eastern corner of Berks County. Some of the most fertile farmland in the country is located right here in the valley. It is also home to a large group of German ancestry called the Pennsylvania Dutch.

They say around here, "If you ain't Dutch, you ain't much!" and many believe it, too.

After the first few months, everyone soon knew who I was, but few would speak to me unless I spoke to them first. The post office is right across the street from the Inn. It's not unusual to stop in and hear several people conversing in Pennsylvania Dutch or to see, and smell, the farmers who've strolled right out of their dairy barn. Many of these folks grew up here and lived their whole lives on the farm. Change was one thing they were not accustomed to. Outsiders, "who ain't Dutch," often get the Amish, the Mennonites and Pennsylvania Dutch confused.

There are some Old-Order Amish, who are strict and wear all black. The men have beards and don't use any motorized farm equipment. They go to school in one-room schoolhouses until eighth grade, then work on the farm. At the age of eighteen, they are given the opportunity to become baptized and join the church. Horse-drawn black buggies can still be seen, especially on Sundays when many go out visiting. Many of the Amish in the area have gotten into construction and furniture building because of the lack of available farmland.

The Mennonites are not nearly as strict as the Amish, but some are more conservative than others. Most women wear a small prayer cap or white-net hat over their long hair, which is tucked under their cap.

Some Mennonites drive black cars or trucks with the chrome painted flat black. Here in the Oley Valley there are far more Mennonites than Amish. Many of them are farmers or successful businessmen.

The annual Oley Valley Community Fair is held on the third weekend of every September. You can hear the Pennsylvania Dutch spoken there. I'm proud to say I've learned to speak Dutchified English as well as the best of them.

The cuisine of this area can best be described as meat and potatoes. Most of the natives lived off of the land. Since most were originally farmers, pork, beef and poultry played a large part in their diet. Pork is by far the staple food.

Many of the locals would raise their pigs though the summer months, then slaughter in the winter. The choicer cuts were used for roasts, chops and hams. Hams and bacon were cured and often smoked in buildings right on the farm. The rest of the other bits of meats were ground and seasoned with pepper and coriander to make the local sausage. A large amount of sausage was also smoked to preserve it through the winter months. Everything that was left (the head, tail, feet or "trotters," and sometimes the liver and kidneys) were thrown into a pot of simmering water along with spices and cooked until it fell apart. The bones were removed, cornmeal was added to the mixture, it was ladled into pans to cool, and that's how Scrapple was made. It was sliced, then fried and served as breakfast meat or often for dinner.

Mom once said the Pennsylvania Dutch used everything from the pig except the last squeal of the pig and she was right!

The blood of the pig was used to make blood pudding or a sausage-like preparation. The fat was rendered into lard for cooking or soap making. Nothing went to waste.

Most farmers kept cows for milking. Calves became the next generation of females or "heifers" for milking, or they were sold along with the males that were raised for veal or castrated. The steers were raised for meat-production.

Chickens and ducks were raised for their meat and eggs. "Pullets," or female chicks, were kept for egg production. The roasters were often raised just until the fall, then slaughtered while they were young and tender. The old laying hens were slaughtered and used for soups and stews. Duck eggs were prized for baking.

Most of the farmers grew enough vegetables to sustain themselves through the winter. They were experts at drying and canning their crops. Cabbage was grown for eating in salads, and especially for sauerkraut. Many kinds of potatoes were grown, usually enough to store through the winter.

With all this abundant, fresh-grown produce, and meat that was readily available, a cuisine developed. It is still very popular amongst many in the area, especially those of us who grew up on this food. My own family still enjoys many of these dishes.

Pot Pie or *Bot Boi* in Pennsylvania Dutch is one of the dishes. It is usually a stew of poultry simmered in a rich broth with potatoes, onions, celery and egg noodles, which are more often like dumplings. Salt, pepper and parsley are often the only seasonings used, although many cooks do use saffron (of all things) in their chicken dishes.

Pork and Sauerkraut is another dish, probably one of my favorites. Usually, a less-tender cut of pork (Shoulder or Boston-butt works very well) is braised in sauerkraut. It is served with mashed potatoes and applesauce or apples of some kind. I have prepared many variations of this dish, some more German or Alsatian than Pennsylvania Dutch.

I must mention one more dish to show just how resourceful these people are. It's a dish called *Hog Maul* or in everyday English, Stuffed Pig's Stomach. The pouch is sewn shut at one end, then filled with a mixture of cooked potatoes, onions, carrots and celery mixed with cooked, fresh and smoked sausage. The other end is sewn shut, and it is roasted in the oven until the outside is very crisp. It is really quite good, if you can get past the thought of what you're eating.

Most locals brought up on real Pennsylvania Dutch food are used to eating many one-pot meals, which are often eaten with a wide variety of sweet and sour preserves, pickles, relishes and salads. (*Not* green, leafy salads that most of us know.) Plenty of bread with lots and lots of butter is eaten with them. This was hearty fare to feed hard-working people. Dessert always followed dinner. The locals are incredible bakers, but if there isn't pie or cake, puddings or canned fruit is often served.

I have often heard it said that gravy is a food group here in Berks County. This is some very substantial food that can easily lead to obesity.

A small community grew up around the Main Street of the village of Oley. There was a bank, general store, butcher shop and then, in 1881, J.R. Mensch built the Hotel. He also built the building directly across the street which was, for many years, the general store. Across the alley from the hotel, a large block building was erected for indoor basketball, the first in the area. It also served as a banquet hall. The food was prepared in the hotel kitchen, then transported across the alley to the banquet hall.

A Culinary Journey with Chef Steve Yeanish

Buying the Inn

We made a reservation for Sunday Brunch at the Inn at Oley, and a curious group of us went to see what it was all about. The property was much larger than expected because it is long and narrow. We wandered for what seemed like hours and I started to see more of the potential of the project. We talked endlessly about what we could do. The entire kitchen was intact. There was a stainless chef's table with warmers and steam table, a 20-quart Hobart mixer, a walk-in cooler, freezer, two reach-in coolers, double range, griddle top and vertical broiler, all in good working order. There was enough china, glassware and silver scattered throughout the three floors and basement to get us started.

We met the owner, and he took us through the whole building, explaining things as we went. We agreed on a price, but there was one major catch. A previous owner had departed taking the liquor license with him. This was a hotel liquor license, which meant it could only be used in a facility that operated a restaurant and had six bedrooms for overnight lodging. (The Pennsylvania Liquor Control Board had created these licenses after Prohibition.) Transferring licenses from another municipality wasn't possible then. That meant that this license could only be used in Oley Township, and only in a building that had six rooms to let. To make a long story short, the license was really only viable for this property. The only problem would be getting the license from the former owner.

We agreed to proceed with the purchase. It was a very scary, but exciting time. A friend referred me to a bright, young legal associate in his office, Thea Block. She worked diligently to sort out my sales agreement and the liquor license. We quickly got to know each other well and this tall, elegant Irish blonde is still one of my best of friends some twenty years later.

I was only thirty three years old at the time and wary of the risks, but I took the plunge. Down deep, this was my dream and I knew it was attainable because I was willing to make the sacrifices.

Plans began to fall into place. Settlement was scheduled for August 31, 1987. The Inn continued to operate as the Oley Valley Hotel until about a week before settlement.

I couldn't wait to get started. I was so impatient, I borrowed a sewing machine and some fabric from Phil and we started making new draperies for the dining room. They were finished before settlement. The final days were getting nearer.

Saying Good Bye

There was a surprise going away party for me in the ballroom on my final Friday at Brookside Country Club. The entire staff was there, about forty people. Distracted by phone calls, I didn't even see it coming. I thought we had a luncheon party that day. The pantry staff had prepared a cold buffet for everyone.

This was not an easy time for me. It was hard to leave a good thing like the Brookside. Many of the people I worked with had become like family to me. After fifteen years, we kind of grew up together. I was a teenager when I first started working there.

Food service people often see more of their co-workers than they do of their own families. Now at the age of thirty-three, I was leaving most of my best friends.

They presented me with a beautiful print, *The Huntsman's Courtship,* that still hangs in the bar of the Inn today. It was framed and matted and looked like I had hand-picked it myself. The Board of Governors presented me with a swivel arm brass table lamp, which is still in use to this day. I was very touched by their generosity and was glad to leave on good terms. Their support and well wishes were much appreciated during this exciting, but scary time.

There are people you always genuinely enjoy working with. They do their job, are low-maintenance, and you can't help but like them. Saying goodbye to Thelma was like saying goodbye to my mother. I'll always remember her kindness and generosity. Dennis is still a great friend. He often helps me with catering functions, or as a fill-in line chef when necessary.

Working with Fran was always fun, but she never had any luck with cars. Every car she owned had problems. She often parked behind the clubhouse. One slow night, we took old lemons and mounted them all over her car. They were stuck on the hubcaps, in the grillwork, on the front, everywhere. We found some yellow washable paint, and wrote *Sunkist* across the windshield.

Another time, we filled her car full of empty cardboard boxes from the floor to the ceiling. They were wedged in as tight as they possibly could be arranged. The only time she ever got really angry with us was when we took off her hubcaps and put rocks inside. As soon as she backed up, it sounded like her car was rattling apart. We couldn't believe that two small stones would make so much racket!

Fran was Hungarian and she always loved to make Christmas cookies. Her favorite were Kipfel, which are almost the same as Rugalach, except they are shaped differently. Kipfel is one of those heat-sensitive doughs that need to be worked cold, and her recipe called for two-three folds. She could never get the dough right, so we struck up a deal. I made the dough for her, and she supplied me with the cookies. They're outrageously good. I especially loved the lekvar (prune), raspberry, apricot and walnut. Whenever I eat them, I think of Fran, then I chuckle out loud.

Kipfel

There are many variations of this Eastern European filled cookie. I've tried many, but I really like the richness of this one. Filling options range from raspberry or apricot preserves, lekvar (prune, my favorite), poppy seed, to walnut and pecan. Fillings can usually be found in the baking aisle of the market. A marble surface is wonderful for rolling out these cookies!

Preheat oven to 350 degrees
Yield: about 10 dozen small cookies

In mixer with a paddle attachment, combine:
8 ounces or 1 cup **soft unsalted butter**
4 Tbs **granulated sugar**
3 **egg yolks**
¼ tsp **salt**
Zest of 1 lemon *(the yellow part only)*
1 cup **dairy sour cream**
1 cup **half and half**

Mix until just combined.
Add 4 cups **flour** *sifted with:*
2 tsp **baking powder**
1 tsp **baking soda**
Turn mixer on low speed.
When dough is thoroughly mixed, turn off mixer.
Divide dough into 2 pieces.
Flatten dough into discs, wrap each in clear plastic wrap and refrigerate at least one hour or overnight.

To roll cookies:
Roll dough out on a cool, flat surface until dough is about ¼ inch thick.
Cut dough into small 1½-inch squares.
(Unused pieces can be added to the next batch and re-rolled.)
Place a drop of filling the size of a dime into the center of each square.
Bring one corner of dough ⅔ of the way diagonally across the dough to cover the filling.
Then, bring the opposite corner of the dough back across the dough-covered filling.
Pinch the dough at the edge where the corner overlaps the filling.
This makes a cookie with open ends and the filling is just barely visible in the openings.
Place on ungreased cookie sheet or Silpat®-lined sheet. Keep one cookie space between cookies. Sprinkle a dusting of **confectioners sugar** on the Kipfel after cookies have baked and cooled.

On August 31, 1987, settlement for the Inn was held at Thea's office, and as soon as it was finished, I headed right for the Inn with tools and work clothes in tow. My parents met me there. When we opened the door of our new adventure, it was such an incredible rush! Dad hadn't seen the interior and he was totally blown away as he walked through and saw the original bar, tin ceiling, and all the old woodwork. He paused at the bottom of the spiral staircase and said he felt like he was standing still in time and it was more than he ever dreamt it would be. He was ready to get started!

For the next six months, Mom and Dad traveled to Oley most every day, sometimes spending the night. And my family helped as well. They rarely showed up empty-handed and worked tirelessly on the almost-overwhelming amount of work we tackled. Ruth Ann and Jayne always brought cakes, cookies or other goodies they had baked. Many weekends I spent most of the day feeding the work crew.

The first major job we tackled was to organize everything. Silverware, glasses and dishes were scattered throughout all four levels of the building. We gathered everything together into one area and started counting. We had to establish which glasses were going to be used for what drink and what china was available. We found treasures, and we found trash. Lots of it. It seemed like people had come, done their thing, and left everything where they dropped it.

We finally saved everything of any real value, then called a flea market person to take the rest. We filled Dumpster® after Dumpster®, then burned all cardboard, scrap wood and paper.

On the first day it rained, I literally stood in shock and cried. Every one of the five different roofs on the building

Setting Up Shop

Before we renovated

leaked. Each one was a different material and some were worse than others. Once I got over the initial shock, we put empty buckets under every leak until we ran out of buckets. As soon as money was available, the worst roofs were replaced. The others simply had to wait if they weren't causing any major problems.

The front room beside the bar/pool table room was an ice cream parlor with dipping cabinets and a refrigerated display case for desserts. I quickly liquidated this equipment into cash to fund new improvements.

Thea insisted we move the public restrooms to the first floor. The American Disabilities Act had just come into law. Compliance was no longer a choice, so we changed the entrance door to the side, level with the driveway for wheelchair accessibility.

The new restrooms were roughed in with new plumbing, but the plastered walls were in such bad condition that the plaster-on-lath had to be removed down to the studs. The room was sealed off. We wore masks and demolished two entire walls, while removing bucket after bucket of plaster debris. The dust from that job traveled up two stories so it looked like a powder bomb went off. The restrooms were tiled and ready for fixtures. Phil offered me a pair of antique oak French doors with opaque glass that suited perfectly.

My brother Ray and brother-in-law Jerry volunteered (willingly!) to tackle the basement. They filled a stake-body truck with nothing but scrap iron pipe that was left in the basement. When they finished, they reappeared that evening looking like coal miners, but the entire floor was empty and washed clean with a hose. It is hard to find people to work like those guys did; God bless them! They did it for a heart-felt thank you.

My sister Jayne and her husband David came every weekend and cleaned up after the workers of the previous week. There were contractors, Dad, plumbers, tilers or electricians. They even cleaned the entire kitchen from floor to ceiling.

We set up a bedroom for them on the second floor. They called it the Beirut Suite. It had a real mattress and box spring with a metal headboard with a pipe-like arched frame, and bleak furniture. The room was papered in gloomy shades of tan and brown.

Every wall surface on the first floor was stripped of wallpaper, patched, sanded, primed and painted or wall papered. Every window was cleaned, and new drapes and sheer curtains were hung. New light fixtures were placed in every room.

The old Sunshine wood stove and Olympic coal stove in the bar were taken apart and cleaned. Every ceiling, including the bar, was washed, patched and painted. What eventually became the Rose Room had the floor tiles stripped and was carpeted.

Dad put a trap door into the basement from the place where the old beer kegs used to be delivered. We now had a way to remove large pieces from the basement. Then he built a workshop in a corner down there.

There were many, many doors in this old building. We played musical doors. A leaded glass panel was removed and moved over to the former front door. Phil provided a beautiful, old leaded clear-and-opaque-glass oak door. Dad and my brother Charlie installed this and built a small transom above it to fill in the tall space. More Jacobean stain and several coats of polyurethane finished the job. We placed the first cloak room behind an old doorway inside the newly created lobby. There were two odd looking cabinets on the wall, one on either side of a five-foot counter top.

I was always the demolition person. My father once watched me attempt to drive a nail into a piece of wood. He patiently watched then said, "Thank goodness you can cook!" The carpenter framed the wall of the coat room and there now was room to hold heavy coats on a busy winter night.

The mystery of the shelves that had been held by several wood screws intrigued me. They were oak, with the original finish, and one had a curved back. They were obviously from somewhere else. Then one afternoon while working in the bar, I realized their curved back fit into a curved wall behind the bar. Bingo! These were the old shelves of the bar-back and the holes in the stripped plastered walls even lined up. Phil even remembered where the old oak bar top was located and sure enough, the solid oak 14"x12' plank was still there.

He returned the oak plank to its original home and Dad used photographs to rebuild the entire bar. The oak plank was used to top and face the bar and drawers were built into the sides. While scavenging in the basement, I found the missing pieces of carved molding of the frame and sides at the back. Measure-

The Oley Valley Inn

The original kitchen's Sunshine stove in the current Garden Room before we renovated.

The Garden Room after we renovated, featuring my antique kitchen tools.

ments were taken, a new mirror was ordered, and I was able to stain it all the same dark Jacobean stain as the rest of the bar. Then I found the original wooden foot rail and eventually the finial that topped the crown of the back-bar mirror was discovered in a utility closet on the second floor and it was eventually restored in one piece.

Phil had a bolt of fabric with a hunt scene and we covered the walls with this beautiful fabric. Now, some twenty years later, despite the smoke from the fire, it still looks as good as the day we put it up.

The doors in the original part of the building were all very tall, with a movable glass transom above each door. We created a display cabinet lined with mirror, added glass shelves and a light. It became a focal point and housed my collection of Sadek native Pennsylvania birds and wildlife.

We installed central air conditioning the following spring. The attic held two treasures: a pair of rectangular wine racks with individual bottle holders. A glass shelf was placed in the center for additional displays of bottles and my decanter collection.

We did inherit one real treasure. Back in the late 1970s, the internationally-renowned artist Keith Haring was employed here as a dishwasher. Keith came from the Kutztown area. His works, which frequently show outline figures in expressive poses, are in major collections around the world. While working here, he painted a figure of a character standing on his head at the dishwasher directly on the wall. This was later covered with Plexiglass® along with a photo from *The New York Times* of him with a sculpture he had just created. Fortunately, we removed the piece from the wall while remodelling the kitchen,

Steve renovating and hanging wallpaper.

Dad, Ruth Ann, Megan and David getting ready for opening day.

so it survived the fire that nearly destroyed the entire building.

Finally, it was all coming together. Menus, business cards and announcements were printed. Restrooms with handicapped accessibility were completed. Paint was drying. Chairs were reupholstered. The few treasures that came with the purchase were used to decorate the dining rooms along with my collection of David Larson paintings. Carpets were cleaned and installed. An upstairs bedroom was painted from floor to ceiling and drapes were made to convert it into an additional dining room to sit fourteen. My friend, Jan, even came up to create two magnificent floral pieces for the main dining rooms.

The final days were spent cleaning up all the leftover lumber and putting away all the tools, paint and cleaning supplies.

The date of October 31, was set for our opening. We made our renovations in exactly two months!

Unfortunately, the liquor license transfer was not yet in sight, so we opened BYOB. There were still no guarantees on the license, but things were moving along.

When we bought the place, the pantry was bare except for some salt, cornstarch, a few frozen pork tenderloins in the freezer, and salt and pepper in the shakers. My first food order to stock the shelves cost over $3,000.

Rows of cases lined the kitchen, then Mom walked through and spied a box. One of my fondest memories was when curiosity got the best of her, and she asked in astonishment, "Snails! Who the heck eats snails?"

Eventually, food began arriving, so we could start to cook. We were a new team, just getting to know each other and our cooking methods, so we did a trial run the first Friday evening. Everyone was in position. The entire wait staff was there. Phil was our first customer and he and his guest both ordered steaks. We were officially open!

Phil and Jerry hanging wall fabric in the Bar. This fabric survived the fire, and it still looks great 20 years later!

Amazing, but it took only two months of hard work to renovate and create the Oley Valley Inn.

The vertical broiler was turned on for the first time to actually cook a steak. As soon as the fat started to spit and sizzle (as it should to get a good crust to hold in the juices), the entire pan under the sliding grid caught fire and flames shot out of the top of the broiler into the exhaust hood.

Our nervous buzz quickly changed to horror. Professional kitchens have fire suppression systems built into any hood where an open flame could cause a fire. There are heat sensors built in that automatically dispense a dry powder to extinguish a flame. The hood airflow should also be turned off because the air will be sucked into the duct-work, which may be greasy, and a fire then spreads inside the hood and you have an even bigger problem on your hands. I acted quickly and calmly, turned off the hood, and grabbed the fire extinguisher to douse the flames until they were out. There was a lovely haze of gray powder over the whole kitchen. Everyone helped or grabbed a bucket of hot soapy water. We cleaned up the mess in no time flat. When the broiler was clean, we were back in business. The customers never knew what happened, and the night went on. Our first guests enjoyed their first meal from the new Oley Valley Inn.

Our serving crew on the Opening Night of the Oley Valley Inn, October 31, 1987.

Furnishing the Inn

John Phillip "Phil" Crowley is a very kind, friendly man. He has been my friend for more than thirty years. He owned The Bashful Barn on Philadelphia Avenue in Boyertown. His store was originally a cigar factory, and then it later became the Upholsterer's Union Hall for the Boyertown Casket Company.

Over the years I've purchased many beautiful pieces of furniture from him. I've always enjoyed discussing projects with him, in fact it was Phil who helped me find the Inn.

A local water color artist, David Larson, had a studio in Phil's building and Phil had the watercolors framed and sold them in his shop. I started collecting his watercolors and many of them are displayed in our restaurant.

One of my many interests has always been antiques. I have inherited many family pieces, and purchased many from auction and flea markets. Refinishing old pieces of furniture is a really relaxing project for me. The stripping of layer after layer of old finish unveils the history of a piece—gradually revealing how it was used, where it was placed and how it looked when new. The final reward comes when it is again displayed in all its glory.

My father gave me an old dry sink that was in the basement of our home for many years. It was a primitive piece in bad repair, so I completely dismantled it, then stripped, refinished and reconstructed it. Aunt Joan was visiting me one day and recognized it as Grammy's. She couldn't believe it still had Grammy's rolling pin in the drawer when Dad gave it to me, so I gave it to Aunt Joan.

I bought an old oak icebox for $150. It was all original, from the finish to the wire racks. There was just a small crack in the interior. It now sits in the Garden Room, which was the original old kitchen of the Inn,

Phil was using old pieces of furniture for bathroom vanities long before anyone else was. We used several here. Some real treasures came our way. In many cases, the pieces were solid wood, originally finished, but occasionally damaged in transit or removal. Being made of *real* wood, they were easily modified to accommodate new composite sink tops. Most of the antiques we used here were either from Phil, or family heirlooms I rescued from basements, attics and garages. It takes an eye to envision them sometimes, but the effort has always been well worth it. And then, as Phil says, you have an original.

Finally it was time to unpack and display collections.

The Oley Valley Inn

Mother's Frozen Lemon Soufflé

My good friend Phil's mother inspired this recipe!

Yield: 8 individual or 1-2 quart dish
Lemon Curd:
Zest and juice of 4 **large lemons**
6 **large eggs**
2 Tbs **cornstarch**
2 cup **sugar**
½ cup (1 stick) **butter melted**

Remove zest *(just the yellow part)* of the lemon with a zesting plane or fine grater.
Juice lemons, strain the seeds and place lemon zest, juice, eggs and cornstarch in blender.
Mix until zest is thoroughly mixed in and smooth, then pour into a heavy saucepan.
Add sugar and melted butter, then cook over medium heat until mixture bubbles.
Stir continuously until it thickens. **This must fully boil to set the cornstarch.**
Most recipes use a double boiler, but I've not broken a curd yet!
Remove from heat.
Cover with a thin film of melted butter on top to prevent a skin from forming.
Allow to cool in the bowl.

Frozen Lemon Soufflé:

Prepare a 1-2 quart dish by adding a folded aluminum foil collar that extends three inches above the sides of the dish. This should hold the mousse above sides of bowl.
Secure with transparent tape.
If making individual servings, do the same with eight 6-oz. ramekins.

Place 8 **egg whites at room temperature** in a *very clean* mixing bowl.
Turn mixer on low and mix with the whisk.
Add 1 tsp **cream of tartar.**
Continue whipping on high until soft peaks begin to form.
Slowly add ¾ cup **superfine or granulated sugar**.
Meringue will stand in stiff peaks. Set aside.

Whip one quart (4 cups) of **heavy cream** in a chilled bowl with a whisk until beaten stiffly.
Add a spoonful of the curd to the whipped cream and fold it in.
Add a spoonful of the curd to the meringue.
Fold together.
Combine whipped cream and meringue with the rest of the curd by gently stirring from the sides to the middle while turning the bowl. Continue until there are no streaks and mixture is light and fluffy. Place in individual ramekins or a large dish.
Freeze immediately, for several hours or overnight.

To Serve:
Remove collar and coat sides with cool, toasted, sliced almonds.
Pipe a rosette of whipped cream on top of each portion of soufflé.
Cut a thin slice of lemon slit almost all the way through,
and twisted to separate it. Place the lemon around a piped cream rosette. Add a mint sprig.

W e did some newspaper ads around the time of the opening and were busy right from the start, thanks to the buzz from my Brookside members and local interest. Berks County loves a new restaurant, but keeping them coming back is the trick. We couldn't use the name the Inn at Oley, so we became The Oley Valley Inn. I thought BYOB would be a real drag, but we had many customers who really loved it, especially those who had a wine cellar. Customers arrived with shopping bags of wine and mixers too. We continued to operate like that for months.

We had one final inspection of the premises and were anxious to remove that big orange display card which the state makes everyone post for *any* changes of the license. Thea had prepared a binder containing every piece of paper the state LCB requires. The man toured the "licensed portion of the facility."

We had to submit the measurements of every room where beverages would be consumed or stored, the kitchen and cooking facilities, and in our case, the six bedrooms available for overnight guests and a register since we were a licensed hotel.

A bedroom, by the LCB definition, is a separate room with a bed, dresser and chair. At the time of the inspection five of the bedrooms were all set up and ready to pass the inspection, but we didn't have enough beds for the sixth bedroom.

The third floor at this time was a scary place with one bare light bulb and an occasional bat. Get the picture? When the inspection group climbed the stairs, they found a lovely twin bed, a small chest of drawers and a nice little chair. The bed was neatly made with one of our old comforters. Speechless again, the group departed and our inspection was over. Fortunately they never inspected the bed which was temporarily made out of recycled cardboard meat boxes laid end-to-end!

Christmas at Oley Valley Inn

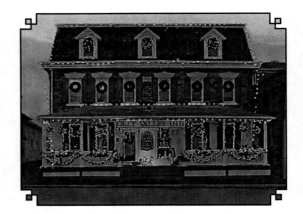

W e continued to be busy through our first holiday season and decorated the Inn with as much as we could afford. It looked very festive. Jayne helped me wrap an artificial tree with grapevine. If you have ever tackled decorating with wild grapevine, you have my blessing. I went to a local wooded area and pulled down what I could manage. I never realized the potential for poison ivy, even in the wintertime. We soaked thick vines in a kiddy pool of warm water to make them flexible. The tree was already illuminated with small white lights. So we started at the bottom, made a loop around the tree, secured it with floral wire and continued until the tree was completely circled with vines of random thickness. The finished tree was a wonderful conversation piece in the bar. It was trimmed with tufts of "snow" and had small feathered birds and realistic icicles.

The staff from Brookside had their holiday employee party here at the Inn that first year. It was fabulous to have the whole gang here and they had a great time dancing on the front porch until the wee hours of the morning.

Every year we go all out decorating for Christmas. Two years in a row, the wreath I had just made and hung on the entrance door was stolen. Maybe it was a repeat customer? I guess I should have been flattered they liked my work so much.

One year at Christmas I made a mannequin dressed in Victorian clothes for the front porch of the Inn. She looked very nice and customers were amazed by how real she seemed. Several diners asked the host on duty, "Do you know you have someone standing at your front door?"

The frame for the figure was easily made out of construction tubes from Home Depot that were mounted on a board screwed into the floor for stability. I made a frame for the arms and shoulders out of chicken wire. A wig stand was attached to the shoulders and the whole thing couldn't have cost more than $25 to build.

After a quick trip to a costume shop and Goodwill for a long dress, winter coat, gloves, mask, wig and hat, our Victorian lady was positioned in front of the door with a holiday wreath under her arm, and a stack of gifts by her side. Her right arm was extended as if she were knocking on the front door.

One Friday night at the height of the busy holiday season, some prankster stole the Victorian lady's head and I had to scramble around on a busy Saturday afternoon to find replacement parts and rebuild her. A year later, I was still annoyed that someone had stolen the lady's head and two wreaths.

That summer I had purchased a small, wooden, hay wagon which was quite old. I got smart and filled it with plants, then chained it to the building by the front entrance. Straw, pumpkins, gourds and chrysanthemums filled it in the autumn.

When it was time for the holiday display, I found a small evergreen tree that fit in the wagon and there was just enough room for a stack of gift boxes beside the tree. I found the perfect boxes in a nicely proportioned stack, but the boxes had to be filled to keep them from blowing away. I wrapped them securely in foil paper to keep them dry and festooned them with ribbons. It was a great look.

The thief got a real surprise when he opened the package, but I had the last laugh. I had written a label for the box: "This gift has been made especially for you by Percy." Percy is my calico cat. The box contained her kitty litter.

A Culinary Journey with Chef Steve Yeanish

Country Chicken Liver and Mushroom Pâté

CHEF SAYS
To draw the blood out of the chicken livers:
Dissolve 1 tsp **kosher salt** *in a bowl with* 2 cups of **water**.
Add the chicken livers, then cover and refrigerate for one hour or overnight.
Drain thoroughly and rinse off the salt water.

1 pound **fresh chicken livers** *(See Chef Says above)*
Place livers in small saucepot.
Add to the saucepot:
2 cups **milk**
Place milk in a pan over medium heat and poach livers **gently** for 15 minutes.
Lazy bubbles are fine, but **do not boil or over-cook**.
When livers are just a bit pink in the center, remove from the heat.
Strain livers and discard the poaching milk.
Allow to cool.

In sauté pan melt:
4 Tbs **butter**
one pound of mushrooms *sliced* (use button, crimini, shiitake or a blend of all three)
3 or 4 **shallots** *sliced*
Add mushrooms and shallots to the butter in the pan.
Sauté over medium heat.
Do not over-brown or burn the shallots.
If the mixture gets too dry, then add more butter.
When they have cooked until tender, transfer them to a food processor or blender.
(A blender usually makes a smoother pâté, however some people prefer a country pâté to be more coarse.)

Add to the shallots and mushrooms in the blender or food processor:
3 Tbs **brandy or Madeira wine**
1 tsp **thyme leaves**
1 tsp **kosher salt**
one stick (4oz.) **butter**
Process, or purée until mixture is a smooth paste.
Season to taste with pepper and more salt, as needed.
Pour mixture into a large terrine OR it can also be made in individual ramekin dishes.
Chill thoroughly.
Serve on crackers, or with French bread slices, Melba toast or croutons.
Accompany with *cornichons* (tiny sour dill pickles), diced onion or onion relish.

The Oley Valley Inn

Crab and Corn Fritters with Jalapeño Butter and Maple Syrup

This is our most popular summer dish here at the Oley Valley Inn!

Yield: 6-8 portions, or as appetizer, about 12

4 **large eggs** *lightly beaten*
1 cup **heavy cream**
½ cup **half-and-half**
¼ cup **granulated sugar**
one 16 oz. box **Cope's® frozen double-cut corn or 2 cups shredded fresh corn kernels**
1 large **shallot** *finely minced*
6 **scallions** *trimmed, washed, sliced thinly*
1 pound **backfin crabmeat** *picked over to remove shells*
2 cups **ground cornmeal**
½ cup **all-purpose flour**
6 cups **corn kernels**, *frozen or cooked and cut off the cob*
2 tsp **baking powder**
Oil for griddle

To make Fritters:
Put all ingredients into a large mixing bowl.
Stir mixture to combine thoroughly.
Heat griddle and grease with oil.
Drop batter by spoonsfuls onto hot griddle.
Cook over moderate heat, browning lightly on each side.
Serve immediately with Jalapeño Butter and pure maple syrup.

To make Jalapeño Butter:
1 large OR 2 small jalapeño chilis, *halved, ribs and seeds removed, chopped finely*
Important:
When chopping chilis, wear rubber gloves and avoid contact with your eyes or skin.
8 ounces or 2 sticks **butter**
3 Tbs **sweet red bell pepper** *finely diced*
¼ cup *confectioners sugar*

Combine all of the above ingredients in a bowl.
Chill until served.
Flavors will develop more if it is allowed to sit.

A Culinary Journey with Chef Steve Yeanish

Curried Butternut Squash Soup with Crabmeat

This is the most popular soup created and served here at the Oley Valley Inn!

Yield: 6 servings

1 large **whole butternut squash**
2 Tbs **butter**
1 **medium onion** *peeled and diced*
2 **celery ribs** *trimmed, washed and diced*
2 **carrots** *peeled, ends removed, diced*
2 **cloves garlic** *peeled and diced (if desired)*
One 48 ounce can **chicken broth (or 6 cups home-made chicken broth)**
2-3 Tbs **curry powder**
8 ounces **crabmeat** *checked and picked through for shells*
1 cup **heavy cream**
brown sugar *as needed*
kosher salt and fresh ground pepper to taste
sliced green onion *to garnish*

Peel butternut squash with a vegetable peeler.
Carefully cut in half-lengthwise with a large knife.
(This is a very densely textured squash, so be careful when you cut it.)
Remove all seeds and discard.
Cut each half into smaller 1 inch thick slices.
Melt butter in a large soup pot or Dutch oven.
Add onion, celery, carrot and garlic, if desired.
Cook briefly to extract flavors.
Add sliced squash and cover with chicken broth.
Heat soup to simmer, cooking until squash is tender, about 20-25 minutes.
Remove from heat.

Using a hand-held purée wand, process the soup until it has blended smoothly.
This can also be mixed in small batches in a blender. Put the blender lid on securely and then drape a kitchen towel over the top of it to prevent splashing or burns.
Return the soup to the pot and heat to simmer.
Whisk in curry powder.
Add crabmeat and heavy cream.
Add brown sugar to taste, depending on sweetness desired.
Finish seasoning with salt and pepper. Garnish with green onions.

The Oley Valley Inn

Baby Spinach Salad with Warm Bacon Dressing

Mom used this dressing on dandelion greens or endive.
It is especially good served over peeled, new red potatoes with the warm salad on top.
I prefer to pass the dressing and allow each person to dress their own salad.

Yield: 6 servings

Two 8 ounce bags **baby spinach** *washed and dried with kitchen towels*
½ cup **crisp bacon bits**
6 **hard-cooked eggs** *sliced*
½ cup **red onion** *finely diced*

The Salad:
Cook about ½ pound bacon in a skillet until it is brown and crisp.
Remove bacon from the pan.
Remove all but one tablespoon of fat from the pan.
Add ¼ cup water to the pan and stir to deglaze or loosen the bacon bits from the pan.
Reduce to about 3 tablespoons and reserve for bacon dressing.
Place salad in one large, or several individual bowls.
Garnish each dish with bacon bits, sliced egg and about 1 Tbs chopped red onion.

Bacon Dressing:

Place these ingredients in a blender:
2 whole **large eggs**
½ cup **granulated sugar**
1 tsp **salt**
2 Tbs **cornstarch**
½ cup **cider vinegar**
2 cup **milk**
1 Tbs **fat from cooked bacon**

Reduced the liquid in the pan the bacon was cooked in to about 2 Tbs.
Add the liquid in the pan to the blender then mix.
Pour mixture from the blender into the saucepan.
Cook over medium heat until the dressing has thickened.
Serve warm.

Fried Artichokes with Asiago and Zesty Lemon Aioli

Yield: 6 appetizer portions

4 cups **artichoke hearts** *quartered, drained, and towel dried*
flour for dusting
4 **eggs** *lightly beaten*
1 cup **milk**
Kosher salt and ground white pepper
Dash of **hot pepper sauce**
3 cups **Panko bread crumbs** *(look for these crumbs in the Asian section of the store)*
1 cup **grated Asiago cheese**
1 Tbs **parsley flakes**
Oil for frying *(a combination of olive and canola oils works well)*

To make Aioli:
Put these ingredients in a blender and blend until smooth, then pour into a squirt bottle.
1 cup **Hellmann's or other good mayonnaise**
2 **cloves garlic** *peeled, chopped finely*
zest of ½ a lemon
1 Tbs **freshly squeezed lemon juice**
dash of hot pepper sauce
pinch of cayenne pepper

To bread the artichokes:
Combine eggs, milk, salt, pepper and hot sauce in a shallow bowl to make an egg wash.
In another bowl, combine Panko bread crumbs, Asiago cheese and parsley flakes.
Dredge artichokes in the flour.
Shake off all excess flour.
Dip artichokes in egg wash mixture.
Lift artichokes out of egg wash being sure entire surface is coated, then coat with Panko mixture.
Remove from Panko mixture and lay artichokes on tray. Arrange in a single layer.
Allow breading to "dry out" for several minutes.
Heat oil in fryer or large skillet.

Fry at 350 degrees until golden brown, turning with a slotted spoon as they brown.
Transfer browned artichokes with slotted spoon to absorbent paper.
They can be held in a 250 degree oven for up to 20 minutes.
Arrange fried artichokes on plates, generously drizzle with Aioli, then serve.

The Oley Valley Inn

Heirloom Tomato Salad

We serve this salad when the first tomatoes of the season arrive. This past summer we grew ten different varieties in our own garden! The more varieties, shapes and sizes, the better.

To Make the Herbal Vinaigrette Salad Dressing:
Good Season's® Italian dressing has been a favorite of mine since childhood.
It makes a great base for this salad dressing.
Follow the package directions, using only a good red wine vinegar and extra virgin olive oil.

Place the **Good Season's® Italian dressing mix** in a blender, then add:
2 **whole peeled garlic cloves** *chopped*
2 Tbs **flat-leaf parsley leaves**
2 Tbs **packed fresh basil leaves**
2 **whole scallions** *trimmed, washed and sliced*

Put all of the above ingredients in a blender with lid on, then blend on high until smooth.
Pour into a squirt bottle or cruet.
Dressing keeps in the refrigerator for several weeks.

The Salad:
Fresh baby arugula leaves
Tomatoes *sliced*
Cherry or mini-plum tomatoes *halved*
Tomato wedges
Red onions, *sliced about ¼ inch thick*, **Grill these ahead of time**
Fresh mozzarella cheese *sliced or in miniature balls*
Freshly ground black pepper
Kosher salt

Arrange an assortment of tomatoes on individual plates or a large platter.
Toss arugula leaves with enough extra virgin olive oil to coat them.
Arrange arugula leaves in the center of the plate.
Place several rings of onion on the arugula.
Place slices or balls of mozzarella cheese over tomatoes.
Season thoroughly with freshly ground black pepper and kosher or sea salt.
Drizzle salad generously with Herbal Vinaigrette Dressing, then serve.

Roasted Garlic Cheese Spread

Preheat oven to 350 degrees

Cut ¼ of the top off a whole head of garlic.
Rub olive oil over the entire unpeeled surface and wrap the head securely in foil.
Bake in a 350 degree oven for 35-40 minutes until cloves are soft and brown.
Unwrap and cool.
Squeeze the roasted garlic cloves into a bowl.
Mash roasted garlic with a fork, then set aside.

In mixer cream together until well blended:
puréed roasted garlic
Three 8 ounce **blocks of cream cheese** *softened*
1 **small bunch of green onions** *clean, then thinly slice the green and white parts*
2 Tbs **chopped fresh parsley** *(can use dried)*
½ cup **diced dehydrated onions**
½ tsp **white pepper**
⅔ cup **Parmesan cheese** *grated*
1 Tbs **Lea & Perrins® Worcestershire sauce**
2 Tbs **minced chives** *(fresh or dried)*
Refrigerate for several hours, or overnight, to allow flavors to blend.

Jarlsberg and Onion Fondue

My friend Ann shared this recipe with me. It is always a big hit!
Preheat oven to 350 degrees
Yield: appetizers for 6-8 people

1 packed cup **grated Jarlsberg cheese OR** *(another Swiss-type cheese may be substituted)*
1 cup **Spanish or Vidalia onion** *diced*
1 cup good-quality mayonnaise *(I prefer Hellman's® or Kraft®)*
Optional: 1 tsp. **Old Bay® seasoning**
Several dashes **hot pepper sauce**
1 cup backfin crabmeat *picked over for shells.*

Combine all ingredients in a mixing bowl, stirring until they are just combined.
Place in a shallow Pyrex® or other baking dish.
Bake at 350 degrees until it is bubbling and golden brown.
Serve hot, or at room temperature with chips, crackers, or Melba toast.

The Oley Valley Inn

Smoked Trout Pâté

2 **fillets of smoked trout** *skin removed*
1 Tbs **fresh dill weed** *lightly chopped*
1 **whole fresh shallot** *quartered*
Chop these ingredients in a food processor until fine.
Then add:
4 ounces **softened cream cheese**
½ cup **mayonnaise**
2 rounded Tbs **horseradish**
Dash of **Lea & Perrins® Worcestershire sauce**
¼ tsp **white pepper**
Process until just combined and season to taste.
Place in large a terrine or in several individual ramekins and chill thoroughly.
Serve on crackers, Melba toast, rye or pumpernickel bread or on Belgian endive spears.

Saffron Risotto

Good with veal. Try this with the Osso Bucco with Gremolata recipe on page 69.
I prefer risotto to be on the loose side, a bit thinner than porridge.
Remember, risotto always thickens as it cools.

Yield: about 6 side dish portions

2 Tbs **olive oil**
1 **medium onion** *peeled, diced*
2 cup **Arborio medium grain rice**
½ cup **dry white wine**
About 5 **simmering cups of rich chicken broth**
generous pinch of saffron threads *rubbed through your fingers and directly into the broth*
2 Tbs **soft butter** *if desired*
Grated Parmesan cheese *if desired*
In heavy saucepan, heat the olive oil and sauté the onion briefly.
Add the Arborio rice, stirring to coat each grain of rice with oil.
Add the white wine.
Stir the wine into the rice.
Begin adding the simmering chicken stock, about one cup at a time.
Simmer on medium heat until the stock has been absorbed.
Continue adding stock gradually, as needed.
When grains have become "tender to the tooth" or *al dente*, remove rice from the heat.
Season to taste with salt and freshly ground black pepper.
Add butter and or cheese, if desired.

Orange and Rosemary Roasted Pork Loin

This is an excellent dish for a large group, especially served buffet or family style. The Savory Leek and Bacon Bread Pudding is an excellent accompaniment, and so is the Sweet Potato Filling. See recipe on the next page.

Preheat oven to 350 degrees
Yield: 8 servings

One 4-5 pound **center cut boneless pork loin** *(not two pieces tied together)*
Kosher salt and freshly ground black pepper
4 Tbs **freshly chopped rosemary leaves (or 2 Tbs crumbled dry rosemary leaves)**
One 12 ounce **jar orange marmalade**

Rub entire surface of the pork loin with salt, black pepper and rosemary.
Place the meat in a roasting pan or Pyrex® baking dish.
Brush the entire surface of the roast with as much orange marmalade as possible.

Place pork in a 350-degree oven and roast approximately 45 minutes or until the surface is bubbly and brown. Instant read thermometer should read 165 degrees.

If the surface of the roast starts to burn, lower the temperature and cover with foil till done.
Remove roast from pan, place it on a warm serving platter and tent it with foil.
Allow roast to rest in a warm spot for about twenty minutes.
Pour any juices from the roasting pan into a small saucepan.
Add any additional marmalade or juices that have run off the pork.
Heat juices slowly until the mixture has reduced and thickened.
To serve, slice roast into thin slices and sauce over it or pour sauce into a gravy boat.

The Oley Valley Inn

Sweet Potato Filling

I like Potato Filling, so I created my own version as an alternative to the White Potato Filling the local Pennsylvania Dutch traditionally make in this area. It goes great with turkey, ham, pork or chicken. This dish can easily be made one day ahead, then baked when needed, so it's great for the holiday season.

Preheat oven to 325 degrees
Yield: 6-8 servings

6 large **or** 8 medium **sweet potatoes or yams**
8 slices **good quality sandwich bread** *toasted and sliced (Pepperidge Farm® or Arnold®are good)*
½ cup **OR** 1 stick **butter or margarine** *melted in a large skillet*
1 large **Spanish onion** *peeled and diced*
5 **ribs celery** *trimmed and washed, then diced*
4 **large eggs**
½ cup **milk or cream**
Kosher salt and freshly ground black pepper
2 Tbs **chopped flat-leafed parsley**

Bake yams or sweet potatoes in a 350 degree oven for 1 hour, or until fork-tender and the skin is loose.

While yams are baking:
Gently sauté the onions and celery in the melted butter until onions are transparent and celery has cooked through, then cool to room temperature.
(Some cooks prefer to actually caramelize the vegetables. I sometimes do, but it isn't necessary.)

When cooked yams are cool enough to handle, peel them and place them in a mixer bowl.
Use the flat paddle or beaters of the mixer to mash the yams.
Add the butter, onion and celery mixture and the toasted bread cubes.
Mix briefly.
Add the eggs, one at a time, while the mixer is running.
Add the milk or cream.
Add the parsley.
Season to taste with salt and freshly ground black pepper.
Place vegetable mixture into a spray-coated baking dish.
Bake uncovered for 30-45 minutes, until puffy and golden brown.

Savory Leek and Bacon Bread Pudding

This is good served with pork, poultry or a stew.

Preheat oven to 325 degrees

1 pound **bacon**
Dice it, fry it, then remove it from the pan.
Reserve **2 Tbs** of the **bacon fat**
3 **leeks** *cut in half lengthways, cut off green ends and root end*
After washing the leeks, slice across them making thin slices.
Sauté the leeks in the reserved bacon fat until they are tender and transparent.
Then set aside to cool.
1 **loaf quality sandwich bread** *about a pound (Pepperidge Farm® or Arnold® are good)*
Cut bread into ½ inch cubes.

CHEF SAYS:
Either allow bread cubes to go stale by leaving them out overnight OR toast bread cubes on a sheet pan in a 300 degree oven for 15 minutes.

Put bread cubes into a large bowl.
Add bacon and leeks.

In a blender mix:
1 quart of **milk or half and half**
6 large **eggs**
Salt
White pepper
Dash of **fresh nutmeg** *if desired*
Dash of **hot pepper sauce**
½ cup **melted butter**

Pour this mixture over the bowl of bread cubes.
Add bacon and leeks.
Stir and set aside for 15 minutes.
Stir again, then pour into a greased two quart Pyrex® baking dish.
Cover with foil.
Place on a rack in the middle of the oven.
Bake for 30 minutes.
Uncover, then bake for 15 more minutes.
This is done when it puffs up, or when a knife inserted in the center comes out clean.

The Oley Valley Inn

Pecan-Crusted Fillet of Red Snapper with Red Raspberry Beurre Blanc

Yield: Serves 4

The Fish:

Four 6 to 7 ounce **fresh red snapper fillets** *(skinned and all bones removed)*

1 cup **pecans** *finely chopped*

⅓ cup **bread crumbs**

3 Tbs **clarified butter**

3 Tbs **canola oil**

In a food processor chop the pecans with the breadcrumbs.

(This will prevent the pecans from turning into a pecan butter.)

Season fish fillets with salt and freshly ground black pepper.

Dip both sides of fish into the pecan mixture and shake off any excess.

Heat clarified butter and canola oil in a large skillet.

Carefully add fillets to the hot skillet.

Cook for 2 to 3 minutes over medium-high heat on both sides until golden brown.

Remove from skillet and drain on paper towels.

If fillets are thick, finish cooking them on a platter in a 350 degree oven.

To Make the Red Raspberry Beurre Blanc:

1 Tbs **butter**

1 **shallot** *finely diced*

1 cup **white wine**

½ cup **heavy cream**

2 Tbs **seedless red raspberry purée**

4 Tbs **sweet butter**

Heat skillet.

Melt 1 tablespoon butter. Add diced shallot and sauté briefly.

Remove pan from heat, then add 1 cup white wine.

Return to heat and reduce mixture to ¼.

Add ½ cup heavy cream and 2 tablespoons red raspberry puree.

When reduced by half, remove from the heat.

Whisk in one tablespoon of sweet butter at a time, until sauce is smooth and creamy.

To Serve:

Place fish fillet on a plate and pour Raspberry Beurre Blanc over it.

Garnish with fresh red raspberries and serve.

Twice-Baked Stuffed Potatoes

I have made thousands of these potatoes during my career!

Preheat oven to 400 degrees
Yield: 8 servings

4 large **Idaho or Russet potatoes**
4 ounce **butter**
½ cup **onion** *diced finely*
1 cup **milk or half and half**
1 cup **instant potato flakes**
¾ cup **sour cream**
½ cup **Parmesan cheese**
4 Tbs **snipped chives**
2 large **eggs** *beaten*
1 tsp **salt**
¼ tsp **ground white pepper**
Garlic powder *to taste*

Scrub potato skins.
Prick skin surface with a knife to prevent the skin from bursting in the oven.
Bake at 400 degrees until the skin is crisp and cooked through, about 1 hour.
Allow potatoes to cool slightly.

Melt butter in a sauté pan and sauté onions until they are transparent.
Add milk.
Heat until simmering.
Add instant potatoes to thicken, then stir.
Remove pan from the heat.

Cut potatoes in half length-wise with a serrated knife to make "potato boats."
Scoop potatoes out of the skins and mash OR put them through a ricer immediately.
Add onion mixture to the mashed potatoes.
Add sour cream, Parmesan cheese, chives and eggs.
Season to taste with salt, ground white pepper and garlic powder.
If the mixture seems too loose to hold a shape, add a bit more potato flakes to thicken it.
(The eggs will help the mixture to "set " in the oven.)
Place potato mixture back into potato skins using spoon or a pastry bag with large star tip.
Bake again in a 350-degree oven for 15-20 minutes or until lightly brown and hot.

The Oley Valley Inn

Roasted Beet Salad with Chèvre and Walnut Croutons

Chèvre, or goat cheese, is easier to cut when it is cold, but it may crumble. Slightly warmer pieces of cheese can be shaped into discs, then coated by pressing the chopped walnuts directly into the cheese.

Preheat oven to 350 degrees
Yield: 6 servings as a salad course

6 **small fresh beets** *tops trimmed to ½ inch, washed*
Olive oil to rub on beets
Lightly rub beets with olive oil.
Place beets, lined up in a row on a 16-inch long piece of foil.
Roll the foil up into a cylinder with beets tucked inside, then twist the ends like a large taffy.
Place foil cylinder on a small sheet tray on the center rack of the oven.
Bake about 1½ hours or until tender when a knife tip is inserted.
Allow beets in the foil to cool to room temperature for at least one hour.
(This can be done several days ahead, while you are making a roast or baking.)
When beets are cool, unwrap the foil.
Wear plastic gloves if you don't want to stain your hands.
The tender beets should slip right out of their skins.
Slice beets, then cut into julienne (match stick size) pieces. Reserve them for the salad.

To Make Cider Vinaigrette:
½ cup **apple cider vinegar**
¼ cup **apple juice concentrate**
1 Tbs **Dijon mustard**
1 medium **shallot** *sliced*
1 cup **light olive or canola oil** *or a blend of both*
Dash of kosher salt and freshly ground black pepper
Place vinegar, apple juice concentrate, Dijon and shallot in a blender.
Liquify ingredients on high speed with the lid on tight.
While blender is running on low speed, pour the oil in a steady stream through the opening on top of the blender lid.
Season finished dressing with salt and pepper to taste.
(This dressing can be made up to 3 days ahead)

Chèvre "Croutons"
1 cup **walnuts**, toasted in a 350-degree oven for 10 minutes, then chopped medium
1 piece **French goat cheese (Chèvre)** cut into six half-inch slices
See note at top of recipe.

Late Summer Succotash

This makes a great vegetarian dinner.
It can be served in a bread bowl and topped with Pepper Jack cheese or cheddar cheese or baked in a casserole and topped with your choice of cheese.
It is also a great buffet dish.

Yield: 8-10 servings

4 **ears corn,** *cooked or uncooked, cut off he cob (you can use frozen corn)*
2 Tbs **olive oil**
1 **medium onion** *peeled and diced*
1 **small green pepper** *seeded and diced*
1 **small red pepper** *seeded and diced*
2 **small** OR 1 **large zucchini** *diced*
2 **cloves garlic** *peeled, diced finely or passed through garlic press*
2 cups **fresh lima beans** *lightly blanched (can substitute frozen beans)*
2 cups **fava beans** *shelled, peeled and blanched (can use frozen beans)*
One 16 ounce can **black beans** *drained and rinsed*
4 **Roma tomatoes** *quartered, then sliced (peeled if desired)*
1 tsp **fresh thyme leaves** OR ½ tsp **dried thyme**
Kosher salt and freshly ground black pepper
10 **fresh basil leaves** *rolled, then cut into thin shreds (chiffonade)*

In a large skillet, heat olive oil.
Briefly sauté onions, peppers, zucchini and garlic.
Do not let the garlic turn brown, or it will add a bitter flavor.
If using raw corn, cut it off the cob, add it now and cook it briefly.
Pre-cooked or frozen corn can be added directly without par boiling
Add remaining ingredients, except the basil.
Season to taste with kosher salt and freshly ground black pepper.

Simmer ingredients on medium heat for 10-15 minutes.
Add chopped basil.
Add salt and pepper to taste.

The Oley Valley Inn

Zesty Lemongrass Dressing

Lemongrass is popular herb in Thai and Vietnamese cooking. For a quick meal, I like to add this dressing to a combination of cooked noodles, leftover shrimp, grilled chicken, sliced scallions and peanuts. Sometimes I add crisp, peppery arugula leaves to this salad.

Yield: about 5 cups

6 **cloves garlic** *peeled*
one 3 ounce **piece of ginger root** *peeled*
*3 pieces **lemongrass**
(Use only the tender center-part of the lemongrass. Each piece should be about 3-4 inches long.)
2 cups **rice vinegar**
¼ cups **soy sauce**
½ cup **cilantro leaves** *loosely packed and chopped*
6 **sprigs fresh mint** *leaves only, chopped*
4-6 Tbs **brown sugar** *to your preferred sweetness*
** 2 **jalapeño peppers** *seeded, ribs removed, finely diced*

CHEF SAYS:
Wear rubber gloves when handling or chopping jalapeño peppers.
Do NOT let them touch your eyes or skin!

1 Tbs **hot oil** *(available in the Asian section of most markets)*
2 cups **peanut oil**
Juice of 1 **lime** *zest removed and added to juice*

Finely mince garlic, ginger root and lemongrass.
(This can be done in food processor.)
Put minced garlic, ginger root and lemongrass in a stainless, or nonreactive aluminum bowl.
Add remaining ingredients and mix well.
Let dressing stand for at least one hour after it is made to allow the flavors to develop.

* Available in most Asian markets
** You can also substitute sareno chilies or 2 tsp crushed red pepper pods

Walnut Onion Bread

Preheat oven to 350 degrees

1 pound and 12 ounces (about 5½ cups) **all purpose flour**
1 Tbs **instant yeast**
1 Tbs **salt**
17 **ounces skim milk OR** 16 ounces **water** plus 3 ounces **instant nonfat milk powder**
3½ ounces **walnut or olive oil**

Combine flour and yeast.
Add salt, then stir again.
Add milk.
Add oil.
Knead for 7 minutes using a dough hook.
Place dough in an oiled bowl, cover with plastic wrap and let it double in size.
Turn dough out onto floured table.

Roll dough out into a rectangle and sprinkle the surface with:
1½ cups **chopped walnuts**
1 cup **finely diced fresh onion**

Fold dough over and gently knead the walnuts and onion into the dough.
Rest dough for 30 minutes.
Shape dough into four long loaves.
Allow dough to rise and proof again.

Mist loaves with water.
Cut several diagonal slashes on top of each loaf.
Place pan of loaves in oven.
Bake for 30-35 minutes or until an instant read thermometer reads 202 degrees.

The Oley Valley Inn

Chocolate Almond Biscotti

Preheat oven to 350 degrees

1½ cup **butter or margarine** *softened*
1¼ cup **sugar**
2 **eggs**
1 tsp **almond extract**
2¼ cup **all-purpose flour**
¼ cup **Hershey's Cocoa Powder or European-style cocoa**
1 tsp **baking powder**
¼ tsp **salt**
1 cup **sliced almonds**

In large bowl, beat butter and sugar until they are well blended.
Add eggs and almond extract.
Beat until smooth.
Stir together the flour, cocoa, baking powder and salt.
Blend this into the butter mixture, beating until smooth. *(Dough will be thick)*.
Using a wooden spoon, work almonds into the dough.

Divide dough in half.
Using lightly-floured hands, shape each half of the dough into rectangular logs that are about 2 inches wide and 11 inches long.
Place log-shaped dough on a large, ungreased cookie sheet, at least 2 inches apart.
Bake for 30 minutes or until logs are set.

Remove from oven.
Cool on a cookie sheet for 15 minutes.
Using a serrated knife and a sawing motion, cut logs diagonally into ½ inch slices.
Discard the little end pieces, or feed them to the cook.
Arrange slices cut-side down, close together on a cookie sheet.

Bake a second time for 8 to 9 minutes.
Turn each slice over.

Bake an additional 8 to 9 minutes.
Remove from oven.
Cool on cookie sheet or a wire rack.

Crab-Crusted Flounder with Scalloped Corn

Preheat oven to 375 degrees
Yield: Serves 4

Four 6 ounce **flounder fillets** *(can substitute Talapia)*
8 ounces **lump or backfin crabmeat** *picked over to remove any shells*
½ cup **mayonnaise**
1 tsp **lemon juice**
Dash **hot pepper sauce**
Dash **Lea & Perrins® Worcestershire sauce**
¼ tsp **dry mustard**
1 Tbs **chives** *chopped*
1 Tbs **parsley** *chopped*
1 cup **dry breadcrumbs**
2 Tbs **melted butter**
4 ears **fresh corn** *shucked, kernels cut off cobs*
2 Tbs **melted butter**
1 cup **heavy cream, half and half or milk**

Spray a cookie sheet or shallow-sided pan with Pam® pan primer or vegetable oil spray.
Place four even portions of fish fillets skin-side up on the pan.
Combine mayonnaise, lemon juice, hot pepper sauce, Worcestershire sauce, parsley and chives and stir well.
Add the crab to this mixture and stir again.
Divide mixture into four equal portions and spread one portion on top of each piece of fish.
Combine breadcrumbs and melted butter, then spread this on top of each fish portion.
Bake fish at 375 degrees for 20-25 minutes until the top is golden brown and the fish flakes when it is tested with a fork.

To make the sauce:
Melt the remaining 2 Tbs of butter until foamy.
Immediately add corn kernels and sautée briefly.
Season with salt and pepper.
Add cream, half and half or milk and continue cooking until sauce has slightly thickened.
Add more salt and pepper to taste.
Add a pinch of sugar, if desired.
If you want a richer sauce, add a tablespoon of soft butter.
Spoon corn mixture on top of plates, top with baked flounder fillet, then serve.

Sesame-Crusted Salmon with Roasted Tomato and Papaya Salsa

Preheat oven to 275 degrees
Yield: Serves 6

6 pieces of **salmon fillet,** each weighing 6-8 ounces *(your fish supplier can cut them for you)*
1 cup **toasted sesame seeds** *(mixed with 2 tsp black sesame seeds, if available)*
1 **lime**
Salt and pepper
6 **Roma tomatoes**
Salt and pepper
1 **papaya** *peeled, seeded and cut in ½ inch dice*
Juice of ½ lemon
1 Tbs **olive oil**
2 Tbs **rice wine vinegar**

To make the Papaya Salsa:
First roast the tomatoes:
Slice Roma tomatoes length-wise.
Arrange the tomatoes on a baking sheet, cut side up.
Season with salt and pepper, and an optional olive oil drizzle.
Bake in 275 degree oven for about 30 minutes or until they start to dry out.
The actual time will depend on the size and ripeness of your tomatoes.
They should not be as dry as a sun-dried tomato.
At this point, Roasted tomatoes can be stored in the refrigerator for up to two weeks in a covered container. They're also great in pastas, as a pizza topping or on sandwiches.
Chop the roasted tomatoes into small pieces.
Place tomatoes in a mixing bowl and stir in papaya, lemon juice, olive oil and vinegar.
Taste for salt and pepper.
Add a bit of sugar or artificial sweetener, depending on your taste.

To make the Salmon:
Squeeze the lime juice on the salmon fillets.
Season fillets with salt and pepper.
Liberally sprinkle sesame seeds on both sides of the fish.
Bake in a 350 degrees oven in a non-stick-baking pan or a pan sprayed with PAM® for approximately 20 minutes.
If you prefer your fish medium or rare-
bake for a shorter time at a higher temperature (10 minutes at 400 degrees).
To serve, place papaya salsa on top of the fish or on the side. Garnish with lime wedges.

In the early days, our policy was all new servers had to work in the kitchen at least one Saturday night to learn how food was prepared, presented, garnished and how orders were called. It was a good introduction for them.

My sister Jayne and her husband David helped me out most weekends. Soon, I advertised for a waiter in the local paper. Barrie, one of the applicants, had serving, bartending and hosting experience, so I hired him.

It turned out to be a match made in Heaven. Barrie and I worked together and accomplished a lot, finishing one project after another. Phil taught Barrie how to upholster and do wall treatments. Soon, entire rooms on the second floor were redone, papered, painted, tiled and finished. The main dining room and other rooms were also redecorated. David taught Barrie bookkeeping and all the ropes of our office procedures.

We tried a new bistro-type approach in the restaurant. Our faithful customers stuck with us, but they requested more and more of our old standard menu items. Before we knew it, we were back doing variations of our original menu.

There are many mushroom farms here in the Berks County area. We got to know Ben, who had a state-of-the-art mushroom farm in nearby Lenhartsville, just a few miles from Dad's Bungalow. Ben dined frequently at the restaurant and we got to chatting. He wondered if we would be interested in doing some product development for him. He told us what that would entail and we agreed. We made trial batches of recipes in their test kitchen and then experimented creating new recipes, as well as developing some they already had. We also did yield tests of various processing procedures for cooked mushrooms that they packaged and sold.

It was very interesting work. We always had a plentiful supply of very fresh, free, top-quality mushrooms to use at the Inn.

In the early days, Ben was my mentor. He told me when his family sat down to dinner, his father would ask, "What did you do today to help your boss make money?" His father emphasized it was important to make a living, but always be sure the boss makes money so you still have a job.

Ben sat me down one day and said, "Steve, listen to me. I'm going to tell it to you straight, like I'm your uncle or father. Your business is like your child. Nobody is going to take care of it like you do. Count on that." Ben's words of advice didn't fall on deaf ears.

Enthusiasm is contagious. My friend had just purchased an old Victorian house on the Delaware River and was renovating it to make a bed and breakfast. Barrie and I spent several weekends helping her out. We saw her potential, and soon realized that we could do the same at the Inn.

One morning, the new manager of our local bank asked if she could do anything for me. I described my plans for a bed and breakfast and told her we wanted to renovate the second floor and convert the empty attic space into an apartment. "Let's talk," she said. "Write it up and start getting some estimates."

It all started from there. We were now an established business, with a liquor license. We had put so much sweat equity into the property, while continuing to improve it. Our real plans for expansion could now begin in earnest.

Berks County Mushroom Chowder

I created this soup for a very dear friend of mine, Ben Penturelli. He was a great mentor in the early days of the Inn.

1 pound **bacon** diced into ½ inch dice
1 **large Spanish onion** peeled and diced into ½ inch dice
5 **ribs celery** trimmed, washed diced into medium dice
2 pounds **sliced mushrooms** (use any combination of button, shiitake or crimini)
1 tsp **dried thyme leaves**
2 **large bay leaves**
one 48 ounce can **chicken broth OR** 6 cups **home made chicken broth**
6 **large potatoes** peeled and cut into ½ inch cubes
Water or chicken broth to cover potatoes
1 tsp **salt**
Roux or other thickener (Roux see page 87)
1 quart **half and half or milk**
3 Tbs **fresh flat leaf parsley** chopped

Place diced bacon into a heavy-bottomed deep pot.
On medium heat, crisp bacon, stirring frequently to brown evenly.
When crisp, remove bacon with a slotted spoon and drain it on paper towels.
Remove all but ¼ cup bacon fat.
Add to the pot: diced onion, celery, thyme and bay leaves.
Over medium heat, cook for 3-4 minutes to extract the flavors, stirring often.
Add sliced mushrooms and stir.
Cover pot with lid and steam on low heat for 5 minutes.
Add chicken broth and bring to a simmer over medium heat.

Meanwhile, place diced potatoes in another pan, cover with water or broth.
Add salt and simmer until potatoes are fork-tender.
While soup is simmering, thicken it lightly with roux.

CHEF SAYS:
Heat roux in the microwave until it is hot to prevent lumping, or as an alternative, whisk in slurry of water and a tablespoon of cornstarch or flour.

Cook soup stirring briskly for several minutes to fully incorporate the thickening agent.

Cooked potatoes can be added directly to the soup.
The potato water or broth will contain starch and salt, which can add flavor and also help to thicken the soup.
Add half-and-half or milk and return to simmer.
Season to taste with salt and pepper.
Finish with chopped flat leaf parsley and reserved crisp bacon bits.

A Culinary Journey with Chef Steve Yeanish

Brunch at Oley Valley Inn

You can't describe the Oley Valley Inn without talking about our brunch. We've had brunch here since the very beginning when we first opened. We were never a lunch place, but brunch is always the clever chef's way to get customers in the door. It required very little extra equipment, just effort. Brunch buffets were the rage here in Berks County, so a sit-down, served brunch was quite a shock to many of the locals at first.

I'm often asked the cost of our brunch. When I explain the price range, most people get the idea, but some don't. Many times people ask me, "How do you know how much to charge?" I'm sometimes tempted to respond, "We'll weigh you when you come in, and then again when you leave," but unfortunately, I think somebody might actually believe me!

Brunch is often the busiest service of the week here. There is a real rhythm and tempo. We're packed when we open at 11a.m., then we get another wave at noon, followed by another at 1p.m. We really are moving fast. It often takes four people in the kitchen to handle the hundred or so customers that come through the doors during that short period of time.

The brunch menu was a bit of a trial and error process to start with. We quickly learned that many people were looking for breakfast-type items, but the after-church crowd and senior citizens wanted a hearty dish that would be their main meal of the day. We soon started serving dinner-type entrées as well. Pasta dishes and entrée-type salads have always been popular, too.

I have done every version of Eggs Benedict you can imagine. Often a new recipe is the result of a quirk of fate. We once unexpectedly had an extra very nice whole, rare, roasted tenderloin of beef, so the Brunch Egg Special became Eggs Henry VIII: toasted brioche slices, topped with warm slices of roast tenderloin, poached eggs, and Béarnaise sauce. We sold out.

A chef's own personal tastes are reflected in their menus, and freshly-squeezed orange juice has always been a passion of mine. In the early days, I was squeezing a case of oranges every Sunday morning and getting more and more frustrated. I tried every kind of orange imaginable, including blends. I was using a juicer attachment that came with a commercial food processor. This thing was a dangerous weapon. The juicer attachment fit over the motor and there was a spinning hub with a basket and a strainer for the seeds. It worked well, but there was one problem. This was a *very* powerful machine. Holding on for dear life, you pressed the orange onto the motor as it ran at full speed. If you lost your grip on the orange, especially if it was wet, the orange would fly soaring into the air. Or else the centrifugal force threw the entire machine out of control. It could crash to the floor if you weren't holding on tightly for dear life. It was quite a chore, and it made one heck of a mess. To top matters off, after all this effort, the juice never tasted the same way twice. Sometimes it was really good (winter season) and others it was weak or sour. I finally gave up when I found a product that tasted consistently good.

As Chef Saucy once said to me when I was a student at the CIA, "So long as it tastes good, who really cares?"

The Oley Valley Inn

Aunt Marie's Sticky Buns

Our warm, Sticky Buns have always been a staple. Sticky Buns are presented to all diners at brunch with our compliments, along with our home-made muffins, biscuits, croissants and the occasional Moravian Sugar Cake.

I tried baking the Sticky Buns fresh on Sunday morning. It started as a noble effort, and then it just became one more thing I had to do really early on Sunday morning after a *very* long Saturday night.

We didn't have a proof box back then either, so I had to work in either an unheated kitchen in the winter or an overheated sweatshop in the summer. You get the picture.

The dough always rose too fast or too slowly. I even tried going through the entire process except for the final rise and baking. Then I realized if they were baked and frozen immediately, they could be warmed in a 350 degree oven for about four minutes. We keep them under a carving light so they are warm when served.

Aunt Marie, my father's sister, was always very special to me. She married her teenage sweetheart, Mick, who died young. She remained a widow for the rest of her life.

Aunt Marie's Sticky Buns were her claim to fame. She was often asked to make them commercially, but she refused. I'm happy that she gladly gave me her recipe.

Marie's secret was to dissolve the yeast in potato water. The result is a wonderfully light and flavorful roll. This recipe is based on her original dough recipe, but I have found a glaze that works better.

Just before the Inn opened, I invited Aunt Marie over for Sunday dinner and prepared a roast beef for the ten of us. We had a memorable meal together. She was so proud that I was inspired by *her* recipe.

Over the years several people have driven INTO the Inn instead of TO the Inn.

Sticky Buns

Our Sunday Brunch here at the Inn features these wonderful sweet rolls served warm, dripping with pecans, raisins and cinnamon goo. This recipe is for the more experienced baker!

Preheat oven to 325 degrees
Yield: about 28 individual cup cake size buns or four 9"pans

The Yeast Mixture:
1 **large potato** *peeled, cut into large cubes*
water to cover potato *(unsalted)*
2 packages **instant dry yeast**
½ cup **granulated sugar**
Cook the potato in a pan of boiling water.
Remove cooked potato from the water and **keep 1 cup of the potato water.**
(If you don't have enough water, add some mashed potatoes to make it up to one cup.)
Mash the cooked potato or put it through a ricer.
Measure 1 level cup of potatoes. *(Use the remainder for something else.)*
Put the cup of cooked potato back into the potato water and cool to lukewarm.
Sprinkle yeast into the potato water and stir thoroughly.
Cover with plastic wrap and allow the yeast mixture to double in a warm part of the kitchen.

Add these ingredients to the yeast mixture:

1 cup **milk** *room temperature*
3 cups **all purpose flour**
1 cup **granulated sugar**
2 **large eggs** *lightly beaten*
½ cup **butter or shortening**
½ tsp **salt**
Up to 6 cups **all purpose flour**

Mix briefly until the dough is formed. The dough should be supple, not stiff.
Allow the dough to double again.
Cover with plastic wrap.
During the final rising of the dough, prepare the glaze.
(Recipe continues on the next page.)

The Oley Valley Inn

Sticky Buns
(continued)

To make the glaze for the Sticky Buns:

¼ cup **melted butter**
2 cups **dark Karo® syrup**
3 cups **light brown sugar**

Heat butter, Karo and brown sugar in a saucepan until bubbling and sugar has dissolved.
Divide glaze into four 9-inch pans,
OR fill 28 individual cupcake-sized tins with about 2 Tbs per cup.
Sprinkle glaze with raisins, pecans or walnuts.

To prepare the Sticky Buns:

Place the dough on a surface dusted with flour.
Roll dough out into a large rectangle, about 12"x28."
Sprinkle entire surface of dough with:
2 cups of granulated sugar mixed with 2 Tbs of cinnamon.

Beginning at the side nearest to you, roll the dough away from you until you have a cylinder-shaped log.
Cut the log into 28 one inch thick slices
Lay the dough slices on top of the glaze in the pan or the cup cake pan
Let the dough rise again until it has doubled.

Put your pan on a cookie sheet to catch any cook-over spills.
**Bake individual buns in a 350 degree oven for 15 minutes OR
bake the round pans for 20-25 minutes.**

After the buns have finished baking, immediately invert the buns onto a serving dish.
Use a rubber spatula to collect all the nuts or raisins that have adhered to the pan.

Bananas Foster Oley Valley Inn

Yield: 6 servings

6 **small to medium ripe bananas**, *use bananas that are just starting to get brown spots*
6 **Lace Cookies shaped into bowls** *(See recipe on the next page.)*
6 scoops **cinnamon ice cream** *(recipe follows)* **OR**
store bought vanilla ice cream sprinkled with ground cinnamon
one 12 ounce jar **caramel sauce** *warmed*
confectioners sugar *for sprinkling*
6 **mint sprigs and fresh berries** *to garnish, optional*

Peel the bananas.
Cut in half, lengthwise.
Spray the cut side of the banana with a pan primer like Pam®
Grill bananas on a lightly-oiled grill pan for about 3 minutes, or until the bananas are warmed through and the hash marks from the grill are visible.
Be careful! Over-grilling will make the banana mushy and difficult to handle.

To assemble the Bananas Foster:
Spoon about 2 tablespoons of warm caramel sauce into the center of 6 large dessert plates.
Carefully place a lace cookie bowl on top of the caramel sauce.
Place a scoop of ice cream into the center of each lace cookie bowl.
Arrange two grilled banana halves on top of the ice cream.
Drizzle each dessert with more caramel sauce so the banana and the ice cream are coated.
Decorate the plate rim with confectioners sugar.
Sprinkle fresh berries of your choice around base of the cookie bowl.
Top with a mint sprig and serve.

Cinnamon Ice Cream

2 **large eggs**
1½ cups **half-and-half**
1 cup plus 2 Tbs **granulated sugar**
2½ Tbs **ground cinnamon**
1½ Tbs **vanilla extract**
4 ½ cups **heavy cream** *(at least 38% butterfat)*

Combine the above ingredients in a blender until the sugar has dissolved.
(If raw eggs are an issue, they can be omitted.)
Add heavy cream and freeze the mixture in an ice cream maker until firm.
(Follow your manufacturer's instructions)
Place the container of ice cream in the freezer for at least 8 hours, or over night.

Lace Cookies
Almond Tuille

I strongly recommend using a Silpat ®liner when making these.
They are usually available at gourmet or cookware stores like
Reading China and Glass or Williams Sonoma.
This recipe may be a challenge for the inexperienced baker.

Heat oven to 350 degrees
Select two 4" shallow bowls to use for shaping the cookie bowls.

4 ounces (1 stick) **sweet unsalted butter**
1 cup **heavy cream**
¼ teaspoon **vanilla extract**
1½ cups **blanched almonds** *sliced into different size pieces, not too small*
1⅓ cups **granulated sugar**
¼ cup **all purpose flour**
½ cup **shredded coconut**
zest of one orange

Melt butter in a small sauce pan.
Add cream and heat until lukewarm.
Remove from heat.
Add vanilla, ground almonds, sugar, flour, coconut and orange zest.
Stir until all the ingredients have just combined.
Refrigerate at least one hour.

Lightly oil a non-stick baking sheet,
or use a baking sheet lined with Sipat® liner
for quicker clean up and easier removal from the pan.

Visually divide the pan in half.
Place ¼ cup of batter on the center of each half.
This batter will really spread!
Bake for 6 minutes, then turn pan 180 degrees and bake about 6-8 minutes
longer or until the cookie is evenly baked and golden brown.
Place pan on a wire rack to improve air circulation.
Use a metal icing spatula to loosen the outer edges of the cookies as they cool.
The cookie will become more solid as it cools.
When you can run the spatula under the cookie and it remains intact,
then carefully lift it from the tray and center it over the 4" bowl.
Gently press the cookie on to the bottom of the outside of the bowl and let it cool.

A Culinary Journey with Chef Steve Yeanish

Bananas Foster French Toast

One of our Bed & Breakfast guests' favorites. This dish is nice served with sausage links or bacon.

Yield: 4 servings

1 loaf **French bread**
2 **very ripe bananas** *mashed*
6 **large eggs**
2 cups **milk**
¼ cup **brown sugar**
1 tsp **vanilla extract**
½ tsp **cinnamon**
Pinch of salt
2 Tbs **melted butter**
2 **bananas** *(sliced for garnish)*
1 cup **warm caramel sauce** *(homemade or use a ready-made ice cream topping)*

Slice French bread on a diagonal, cutting slices about 1-1½ inch thick.
(It's best if the bread is left out overnight to dry a bit).
Place mashed bananas, eggs, milk, sugar, vanilla, salt and cinnamon in a blender.
Purée until smooth.
Pour mixture into a glass dish that is large enough to hold all the slices of bread.
Allow a few minutes for the bread to soak up the batter, then flip the bread over.

On a medium-hot griddle or in a large nonstick frying pan melt the butter.
Do not let the butter burn.
Fry bread on both sides until the batter has set in the center and it has browned evenly.
(Bread slices can be finished by baking in a 350 degrees oven.)

To serve, top each slice of French Toast with sliced bananas, then drizzle with warm caramel sauce, or maple syrup, then dust with powdered sugar and serve.

The Oley Valley Inn

Banana Surprise Muffins

Preheat oven to 350 degrees
Yield: 24 muffins
Line a 24 cup muffin tin with paper liners

1 cup plus 2 Tbs **soft butter**
2 cups **light brown sugar**
4 **eggs**
2 tsp **vanilla extract**
4 cups **flour**
2 tsp **baking soda**
2 cup (about 6) **really ripe, mushy bananas** *puréed*
2 **yellow bananas**
1 cup **creamy peanut butter**
1½ cups **mini semi-sweet chocolate chip morsels**

Cream soft butter and brown sugar until it is light and fluffy.

Beat in one egg at a time, and scrape down the bowl often.
Add vanilla.

Sift together flour and baking soda.
Add half of the dry ingredients and mix until combined, scraping the bowl often.
Add half of the banana purée until combined.
Add remaining flour.
Add remaining banana purée.

Cut and dice the yellow bananas.
Fold the cut bananas into the batter.

Combine peanut butter with mini chocolate chips.

Spoon or scoop batter into the bottom of the paper-lined cups in the muffin tin.
Place a small scoop of the peanut butter mixture into the center of each liner.

Top with more batter, until each liner is ⅔ full.
Bake for 20–25 minutes.

Chilled Strawberry Soup with Amaretto

This is a refreshing soup on a warm June day! This soup looks especially nice when served in an oversized wine glass, preferably one with a wide-mouthed rim for easier eating. The rim can also be coated in advance with egg white and sugar for even more visual appeal.

Yield: about 2 quarts, or 8 servings

1 quart **fresh or frozen strawberries**
½ to 1 cup **Simple Syrup**

CHEF SAYS:
To make Simple Syrup: boil equal parts of sugar and water, then let it cool.

2 tsp **fresh lemon juice**
1½ cups **dairy sour cream**
¾ cup **Amaretto** *a sweet almond-flavored Italian liqueur*
Almond extract *as needed*
Sour cream to garnish
Fresh mint sprigs
Strawberry slices

Place strawberries, Simple Syrup, lemon juice, sour cream and Amaretto in a blender.
Pulse until completely smooth.
Taste soup, adding more sugar, lemon and almond extract to your taste.
Serve in chilled bowls garnished with a dollop of sour cream, mint leaf and
a slice of strawberry.

The Oley Valley Inn

Sour Cream Streusel Muffins

These muffins freeze well in an airtight container.

Preheat oven to 400 degrees
Yield: 12 muffins

2 cups sifted **all purpose flour**
½ cup **granulated sugar**
1 Tbs **baking powder**
1 **egg**
½ cup **melted butter**
8 ounces **sour cream**
1 tsp **vanilla extract**

In a large bowl, sift together the flour, sugar and baking powder.

In another bowl, lightly beat the egg.
Add the melted butter, sour cream and vanilla extract.
Combine well.
Add the sour cream mixture to the flour mixture and mix just until combined.

CHEF SAYS:
Over-mixing will make the muffins heavy and dense, not light and fluffy.)

Fill greased or paper-lined muffin tins with batter.

To Make the Streusel Topping:

⅓ cup **granulated sugar**
¼ tsp **cinnamon**
3 Tbs **butter**
⅓ cup **chopped walnuts**

Mix the sugar and cinnamon together.
Cut in the butter with a pastry blender.
Stir in the walnuts.

Sprinkle Streusel Topping over the batter.
Bake muffins 15 to 20 minutes
or until a tester inserted into the center of a muffin comes out clean.

Eggs "Inn Style"

Yield: 2 servings

Make Hollandaise Sauce *(Recipe is on the next page.)*

4 whole **extra large eggs**, *cracked into a shallow bowl*
1 Tbs **salt**
2 Tbs **white vinegar**
2 **English muffins** *fork-split and toasted*
four slices **ripe tomato cut $^3/_8$ inch thick,** *seasoned with kosher salt and ground black pepper*
Flour for dredging
Egg Wash *(1 egg beaten with ¼ cup milk)*
Breadcrumbs preferably Japanese Panko-style*
Oil for frying
3 **strips bacon** *cooked until crisp then crumbled*
2 **scallions** *trimmed, sliced thinly*

Dredge sliced and seasoned tomatoes in flour then shake off any excess flour.
Dip tomato in egg wash and coat thoroughly, then place in breadcrumbs.
Gently press crumbs into tomato slice.
Place on plate and let it dry for several minutes.
Meanwhile, heat 2 inches of water in a deep-sided pan until water just begins to simmer around the edges.
Add salt and white vinegar.
In a sauté pan, with enough room to fry all four slices of tomato at one time, heat ¼ inch of salad oil.
Fry the tomatoes on medium heat until golden brown on each side.
Remove from pan, drain on paper towels, and keep warm.
Place two halves of toasted English muffin on each plate,
then top with warm sliced fried tomato.

To Poach Eggs:
Stir water in a circular motion until it makes a whirlpool.
One at a time gently pour an individual egg into the center of the whirlpool in the pan.
The motion of the water will help to keep the egg together.
Let the egg cook for a minute, then gently lift it out with a slotted spoon.
Depending upon how firm you like your poached eggs, remove drain thoroughly, and then top each muffin with an egg. Continue until each egg has cooked.
Spoon warm Hollandaise Sauce over each half of the muffin.
Top with crumbled bacon and scallions and serve at once.
Accompany with home fried or hashed brown potatoes.

The Oley Valley Inn

Easy Hollandaise Sauce

2 sticks **OR** ½ pound **butter**
1 **whole egg**
3 **egg yolks**
Dash of cayenne pepper or few drops of hot sauce
Juice of ½ fresh lemon
½ tsp salt *if using unsalted butter*

In a small saucepan melt **2 sticks OR ½ pound butter**.
Continue melting until butter is bubbly and begins to separate.
Keep butter very warm.

Put these ingredients in a blender:
1 **whole egg**
3 **egg yolks** *reserve the whites for another use*
Dash of cayenne pepper or a few drops of hot sauce
Juice of ½ fresh lemon
½ tsp salt *if using unsalted butter*

Place the lid on the blender.
Mix briefly on low speed with the lid on,
then remove the center portion in the top of the lid.
While machine is running slowly, pour hot melted butter into the egg mixture,
and continue blending until sauce thickens.
Milk solids can be added to thin out sauce.
Taste for final seasoning, adding salt, pepper and lemon as needed.
Keep sauce in a warm place or in a Thermos® or other insulated jar until ready for use.

Eggs Henry VIII

Yield: 4 servings

4 **English muffins** *toasted and lightly buttered*
8 slices **rare filet of beef, or raw slices of filet**, *about ³⁄₈ inch thick*
8 slices **beefsteak tomato** *approximately the same size as the muffin*
8 **large eggs** *poached and drained thoroughly*
1 Tbs **salt**
2 Tbs **white vinegar**
about 1 cup **Béarnaise Sauce** *(See recipe on the next page.)*

To Poach Eggs:
Simmer water in a sauce pot. Add salt and vinegar.
Stir water in a circular motion until it makes a whirlpool.
One at a time gently slide an egg into the center of the whirlpool in the pan.
The motion of the water will help to keep the egg together.
Let the egg cook for about a minute, depending upon how firm you like your poached eggs, then gently lift egg out of the pan with a slotted spoon.
Drain each egg thoroughly, and then place each on top of a toasted muffin.
Continue until each egg has cooked.

While eggs are poaching:
Heat a large skillet.
Place English muffins, buttered side up, on individual plates
Season tomato slices with kosher salt and freshly ground black pepper, then quickly heat tomato slices in the pan, turning once, then place one tomato slice on each muffin.

Season beef filet slices the same way.
Add a small amount of oil to hot skillet.
Place beef slices in the pan, turning as meat is heated and just about cooked through.
Most people prefer their beef rare for this dish.
Place the beef on top of each tomato.
Place a warm poached egg on top of the beef.
Top each with a generous dollop of Béarnaise sauce.
Serve with any kind of fried potatoes.

The Oley Valley Inn

Béarnaise Sauce

Yield: 4 servings

¼ cup **finely diced onion, shallot OR a combination of the two**
2 Tbs **fresh tarragon leaves, chopped OR** 2 tsp **dried tarragon leaves**
¼ cup **dry white wine**
¼ cup **red wine vinegar**

Combine all of the above ingredients in a small saucepan.
Place saucepan over medium heat.
Simmer slowly until reduction is almost dry.
Remove pan from heat.
Allow to cool to room temperature.

Prepare a quick Easy Hollandaise Sauce. *(See recipe on page 145)*

Instead of lemon juice, add the tarragon-onion reduction to the Hollandaise Sauce in the blender as soon as the sauce is finished.
Stir in 2 tsp. fresh chopped parsley and additional chopped fresh tarragon, if desired.

Pumpkin Mushroom Soup

6 Tbs **butter or margarine**
1 cup **onion** *diced finely*
½ cup **leeks** *wash thoroughly and finely dice the white part only*
½ cup **celery** *diced finely*
½ cup **carrots** *diced finely*
1 **clove garlic** *finely chopped (optional)*
1 pound **button mushrooms** *sliced*
1 quart **chicken stock** *(can substitute vegetable stock or water with bullion cubes)*
2 cups **cooked puréed pumpkin**
4 Tbs **all purpose flour**
2 cups **heavy cream** *(can substitute half and half or milk)*
Salt *to taste*
Freshly ground pepper *to taste*
Curry powder *to taste*

Heat 2 Tbs butter in large heavy sauce pan.
Sauté onions, leeks, celery, carrots and garlic over medium heat for 3-4 minutes **without browning.**
Add sliced mushrooms.
Sweat by covering pan with lid and cooking vegetables gently in their own juices until tender.
Season with salt and pepper.
Add stock and pumpkin.
Stir to blend thoroughly, then simmer.

In a small saucepan make a roux: *(See Roux page 87.)*
Melt remaining 4 Tbs butter.
Add flour and cook, stirring over low heat until flour cooks, is blonde in color and gritty.
Slightly cool.

Add roux to simmering stock.
Whisk to blend and allow stock to thicken.
Add heavy cream.
Bring to boil.
Season to taste with salt, pepper and curry powder.

The Oley Valley Inn

White Chicken Chili

Yield: about 6 servings

1 pound **dried Navy or Great Northern beans** *picked over*
OR three 20 ounce cans **Navy or Great Northern beans** *(reserve the liquid from can)*
2 **whole chicken breasts** *with bone and skin OR 4 split breasts*
Water to cover chicken breasts OR one 48 ounce **can chicken broth**
1 **medium onion** *sliced*
2 **ribs celery** *trimmed, washed sliced*
4 **cloves garlic** *crushed*
1 **bay leaf**
1 **large Spanish onion** *diced*
2 **ribs celery** *trimmed, washed, diced*
1 large **bell pepper** *diced*
two 4 ounce cans **chopped green chilies**
Several dashes of hot sauce *(to taste)*
1½ tsp **chili powder**
1-2 tsp **cumin** *(to taste)*
Salt *to taste*
Diced cooked chicken breast
½ cup **sour cream**
1½ cups **Monterey Jack cheese** *grated*
¼ cup **cilantro leaves** *to garnish*

CHEF SAYS:
*If you're using dried beans, then soak the beans in two quarts of water over night. The next day, drain the beans, place them in a heavy pot, and cover them with four quarts of water. Bring water to a boil, then simmer about 1 hour, or until beans are tender. Do **not** add salt to the water or it will toughen the beans. When beans are tender, remove from heat, and cool in cooking water.*

Prepare the chicken:
Place chicken breasts in a saucepan and cover with water or canned chicken broth.
Add sliced onion, celery, garlic and a bay leaf then simmer until chicken is tender.
Remove chicken from broth and allow to cool.
When chicken is cool remove skin and bones, then dice remaining meat into ½ inch pieces.
Remove excess fat from stock by skimming with a spoon.
Remove bay leaf.

In a large pot:
Sweat (p.87) the diced onion, celery, and peppers in 2 Tbs oil.
Add stock or broth and bring to a boil.
Add chilis, hot sauce, chili powder and cumin.
Purée one cup of beans and add it to the pot to thicken the stock or broth.
Add diced chicken, remaining beans and any reserved bean liquid. Heat to simmer.
Garnish with a generous portion of sour cream, grated cheese, and fresh cilantro leaves.

Pumpkin Crème Brûlée

This recipe uses a water bath, which will provide a low, even temperature so the custard can set properly. (see p.87) You'll need a clean cotton kitchen towel and a baking pan with high sides that is large enough to hold all the ramekins

Preheat oven to 325 degrees
Yield: 12 servings
Grease 12 ramekins

CHEF SAYS
How To Use a Vanilla Bean:
Split vanilla bean in half, length-wise. Scrape inside of vanilla bean with tip of paring knife to remove as many seeds as possible. Place vanilla bean halves in a shallow bowl then cover with ½ cup of granulated sugar. Rub the sugar over the center of the bean to extract as many vanilla seeds as possible.

3½ cups **heavy cream**
1 cup **milk**
½ tsp **cinnamon**
¼ tsp **allspice**
½ cup **granulated sugar**
½ tsp **ground ginger**
1 **whole vanilla bean**
½ cup **granulated sugar**
14 **egg yolks**
1 cup **cooked pumpkin purée**
½ cup **raw or turbino sugar**

Whisk egg yolks into vanilla-sugar mixture.
Add the other ½ cup sugar, the cinnamon, allspice and ground ginger.
Scald heavy cream and milk together in a heavy sauce pan. **Do not boil!**
Slowly add a bit of the scalded cream mixture into the yolks to temper the mixture.
Add remaining heated cream, and keep stirring as you go.
Stir in pumpkin purée.
Strain mixture through a fine sieve.
Divide mixture into equal-sized ramekins.
Place a clean cotton kitchen towel in the bottom of the baking pan. Fold the towel to fit.
Place the filled ramekins on the towel in the pan.
Carefully create a Water Bath (p.87) by filling the baking sheet halfway up the side of the ramekins with boiling water. *Don't get the water in the ramekins!*
Carefully place the baking pan in a 325-degree oven.
Bake for approximately 20 minutes, or until a clean knife inserted into the center of each ramekin comes out clean.
To finish, pour a thin layer of turbino sugar over the surface.
Place ramekins under the broiler or finish with a torch until golden brown, but not burned.

The Oley Valley Inn

Pumpkin Pancakes Oley Valley Inn

2 cups **all purpose flour**
2 Tbs **sugar**
4 tsp **baking powder**
1 Tbs **cinnamon**
¾ tsp **salt**
½ tsp **ground coriander**
1½ cups **milk**
1 cup **solid-packed pumpkin**
½ cup (1 stick) **unsalted butter** *melted*
4 **large eggs** *beaten*
1 Tbs **vanilla extract**

Vegetable oil or spray for griddle surface.
In a large bowl, whisk together the flour, sugar, baking powder, cinnamon,
salt and coriander.

In another bowl whisk together milk, pumpkin, melted butter, eggs and vanilla extract.
Stir milk mixture into flour mixture, mixing until it is just combined.
Heat griddle or large cast-iron skillet over moderate heat until it is hot enough to
make a few drops of water scatter when dropped on to the griddle surface.
Lightly oil the surface of the griddle.
Use a ¼ cup size measuring cup to drop batter onto the pan, forming four inch rounds.
Cook pancakes for 1-2 minutes on each side until golden brown.
Transfer pancakes to a heat-proof platter as they are cooked.
Keep them warm in an oven until they are ready to serve.
Serve warm with sweet creamy butter and maple syrup.

Apple Dumplings Oley Valley Inn

This is a three part recipe: First prepare the pastry, then the apples, and then the syrup.

Preheat oven to 350 degrees
To make the pastry:
2 cups **all purpose flour**
2 tsp **baking powder**
1 tsp **salt**
¼ cup **vegetable shortening**
¼ cup **butter** *chilled, then cut into small pieces*
Place all ingredients into the bowl of a food processor.
Pulse several times until the mixture looks evenly mixed.
Place dough on a lightly floured surface and combine it into one smooth ball. Divide dough into six pieces.
Roll dough into 6 squares, about 6 inches square.

To prepare the apples:
Peel 6 **apples**, *They should be about 3 inches in diameter.*
McIntosh produces softer texture; Red Rome will be as good, but with more texture.
Cut each apple in half and remove the core with a melon-baller.
Sprinkle inside surface of the apple with **cinnamon sugar.**
Fill with **raisins**. *(if desired)*
Place apple halves back together to make a whole apple.
Place each apple on top of a dough square and sprinkle with cinnamon sugar.
Top each apple with a piece of **butter the size of an acorn.**
Prepare an egg wash *(a mixture of 1 egg beaten with 2 Tbs milk)*
Use a pastry brush to brush the egg wash over the entire surface of the apple.
Pull dough up from each of the corners to meet on the top of the apple.
Press edges together using a light pressure to seal the dough.
Place dumplings in a greased pan or glass baking dish.
Bake dumplings in a 350 degree oven for 30 minutes.

To prepare the Apple Syrup:
Combine these ingredients in a saucepan and bring to a boil:
1 cup **apple cider or juice**
½ cup **light brown sugar** *packed*
½ cup **butter**
1 tsp **cinnamon** and ¼ tsp **nutmeg**
Pour the syrup over the dumplings and bake an additional thirty minutes.
Use the tip of a knife to test the apples, which should bake until tender.
Serve warm with Apple Syrup. This is really good served with vanilla ice cream.

Coconut Ice Cream

This is used as the base for many of our desserts here at the Oley Valley Inn.

Yield: about 2 quarts

In blender, combine:
1 **large egg**
1 **egg yolk**
1 cup **granulated sugar**
1 Tbs **vanilla extract**
1 Tbs **coconut extract**
one 15 ounce can **Coco Lopez® Cream of Coconut** *(as used in Pina Coladas)*
one 16 ounce can **coconut milk** *(usually available in the Thai or Asian section of market)*

Combine all of the above ingredients in a blender covered with a tight lid.

Add to the blender:
2 cups **heavy whipping cream**
2 cups **half and half**
2 cups **finely-grated sweetened coconut**
OR pulse **Baker's® Angel Flake® sweetened coconut flake** *in food processor until fine*

Place all the ingredients into an ice-cream freezer.
Freeze according to your manufacturer's directions.
Store frozen ice cream in an airtight container with a tight lid.
Freeze ice cream overnight until frozen firm before serving.

A Culinary Journey with Chef Steve Yeanish

Pâté à Choux

Fill with the ice cream flavor of your choice. Top with warm Caramel or Chocolate Sauce.

Cream Puff Pastry or Profiteroles
sheet pan sprayed with Pam® pan primer

½ cup 1 stick or 4 ounce **butter or margarine**
1 cup **water**
1 cup **flour**
3 **eggs**

Melt butter in a heavy pot, add water and bring to a rolling boil.
Remove from heat, turn burner to low and add flour.
Return pot to burner stirring constantly
until mixture forms a ball, and pulls away from the sides of the pot.
Move mixture to a mixer bowl.
Beat on low speed adding 1 egg at a time until they are all incorporated into the mixture.
Either put mixture in a pastry bag and pipe it onto a pan sprayed with Pam®
OR drop by tablespoonfuls onto a lightly greased sheet pan sprayed with Pam®
Bake at 350 degrees until puffed up and firm.
Do not under-bake.
Turn oven off and let the pastries cool in the oven with the oven door slightly open.
Pastries should be crisp and cooked through.

Lemon Curd

4 ounces **OR** 1 stick **unsalted butter**
juice of 2 lemons
zest of 1 lemon
1 cup **granulated sugar**
2 **large eggs** *lightly beaten*

Melt butter in a heavy sauce pan.
Remove from heat.
When cooled, add eggs, sugar, lemon juice and zest.
Beat lightly and return to heat stirring constantly, cooking until just boiled and thickened.
Cool completely.

For Lemon Mousse

Whip 2 cups of heavy cream until stiff. Fold in lemon curd until just combined.
Add lemon extract or grated lemon zest for more lemon flavor, as needed.

Coconut Cream Cheesecake

Preheat oven to 300 degrees

one 10 inch Springform pan
one larger pan with high sides to use as a water bath

1½ cup **chocolate cookie crumbs**
½ cup **ground pecans**
½ cup **granulated sugar**
½ cup **melted butter**
Mix all the above ingredients until combined.
Pat mixture into the bottom of a 10 inch Springform pan.
Bake for 5 minutes at 300 degrees.

3 pounds **cream cheese**
12 ounces **confectioners sugar**
½ cup **corn starch**
4 **egg yolks**
4 **eggs**
1 can **Coco Lopez® Cream of Coconut**
1 Tbs **coconut extract**
1½ cup **shredded coconut**
Cream together cream cheese and confectioners sugar.
Add cornstarch, yolks and eggs beating in one egg at a time.
Add Coco Lopez®, coconut extract and shredded coconut.
Pour mixture into Springform pan.

To create a water bath: *(see p. 87)*
Wrap foil around the bottom and up the sides of a Springform pan.
Place this pan inside a larger pan with high sides.
Add boiling water to the larger pan until it comes halfway up
the sides of the Springform pan.

Bake for one hour at 300 degrees
Test with knife blade. When it comes out clean, it is done.

A Culinary Journey with Chef Steve Yeanish

Chocolate Fudge Cake with Peanut Butter

Steve's 1st Place Award Winning Hershey's Chocolate Cake Recipe from the 1997 Oley Fair

Preheat oven to 350 degrees
two 10 inch cake pans greased and dusted with cocoa

To make the cake:

²⁄₃ cup **hot coffee**
²⁄₃ cup **Hershey's chocolate syrup**
²⁄₃ cup **milk**
3 **eggs** *room temperature*
¾ cup **canola oil**
1 cup **light brown sugar** *packed*
1 cup **granulated sugar**
1 cup **Hershey's cocoa powder**
2 cups **all purpose flour**
2 tsp **baking soda**
1 tsp **baking powder**

Beat together coffee, chocolate syrup and milk.
Add eggs, oil and sugars, then mix for two minutes on medium speed.
Sift together cocoa, flour, baking soda and baking powder.
Add dry ingredients to the liquid ingredients.
Mix on low for 15 seconds.
Scrape bowl.
Mix on medium speed for an additional minute.
Pour batter into two 10 inch greased and cocoa-dusted cake pans.

Bake at 325 degrees for 25-30 minutes or until a cake tester comes out clean.
Recipe continues on the next page.

The Oley Valley Inn

Chocolate Fudge Cake with Peanut Butter
(continued)

To make the Peanut Butter Filling:

¾ cup **creamy-style peanut butter**
4 Tbs **soft butter**
2 Tbs **vegetable shortening**
1 tsp **vanilla extract**
2 cups **confectioners sugar**

Cream peanut butter, soft butter and shortening.
Add vanilla, then gradually add sugar.
Beat until light and fluffy, then divide in half.

To make the Chocolate Glaze:

12 ounce **Hershey's semi-sweet chocolate morsels**
¾ cup **heavy cream**
2 Tbs **butter**
2 Tbs **Hershey's cocoa powder**

Melt butter and heavy cream in a sauce pan.
Remove from heat and stir in chocolate morsels and cocoa powder.
Allow to cool.

To Assemble the Cake:

When cake layers have cooled to room temperature, spread half the peanut butter filling on to the cake layer.
Place second cake layer on top, then spread the remainder of filling on top of the second layer.
Spoon Chocolate Glaze over the top and continue spreading it around the sides of the cake.
If the glaze is too runny, put it in the refrigerator until it thickens.
Stir Glaze frequently to keep the consistency workable.
Sprinkle with chopped peanuts.

Chocolate Chambord Torte Oley Valley Inn

Preheat oven to 325 degrees
two 10" round cake pans, greased and dusted with cocoa

To make the cake:

Combine in a mixing bowl:
1 cup **light brown sugar**
3 **large eggs**
²/₃ cup **hot coffee**
²/₃ cup **milk**
²/₃ cup **Hershey's chocolate syrup**
1 tsp **vanilla or raspberry extract**
¾ cup **melted sweet butter** *(cooled to room temperature)*

Mix well until combined.

Sift together in a medium bowl:
2 cup **all purpose flour**
1 cup **cocoa powder**
1 cup **granulated sugar**
1 tsp **baking powder**
2 tsp **baking soda**
½ tsp **salt**

Add sifted ingredients to liquid mixture.
Mix on low speed for one minute.
Scrape bowl down often.
Then mix for one more minute on medium speed.

Pour into the greased and cocoa-dusted cake pans.
Bake 20-30 minutes until the cake pulls away from the sides of the pan and a cake tester comes out clean.
Place cake on a cooling rack and cool to room temperature.

Refrigerate one hour before serving.

The Oley Valley Inn

Chocolate Chambord Torte Oley Valley Inn

(continued)

To make the Chocolate Ganache Glaze:

2 Tbs **sweet butter**
1 cup **heavy cream**
12 ounces **semi-sweet chocolate**
1 Tbs **butter**

Melt 1Tbs butter in a saucepan.
Add heavy cream and bring to boil.
Remove from heat.
Add semi-sweet chocolate.
Add ½ cup **Chambord®-the French black raspberry liqueur**.
Stir until smooth.
Cool until it can be spread.
If it gets too runny, you may need to refrigerate it or stir occasionally if it gets too thick.

To Assemble the Torte:
½ cup **Chambord®-French black raspberry liqueur**
10 ounces **seedless red raspberry preserves**

Invert both cooled cake layers so topside is down.
Generously sprinkle both layers with Chambord® liquor.
You can use up to ¼ of a cup on each layer, depending on your taste.
Place one layer of the cake on a serving plate,
then spread a thick layer of seedless red raspberry preserves on top of it.
Invert the other layer of cake on top so both saturated sides are together.
Spread chocolate glaze over sides of the cake, then cover the top of the cake with the rest of the glaze.

Our Bed and Breakfast Begins

Our plans were coming together for the second and third floor projects. When we bought the Inn everything *kind of* worked. There was a leak in the corner of the bathroom ceiling above the bathtub, which got so bad that you could see day light up there. A new roof fixed that problem.

We decided to have four guestrooms, one with a private bathroom, and the other three shared one bath. The room, formerly known as the Beirut Suite, where Jayne and David had spent so many nights, was transformed into a luxurious bathroom with all the amenities. The two largest rooms were open and sunny. We created a cozy sitting room for our bed and breakfast guests. It had a television, a little library, a coffee maker, a selection of soft drinks and bottled water.

We used *3-D Architect* to design the entire space. It allowed us to create walls and keep mistakes to a minimum. The plan was basically straightforward, and it all fell into place with few structural changes. The design came out great. The only thing I'd add is more closet and storage space.

The attic was stripped to the bare walls. We were able to connect pipes relatively easily. We wound up with a full kitchen, huge bathroom with tile shower and whirlpool tub, two large bedrooms, a laundry, and a great room with a gas fireplace, skylights, lots of natural light and enough room for a dining area, television viewing area and home office. It overlooked the back of the building and provided a 360 degree view from the third floor. Being able to see all that way literally saved our lives!

Then, the obstacles started. We needed a way for overnight guests to get out of the building in case of a fire, so we created a flight of stairs at the end of the portico. Fine. That plan would work, but the zoning ordinance called for a minimum setback of 15 feet for any new construction. We needed a variance, and it was a commercial project, so we had to have the steps designed by an architect to meet the requirements of OSHA, the federal health and safety laws. The zoning variance cost $700, the design for the steps cost another $400, and building and painting the steps was another $1,000.

The next obstacle was I had to go in front of the Zoning Hearing Board to ask for my variance. I presented my case at the meeting and they reviewed my plans. I explained I was meeting the demands of my insurance company and the Inn had been a licensed hotel since it was built in 1881. There was a unanimous vote, and my plans were approved.

The project rolled along and our first rooms were finished. Furnishing them was the fun part. While we were painting and doing the rough work, we decided to name the B&B rooms after places we had visited.

We called our first B&B room *Montreal*. We loved that beautiful old city, its architecture and the Old World feel of it was very appealing. We used lots of carved wood furniture, marble-topped tables and lush tapestries with burgundy and red accents.

In *Brewster* on Cape Cod, we stayed at a beautiful old Inn with a nautical theme. Our second room was done in soothing shades of blue. The carpet was lush and the room was pulled together by the colors in the wallpaper. Nautical pieces and paintings finished it off.

Newport was another favorite place. We admired those extravagant mansions by the sea and used a hydrangeas of summer theme to decorate the third room. Then we splurged on coordinating linens, drapes and accessories. We found a beautiful inlaid headboard, an armoire in burled maple and a dressing table for the room. Then, I found a set of Gorham china plates decorated with roses and some Edwardian hats to decorate the walls.

Our fourth room is called *Calistoga* after a place in the Napa Valley where we stayed while touring. We found an old Victorian iron and brass bed frame. Then we added a floral border around the room, an antique dresser that we restored, and finally a pair of funky lamps Barrie's aunt gave us, which captured the look we were going for.

The third floor came together quickly. We did all the priming, painting and staining ourselves. We ran the Inn during the day, then painted at night, cooked, painted some more, served the customers then often continued painting long into the wee hours of the morning. Barrie stained and finished what seemed like miles of trim and woodwork.

One Sunday morning, my family arrived and we primed and painted the whole attic in a day. It was amazing. Mom had heard so much about what we were doing that Dad insisted she come to see it all for herself, even though it wasn't finished yet. Mom's health wasn't good, so we were happy she could spend the day with us.

As soon as brunch was over, I joined in the fun. I admit to being a lousy painter. I start out okay, but get more and more careless. Dad couldn't bear to watch me. He often said, "You waste so much paint!" or "You put it on too thick!" or "You don't have to dip your brush in so far!" I was somehow elected to paint the ceilings, probably because I was the tallest person in the room. Painting a 1,600 square foot ceiling three times is a lot of back-breaking work.

Finally, our third floor apartment was finished. Of course, being the well-organized shoppers we were, everything was ready to go in place, and we moved in smoothly. We only had one major problem. The staircase was very narrow. At the newel post, the staircase only had a 23½ inch clearance. We managed to get everything up there: washer, dryer, stove and refrigerator (both with the doors off), box springs, mattresses and most of the furniture.

The only problem was our upholstered furniture set. We really liked its style and comfort. When it finally arrived, neither the chair, loveseat, or couch would make it up the final staircase and the windows were all too small to get anything that size through.

We finally gave up and returned it to the warehouse. We were really disappointed, so I went back to the showroom to look for another suite of furniture. While I was there I talked to the delivery man and, as we talked, he came up with an idea. An upholsterer could take the furniture apart, carry the pieces up and then reassemble them in place.

The upholsterer arrived and did his thing. In less than two hours, he was finished and it only cost $300! Now we enjoy it comfortably knowing there's only one way to get it out.

Mom's Passing

A group of artists was painting one sunny summer morning. I was working in the kitchen when one of our waitresses stopped in to get her paycheck. She mentioned they were painting the Inn. We walked out to see their work. I was really impressed, so I introduced myself as the building's owner, and asked to see the finished paintings. Around noon they knocked at the kitchen door. Both pictures were beautiful, so I asked if they were for sale. The watercolor by the artist Irene Dobson is on the cover of this book. We also use it for our menu cover, brochures and postcards. I had both watercolors framed, and they can be seen in our dining room and hallway.

Not long afterward, my mother passed away. She had been hospitalized the week before, and we expected to bring her home in a few days. She would frequently rebound, but not this time. She had eaten breakfast (her favorite meal), then took a nap (another favorite of hers) and died peacefully in her sleep. I always thank The Man Upstairs for letting her pass quickly and without pain.

It was Valentine's Day weekend and the restaurant was fully booked with reservations, so I asked to have the funeral on Tuesday. I told the funeral director that I was going to do all of the family floral arrangements. He was somewhat surprised, but I was quite capable.

I spent my days and evenings working through the busy weekend, but the sleepless nights were horrible. I ordered the flowers from a wholesale florist and created the casket spray, the family wreaths, her corsage and the hinge spray for inside her casket. It gave me great comfort to make these for her. The morning before the funeral, my sisters Jayne and Ruth Ann and their husbands arrived with Gail and Sheila, and we prepared all the food for the funeral luncheon. They helped Barrie set up the entire restaurant, too. Mom would have been so proud to see us all working together.

The weeks that followed Mom's death were not easy ones, especially for my father. Mom and Dad were together almost sixty years. Dad still continued to visit us and we enjoyed sitting and chatting while we ate. This was one of the first times I *really* talked to Dad. I opened up and told him things I was never able to say before. I'd been at the Inn for twelve years, and there were so many memories. Mom and Dad had played a huge part in this project. It wasn't just a business to them. It was a part of my dream they shared in as well. They had helped me on occasion, when I needed it, stood by me when I doubted myself, and they always believed in me.

I was grateful that Mom had always been there for us kids. Dad had worked many jobs to provide for us. We never had a lot compared to kids today, but we had so much more than many kids could ever dream of. We were loved and cared for. We enjoyed wonderful food and spent time together as a family. Mom could be tactless and often spoke her mind, which sometimes got her into trouble, but, that was how she was and we loved her for it. And now we all really missed her.

Dad said he'd always be there for me if I ever needed him. When I did ask for help, out of sheer necessity, he said, "I may not have been around that much all those years, but now I'm able to help and I hope that can make up for some of it." I hugged him with thanks. He had worked hard during the first year renovating the Inn, doing any job I asked him to, and he often found jobs on his own. He took great pride in helping me here. It also got Mom out of the house and she loved coming up here, just to be with me.

Mom's Cookbook Collection

Several weeks after Mom passed away, Dad was visiting one afternoon, doing some odd jobs, which he always enjoyed. I sat down to lunch with him and he mentioned he talked with my sisters, and they all agreed I should have Mom's cookbook collection and recipe files. I wasn't expecting this surprise, but I told Dad they'd have a permanent home here in my cookbook library at the Inn.

Dad said they were all packed in boxes, and he'd bring them on his next trip. The next week, he arrived and asked me to help him unload. Much to my astonishment, there were 15 large boxes of books. We took them to the second floor library so I could go through them.

This was a very emotional experience. My entire file of baking recipes, which I had used for the past 30 years, was completely destroyed by the fire at the Inn. While writing this book I searched for Mom's original recipes and was flabbergasted by some of the things I found while I was looking. It was truly overwhelming when I found copies of my recipes that were lost in the blaze. Mom had written *Stevie's Recipe* on her copies. It truly was a gift to find them again!

No one loved to cook or bake like my mother. There were recipes she had handwritten on cards, scraps of paper, envelopes or notebook pages. Complete food section pages from the local newspapers were saved almost every Wednesday. There were cookbooks, old and new. The original orange hardcover *Betty Crocker Cookbook* was there. My sisters and I often used it when we were looking for a recipe. Just paging through it was a trip down Memory Lane.

There was a total of nine recipe files, some of the wooden files were made by Dad. Recipes were stapled on file cards, magazine and newspaper clippings, labels from boxes or bags, you name it. Some were my Grammy's and others were from our neighbor Stella, my sisters or my Aunts.

There were feature articles about me from *The Pottstown Mercury* with my photograph and stories about special events or recipes from the Inn. There were more than 200 booklets put out by manufacturers, such as Spry® shortening, Swans Down® Cake Flour and Crisco®, to name a few. Most are collector's items now.

What amazed me was the variety of recipes I found in her files. Mom was really a meat-and-potatoes kind of cook, but her collection surprised me. There were recipes for court bouillon *(the poaching liquid used especially for fish)*, gazpacho, chutney, croissants, brioche, and many authentic Chinese recipes.

About five years before she passed away, I asked to borrow her copy of *The Whitehouse Cookbook* by Mrs. F.L. Gillette. If you ever get chance to look at this book, it's a great read. It was printed in 1887. Mom bought it for $35, which was a fortune by her standards. The book features recipes from former First Ladies. It has every recipe, remedy and cleaning direction you can think of. The pages were all brown at the edges and very fragile, so Dad made a wooden sleeve box to store and protect it. Mom brought the book with her on her next visit and said, "This is yours now." Inside the cover she had written, *To my dear Stevie, Bushels of Love, Mom.*

Donna

Steve and his Mom enjoy a quiet moment

Almost every room at the Inn has a piece or two of furniture I have refinished. Many have been gifts. One piece, a blanket chest, was given to me by our dear friend and customer, Donna Scalitino, who moved to the Pottstown area from Philadelphia.

Donna was so vivacious and full of life. She loved to sit with a cup of coffee and just talk. Her stories were full of drama, a lot like her. She was always the center of any group.

We were in the middle of renovating the bed and breakfast rooms when she asked if I had any use for an old cedar-lined chest. I said sure and went to pick it up from her house. It was seventy five years old and the original cardboard manufacturer's label was still stapled to the inside, but I was shocked. It had been painted the most awful color blue imaginable and the original feet had been replaced with modern ones.

I set to work and the finish came off slowly, layer by layer, until finally a beautiful, dark cherry wood was revealed. Once it was sanded and refinished, the legs were replaced and the full beauty of the chest became apparent. It now graces one of our overnight guest rooms.

After my Mom passed away, I was very upset and couldn't sleep. On the morning of her funeral I was up early to watch the sun rise on a warm, clear February morning. So I sat down and wrote Mom a letter expressing all my feelings for her, of gratitude and respect for who she was and how much we all benefited from her love. My thoughts just poured out.

At the graveside, the minister, my late Uncle Earl, conducted the service. After he finished, I asked if I could read my letter to my family.

It was very emotional for me and I fought hard to get my composure, then someone put an encouraging hand on my shoulder and I was able to read my tribute in a strong, clear voice. After I finished, I felt an overwhelming sense of accomplishment and satisfaction in expressing that tribute to my mother. A simple encouraging pat on the shoulder from Donna gave me the support I needed at a difficult time. I will never forget her help that morning and every time I see that chest I think of her.

Donna's mother, Violet, taught her to make Sausage Scallopini, a hearty dish for the soul, which I loved. This recipe brings back many happy memories of Donna, who often prepared this dish for me.

Unfortunately, Donna passed away several years ago. Her family let me create the floral pieces for her funeral, which were all done in her favorite colors. I'm happy to say she had a tribute fit for a queen.

Sausage Scalitino

Preheat oven to 325 degrees
Yield: 8 servings

3 pounds **Italian sausage, either sweet or hot**
Olive oil to oil a baking sheet
1 **medium Spanish onion** *peeled, diced finely*
4 **whole cloves garlic** *peeled and chopped finely*
1 tsp **crushed red chili pepper pods**
one 28 ounce can **crushed all-purpose tomatoes**
one 28 ounce can **tomato purée or sauce**
Kosher salt
3 Tbs **olive oil**
1 **large Spanish onion** *peeled, halved, cut into thin slices*
2 **green peppers** *halved, seeded, ribs removed, cut into strips*
2 **yellow peppers** *halved, seeded, ribs removed, cut into strips*
1 pound **rigatoni pasta** *cooked according to package instructions*
½ cup **basil leaves** *lightly packed, coarsely chopped*
Grated Parmesan cheese

Lightly oil a baking sheet with olive oil.
Pierce the casing of the sausages with a knife tip to allow juices to escape while cooking.
Bake sausages in a 325 degree oven for 35-40 minutes until brown and fat renders out.
Set aside and allow to cool, pour off excess fat.
Cut sausages into 2-inch lengths.

Meanwhile, heat 3 Tbs olive oil in a heavy saucepan.
Add diced onion, garlic and chili pepper pods, then cook until lightly browned.
Add tomatoes and tomato puree or sauce.
Bring to a simmer and season to taste with salt.
Simmer 25-30 minutes.

Meanwhile, heat more olive oil in a heavy skillet.
Sauté onion and pepper slices briefly to lightly caramelize.
Cook rigatoni in boiling salted water.
Drain off water.
In large bowl, combine cooked rigatoni, onions and pepper mixture, cooked sausage (add any juices from cooking) and the sauce.
Place mixture into a large oven-proof baking dish and sprinkle generously with Parmesan or your cheese of choice.
Bake for 30-40 minutes until hot and bubbly. Serve with lots of crusty bread.

A Culinary Journey with Chef Steve Yeanish

Speaking Dutch

Betty worked at the Inn for years. She was the fastest dishwasher I've ever seen, and she was always busy doing something. Betty loved to polish silver, clean vegetables, you name it, and she did it willingly. And she was always smiling!

Betty was the eldest child in a family of 23 children. That is *not* a misprint. Betty speaks the *wery* best Dutchified-English I have ever heard. In Dutchy the Vs and Ws are switched, and vinegar becomes *winegar*, as well becomes *vell*.

I once asked Betty where she was born. She replied, *"Vell, it's really Normas Walley, but we call it Voodchoppertown."* (That translates, "Well it's really Enormous Valley, but we call it Woodchoppertown.")

Not long after she left the Inn, her husband, Junior, passed away. His name was Junior George, not George Junior. My Mom died not long after Junior passed away.

Betty soon moved back to the Oley Valley, so we asked her if she'd like to return to the Inn to do the housekeeping for us. She was very happy to return.

My father was quite lonely after Mom died. When Betty returned to the Inn, she and Dad started to see more and more of each other. I am happy to say that they really hit it off and to this day they are living happily ever after. Betty takes such good care of Dad and they love just being together. And to think I set them up. Just call me Chef Cupid!

The best part is I am Dutchified myself now thanks to Betty. When we have guests from other parts of the country staying in our Bed and Breakfast rooms, I can now "speak Dutchy" to them.

A "Dutchy" sampling:

"Vell, it gave rain onest chust the other daya."
"It rained just once the other day."

"I chust knewa dat my germamiums veren't such det yet cause the melumium foil kept um vet."
"I just knew that my geraniums weren't dead yet, cause the aluminum foil kept them wet."

"Vee vent up-srew to Veaver's market cause their newa circlier came onest in the mail."
"We went up to Weaver's Market because their new circular came in the mail."

"They gots such mikerwave ovents, not chust bake ovents."
"They have microwave ovens, not just bake ovens."

"They have such newa raychisters dare, youa knowa, da onest wit I-B-M on 'em."
"They have nice new IBM cash registers."

"Ay, yi, yi, they sure are fansee."
"Oh, they sure are fancy."

"It raint so hardt it nacht don all the lee-afs!"
"It rained so hard it knocked down all the leaves."

"The grount vas tee-totally covert vit em."
"The ground was totally covered with them."

"Ach du lieve nach a mol."
"I can't believe this not again."
Everyone says it!

After the Fire

Soot covered everything!

After the fire, the Fire Chief and the Fire Marshall from the state police arrived. They started their search for the cause of the fire. They could tell it started in the rear corner near the computer by the intensity of the blaze. They searched, sifted through rubble, and found the remains of the trashcan. Rags in the trash self-combusted and caught fire. In less than one hour, the entire corner of the building had been engulfed in flames.

That afternoon, we were allowed to go into the building. The restoration team, whose contract I had signed the night before as the building burned, was ready to start removing the perishables from the site. The local agent from the USDA arrived that morning and condemned all the food, which had to be destroyed.

A makeshift table was setup and the crew started bringing out the contents of every refrigerator, freezer and the walk-in cooler. Everything was inventoried and tallied on sheets. Each table of items was photographed as well. The food contents of a restaurant kitchen are massive, especially when you are ready for a holiday weekend. There were six whole beef tenderloins, two strip loins of beef, twenty-something pounds of jumbo lump crabmeat, racks of lamb, veal tenderloins, boxes of frozen shrimp, and several pieces of grade-A foie gras. This premium food was now all garbage.

It was bad enough to lose all that food, but then we had to inventory it, and carefully go back and put prices on each item.

Now the real fun began. As each item of equipment was carried out of the kitchen, I had to identify it, record it, and decide whether it was trash or salvageable. Broken items had to be accounted for as well.

As the area was slowly emptied, salvageable goods were washed in very strong degreaser and detergent. Scouring pads removed the black soot that clung to everything. It seemed like an endless task. As items were cleaned, they were wrapped, packed in cardboard boxes and stored in other parts of the building. This process went on for weeks. My hands were stained black from handling all the soot. It would be a month before my stains went away.

Demolishing the Kitchen of the Inn

The ruins are demolished.

As each section of the ruined kitchen and bakeshop was demolished, the building debris was cleared away. Finally, the job was finished, and only the cinder block wall from the original 1974 kitchen of the Inn at Oley remained.

There had never been a foundation under this part of the building. Pipes for water and drains were built right into the floor. The gas line for the cooking ranges was a cast-iron pipe. There was a low crawl space between the original building and what used to be the kitchen area. It was an architect's nightmare, but the insurance company's engineer deemed the cinderblock wall fit for reconstruction.

Then it all started to get complicated. It took endless hours to do all the inventories. Each item had to be logged and placed in a file on the computer. Prices had to be found from invoices, or we had to research sources and gather price information about items that were comparable to our loss.

Then we had to make lists of what we needed to purchase to start over again. We wanted to put the Inn back together the right way. I wanted to be my own project manager and use our usual plumber and the electrician we always worked with. These men already knew our old building and were part of the fantastic volunteer crew that helped to put out the fire that night. They knew where to turn our gas and electric off as soon as they got to the site.

I started getting quotes on new construction from contractors and eventually decided to use a firm who worked on my friend's restaurant. They had a lot of commercial experience and were very reputable.

Meetings were set with all the contractors and plans were drawn. We had to build a basement under the new kitchen, but it had to be within the original footprint of the old building. A crawl space would connect the old basement with the new basement.

Digging our new basement.

Building our new kitchen.

Rebuilding the Ruins

Water, sewer and electric lines had to go through the crawl space. An engineering firm had to go over the whole plan and spec out all of the major water, electric, heating, cooling and lighting. Sound expensive? It was.

The old block portion of the building was demolished on August 31, 2005, eighteen years after the date of my original purchase of the building. Work went quickly from this point. Our entire parking lot was full of trucks for almost two months.

The interior of the restaurant was smoke damaged. The sitting room of the Montreal Suite was the only room that had been seriously damaged. Two windows were broken, smoke stains were visible on the walls, and the carpet was badly soiled. Our third floor apartment had little or no damage at all. After a week of open windows, the smokey smell had disappeared. Downstairs was another story.

Every room in the building had to be cleaned from floor to ceiling. Walls were scrubbed. Every piece of fabric, drapes, linens, robes and towels had to be professionally treated and cleaned. Imagine the logistics of unloading an entire truckload of dry cleaning and then getting the right items sent back to their proper room! It was like putting a huge puzzle together.

The bar room of the Inn became our headquarters. We had three square tables set up to use for everything from a conference area, to a design center, work area, tool storage and for paint mixing. There was even a reference area for paint samples, fabric swatches and brochures. It was all going on around there somewhere. We had to continually put this stuff away and clean up as we went along.

I finally got my dream kitchen. The kitchen line stayed much the same, although the chef's table now has two refrigerated sections for á la carte prep, as well as a larger, individually-controlled steam table. There is a double wide pickup window, and built-in, self-contained soup warming pots. It is now an "L" shape that allows the pantry area to be at the end of the line. Each station has its own reach-in refer, too.

The line previously had been broken up into three stations for sauté, grill, and fryer-steamer. Three chefs could now easily work the line. The bakeshop and dishwashing areas were at opposite ends from the original kitchen. The bakeshop was now in a tidy, compact area with its own tables, storage, proof box and convection oven. A self-contained ice cream freezer was added.

The new basement provided much-needed storage space, as well as accessibility to all the mechanical works of the kitchen. There was room for an office, complete with frequently-used cookbooks and Internet access. We wash most of our linens, so there was a large-capacity washer and dryer. We now had a storage room for catering equipment, and I even created another area for my floral projects that are often used when catering. I usually create many of the props that we use for our theme parties.

In the old kitchen, we sometimes ran out of hot water if someone filled the fifty-gallon whirlpool tub in the B&B on a Saturday night. Now we have a separate hundred-gallon hot water heater *just* for the kitchen!

> *The entire length of the time from the day of the fire until we re-opened for business was six months and 17 days.*

Of course, all of this came at a price. Since it was considered new construction, we had to comply with all new regulations of the USDA. Their rules would take pages to explain. Most are well-founded, but again, it all comes at a price. The air return into the kitchen from the exhaust hood was required to be heated or cooled to within 20 degrees. So, we now have an air-conditioned kitchen.

The entire Township of Oley has been designated a National Historic District, the first one in America to be recognized, so we have a Historical Architectural Review Board. This committee oversees any modifications to properties that are more than fifty years old. Most of the building here falls under their guidelines, but the kitchen part of our building was built in 1974, so it didn't qualify. Our architect, Patrick Dolan, did an incredible job of blending the new construction with the old.

The kitchen, as it originally stood, reminded me of a double-wide trailer parked behind a beautiful old building. It was covered with gray siding and all the mechanics of the exhaust system were visible. Not any more!

Patrick's new design for the two-story addition looks like buff-colored clapboard, but it is actually made of cement (not vinyl or aluminum). The second story has a wall-like façade that appears to be a Mansard-style roof with cedar shakes. This conceals the roof-mounted mechanicals (exhaust fans, air handlers, compressors, etc). Arch-topped windows were added to match the rest of the building. Accent lights were put in to illuminate the long planter for my culinary herbs in the warm weather. It's also a focal point for holiday planting and decorating.

All of our many silk flowers, plants and arrangements in the building were coated with dust and smelled like smoke. Each one was completely taken apart, hand washed and rearranged. That was a *huge* job, but it gave me something to do during the time we spent waiting for the new construction to start.

The smoke settled into the carpet after the fire and the odor lingered for many months. The insurance company was only willing to replace the carpet in the Montreal Suite, insisting the rest of the carpet could be cleaned. We decided it was better to just replace all the eight year-old carpet and we had a local installer come in. He did the job quickly and professionally, and low and behold, the smoke odor was gone for good!

We had business interruption insurance. Imagine how surprised I was when I was told that the business interruption payment wouldn't be paid until the end of the claim!

The entire amount of time from the day of the fire until we reopened for business was six months and seventeen days. Moral of the story: You only get what you pay for.

Mom said, "Cheap aspirin is like cheap toilet paper. It doesn't cost much, and it doesn't do much, either." Before the fire, I never really sat down and estimated the actual cost of reconstructing a 120-year-old building, *or* building a new fully-equipped kitchen from the ground up, *or* itemized the exact value of the contents of our building. We businesspeople all worry about liability, be it liquor, product or injury, but fires really do happen, especially in restaurants.

A Culinary Journey with Chef Steve Yeanish

Rebuilding the Kitchen

The old kitchen.

Building the new kitchen.

The new kitchen was designed to work with the style of the old building.

The Oley Valley Inn

Every single item had to be accounted for, tracked, scrubbed then put away.

We spent more than $5,000 on dry cleaning linens and other fabrics.

A Culinary Journey with Chef Steve Yeanish

Reopening

We were finally ready to reopen. It was the beginning of December and we were hoping to get at least a little bit of the holiday season business. The last two weeks of construction were truly amazing. Friends, family, staff—and even customers—came from everywhere to help us get ready.

There were plenty of jobs for everyone: dusting, cleaning, putting away tools, paints and drop cloths, restocking shelves, unpacking china, glassware and flatware, washing and storing it, and restocking the shelves. The walk-in cooler was set up and filled with food. Sometimes, the same box was moved five times until it was finally unpacked and everything was put in its rightful place. And *then* we had to decorate for the holidays!

On December 12, 2005, the Oley Valley Inn was open for business again. We held an Open House Celebration and the bright, shining new kitchen was the highlight of the tour. Everyone was welcome to see what took nearly seven months to accomplish. From the street, it was impossible to see any progress, but as people drove into our parking lot, they were really surprised. Hundreds of invited guests enjoyed champagne and hors d'oeuvres. And we proudly presented our new Chef Luigi.

We made a lot of improvements while we were closed. Along with replacing carpeting throughout the entire building, we added new accent lighting to our main dining room and new draperies. Our beer cooler behind the bar was at least fifty years old, and ran on a remote compressor. Parts for it were no longer made and if it died, we were stuck. So we reconfigured the bar sink and refrigerator for the new cooler, which fit like a glove.

My brother John had just retired and he was an absolute Godsend. He rebuilt the floor that had always squeaked in the Garden Room. Parts had completely rotted, so he dug them out and replaced the floor joists. Then, he spent countless hours hanging new shelves and arranging furniture. His wife, Beverly, came and spent many days helping as well, usually with a paintbrush in her hand.

Even though the Beirut Suite was long gone, Jayne and David arrived to help with last minute holiday décor and clean up. Ruth Ann was always willing to help, too. My entire staff was here and they spent many hours working off the clock. It is at times like these when you really get to know that you are fortunate to have a truly wonderful staff!

Barrie

Quirky Customers

My philosophy has always been, "I'd rather make friends than enemies." These are TRUE stories from my thirty years in this crazy business.

A customer told the manager on his way out of the restaurant, "I have to tell you, those Eggs Benedict were horrible!"
Anxious to please, Barrie replied, "Well what was wrong with them?"
His answer, "The yolks were all runny! They are supposed to be hard inside!"

An angry customer sent Béarnaise sauce back to the kitchen exclaiming, "This sauce is not hot!" (Béarnaise is a warm sauce and heating it would have made scrambled eggs.)

One woman refused to eat her Caesar salad. The server asked her what the problem was. She hadn't even tasted it.
"The lettuce is yellow," she complained.
The server told her we were using the hearts of romaine.
"It's not green, and I am not eating it, so take it away!"

Barely-touched soup was sent back to the kitchen with the comment, "That was onion soup? It was sweet. It's supposed to be salty!"
The server replied: "Chef says he's never tasted a salty onion in his life."

A customer complained that his soup was cold. The server replied, "I'm sorry sir, but Gazpacho soup is supposed to be served cold."
The customer snapped, "I know my Gestapo soup, and I know it is supposed to be served HOT!"

Diet or health-conscious customers order egg white or Eggbeater® omelets, but they still ask for the cheese or Hollandaise Sauce with it.

In the height of asparagus season in May, a customer returned their just-picked, gloriously tender, crisp asparagus asking, "Don't you have any canned? I think it is far better."

We proudly serve local tomatoes at the height of the season. We even grow some heirloom varieties of our own. When served a plate of room-temperature succulent tomatoes layered with fresh mozzarella and basil picked from our own herb garden, a customer commented, before even tasting them, "Those aren't local tomatoes, I can tell just by looking at them."

A very pretentious customer was ordering dessert. He pointed to the Profiteroles on the dessert menu and said, "I'm going to have the pedaphiles."

A connoisseur sent back his prime, domestic Rack of Lamb. He said, "This lamb is so strong tasting, you need to be serving New Zealand lamb."

"Can I have a pair of rubber gloves to eat my duck? I just read that just touching the fat can make you gain weight."

A Culinary Journey with Chef Steve Yeanish

Several years ago there was an emergency and just as I grabbed the telephone to dial 911, the phone rang, so I answered, "Oley Valley Inn."

A woman responded, "I was wondering if I could make a reservation?"

I calmly but assertively said, "Ma'am, there is an emergency and I need to use this phone line to call for help."

"Well, I was just calling---"

"Ma'am, PLEASE, I need you to hang up!"

Later that evening the phone rang again.

A man said: "Yes, my wife called today to make a reservation, and the person on the phone was very rude to her."

"Well sir, that person was me. I am the owner of the Inn. We just had a brand new 500-gallon propane gas tank installed and the valve on it was faulty. At the time your wife called, there was a stream of liquid propane gas shooting 20 feet into the air like a geyser. I had to call 911 before this building and the entire block blew off the face of this earth, so I apologize if I was short with your wife."

"Oh, my! Is everything all right now?"

"Yes, sir, it is. Fortunately with the combined expertise of the Fire Company and the Gas Company, they were able to close the valve safely after the entire street was evacuated."

"There were huge bones in my Osso Bucco. You should call that Osso Bono instead."

"We can't serve the shrimp tonight. We just realized the Rabbi IS coming!"

"I'll have the club sandwich, and there better not be any HAM near it or I'll send it back, and make sure the BACON is very crisp!"

The Ladies Powder Room of the Inn has always been very special. There is a beautiful marble-topped dresser with an arched mirror just as you enter the room. The walls are covered in a rich burgundy floral tapestry and the room is tiled in almond. A pair of French doors with opaque glass separates the toilet portion from the vanity, dresser and an antique wooden chair. The "stall" area of the room is 4 feet wide and at least 8 feet long.

Long before I owned the inn, I purchased a Fitz and Floyd relief of a white porcelain swan. It was beautiful—at least 24 inches wide from tip-to-tip of its spread wings, and the neck and head curved gracefully to the front. It had an open space on either side behind the neck that I had filled with all kinds of silk foliage, and it was on the far wall, away from the commode.

One Sunday afternoon following brunch, we were cleaning up in the kitchen. A loud crash was heard throughout the entire restaurant. Of course, I went to investigate. I knew what had broken. My beautiful swan had taken a dive to the tile floor. A mortified woman came out of the ladies room and nervously asked, "Do I have to pay for it?" I hesitated for a moment, then calmly responded, "No, but I sincerely hope to be seeing you as a regular patron for a while!" Mom always said, "Don't cry over spilled milk."

"I can't eat my soft-shell crabs."
"I'm so sorry to hear that. They have been very popular this evening."
"Well I just don't like them."
"Have you ever eaten them?"
"No, this is the first time I ever tasted them. I'll have the crabcakes instead."

The Oley Valley Inn

"The prime rib is fatty."
Prime rib is easily the fattiest piece of meat on the entire steer. If it didn't have fat on it you probably wouldn't want to eat it. If you saw the fat that was trimmed off before you got it, you would be equally appalled.

"My strip steak is all gristle."
The end of the strip does have gristle. I don't serve those end cuts, not when my menu reads "center cut." There is a strip of connective tissue that runs along the bottom side of the steak and runs about one third of the way up the fat side of the steak. I know that I prefer this to be removed, but on the flip side, if it is removed, it will allow some of the steak's juices to escape before it can be properly seared. I am not alone, and Lord knows it is hardly on the Heart Healthy list, but I enjoy a tad bit of that wonderful charred fat on my steak.

"A customer returns a steak because it is overcooked."
99% of the time it is a strip steak and the tailpiece is cut into first. Cut the steak in the center, and it is cooked perfectly. Do you want it partially pink, or dead? Most people need to explain their preference. "Well-done" folks should let us butterfly your steak. (We slice the steak in half horizontally, leaving it hinged at one end, which allows the steak to cook faster, sear, and at least retain some internal moisture.)

While planning a party I suggested an appetizer of Crab Remoulade. When the client asked what the remoulade was, I said that it was basically a tartar sauce with capers and chopped anchovies. The client insisted I was wrong. She said she didn't know what remoulade was, but she knew I was definitely wrong.

A Culinary Journey with Chef Steve Yeanish

We've Been Part of Many Wonderful Events!

I have had the privilege of being part of many families' happiest moments. For example I have baked every single birthday cake for one of my customers, who is now 22 years old. I have made wedding cakes for parents and then, years later, made their children's wedding cakes, too. I have catered in venues where only the most exclusive caterers were allowed. We even became an exclusive caterer.

We've taken our show on the road and catered a kosher Bat-Mitzvah in the synagogue and then served a gourmet four-course meal prepared in the kitchen of the temple, which was meat, preceded by a dairy luncheon. *(Everything in the kitchen had to be switched over three times to maintain a strictly kosher kitchen.)* We've also catered hundreds of gala parties such as a retirement party for an NBA official, that was attended by 500 guests and all the big names in the league from Larry Bird and Michael Jordan to Magic Johnson.

We continue to cater to our select group of customers, and I especially love our favorites. Gertrude and Bill were in their 80s when they became regular customers. They were truly some of our most treasured friends, and were regulars both at Brookside and then at the Inn.

Gertrude was a petite, white-haired lady, who carried herself like a film star. We all loved Gertrude, she was the kindest, sweetest and classiest lady you'd ever meet and she never had a bad word to say about anybody. She and Bill adored each other. Bill made me promise that, with or without him, there would be a 90th birthday party for Gertrude at the Inn. After Bill passed away Gertrude said, "Steve, I don't know what to do about my birthday."

I asked, "What are you worried about?" Gertrude said, "Well, I don't think I can have it now without my Bill."

I responded, "Well, Gertrude, you have no choice. I made a promise to Bill that there *would* be a birthday party for you, with or without him."

"Well, I guess I'm having a party then!" was all she said.

It was a beautiful June afternoon. The guests were seated for a lovely dinner. With a flute of her favorite champagne, Gertrude stood and toasted, "Here's to Bill!"

Then everyone in the group enjoyed telling one of their favorite stories about our beloved Bill. I made one of my favorite cakes, lemon-scented Génoise with lemon curd filling, frosted in lemon mousse, with toasted almonds on the sides. She was delighted. There is a photograph of me presenting Gertrude with her 90th Birthday Cake on the back cover of this book.

For Gertrude's 95th birthday, we planned a small party for her at the nursing home. I took my personal china, silver and stemware and made special floral pieces and a petite birthday cake for each guest. Gertrude was totally surprised. She couldn't believe Barrie and I were there on our day off, but we said, "Only for you, Gertrude!"

She couldn't say thank you enough and hugged and kissed us as we left. It's never a chore to do something for a wonderful person like Gertrude. We saw her on Christmas Eve and her smile said it all. "I can't believe my boys (that's what she called us) are here to see me on Christmas! I am so thrilled you even stopped to see me. You make me feel so special!" That was the last time we saw her.

The Oley Valley Inn

Our dear friend Gertrude celebrating her 90th Birthday.

Cake is always a favorite!

A Culinary Journey with Chef Steve Yeanish

Pumpkin Pancakes Anyone?

My eldest brother Ray says, "If you can't dazzle them with brilliance, then baffle them with bull."

I missed a phone call one afternoon while out running errands. When I got back, Barrie told me a gentleman had called from London to ask for a recipe he wanted. My curiosity got the better of me, so I quickly returned his call. Barrie came in just as I was saying goodbye.

"Well," I said to Barrie, "I have good news and I have bad news."

Without missing a beat Barrie replied, "Tell me the good news."

"Well, the good news is that man is writing for *Gourmet Magazine* and they're doing an article on biking in Berks County, for next autumn. They stayed at various bed and breakfasts and visited several restaurants. He was here for Sunday Brunch and really enjoyed our Pumpkin Pancakes."

"What's the bad news?" asked Barrie.

"Well, the bad news is those new pumpkin pancakes on the menu were rustled up using Bisquick,® canned pumpkin, brown sugar and my own pumpkin pie spice blend."

Barrie gasped, "Well, what are you going to do?"

"Well, I don't think it would look good for us, or *Gourmet Magazine*, if I sent them the original recipe, so I better start doing some research and recipe testing to come up with a way to recreate them."

I spent a few hours studying my cookbook collection, then made several batches and tweaked a few more, until eventually I came up with a pancake that tasted like the one the writer actually ate, then I faxed the recipe to him. This was printed in the October 1995 issue of *Gourmet Magazine*.

A fellow chef and owner, Jay Schaeffer, once told me there is plenty of room for new restaurants in a given area. We should all share customers and keep them in our own backyards. People shouldn't have to drive to a major city to experience fine cuisine. I have many friends from California and the West Coast who are surprised, then blown away, by the innovative food in our own Berks County.

I recently attended a reunion at the Culinary Institute of America. That afternoon, Master Chef Fritz Sonnenschmidt made a comment that I took to heart. He said we were very fortunate to have been able to attend such a fine school, and learn from the experience of chefs who've worked around the entire world, and cooked for heads of state, royalty and celebrities. He said it's now our responsibility to share that knowledge with the next generation, who are as eager to learn as we were. His comments made me realize how fortunate I am, and how much I still can do.

When I first left school, there were many chefs who were guarded and very careful about sharing recipes or techniques. I always asked one particular chef for a recipe or two, but he always put me off. He never actually said no, but then he never gave me any information either.

I was once warned never to discuss preparations, suppliers, or, God forbid, actual recipes in front of a waitress whose husband was going to be the chef at a new restaurant that was opening nearby. Talk about insecurity!

As Mom used to say, "It's good to know your friends, but it's even better to know who your enemies are."

Restaurant owners in Berks used to keep to themselves, but in cities like New York, restaurants often share waiters, cooks, dishwashers or whatever. It was one big labor pool and you wouldn't lose your job because you were seen eating in a competitor's dining room.

One local old-timer told me I shouldn't hire good employees, I should steal them from other places. Imagine that! Don't get me wrong, rivalry still exists, but I feel welcome in any restaurant in the area.

Most of us chefs know each other by name. We all have a bottom line to look out for, yet we all have something different to offer. It is great to know that I can pick up the phone and call one of my peers when I am in a bind for a new service or to check out the reference of a potential employee.

I do have one policy when dining out, especially in Berks. I know enough to find fault with most *anything* I see or eat, from the service, food, atmosphere or even the outside entrance, but I've learned to just sit back, relax and enjoy the experience, like any other customer would.

Customers come to my establishment for sustenance or to celebrate a special occasion. Others want an experience. Of course they'll compare us to other restaurants! They may not be critics, or chefs, but they all have expectations of their own. As our friend Ben once said, "Your business is like your child. No one is going to take care of it like you do."

Once it's your turn to be on the receiving end of criticism, don't ask what someone thinks unless you're really ready to hear it. Not everyone is kind, and some people really *will* tell you *exactly* what they think!

When I'm dining at someone else's restaurant I always say please and thank you, which are two phrases that are forgotten sometimes. I always leave a good tip of 20% or more. God knows, in this business if you're cheap, the word spreads faster than if you're generous.

There are two things servers do that annoy me. I eat slowly, so I'm always the last person to finish. Please don't rush me, especially by walking impatiently past the table six times. I was taught that the table should never be cleared until everyone has finished eating. And secondly don't *ever* offer my dining companion dessert while I am still eating my dinner!

Servers who are rude or inattentive only get a 10% tip with a tails-up penny on top of the check. Old-time waiters told me that this was considered to be the ultimate insult from a customer, and their final comment on poor service.

Complete strangers come to the Inn expecting an enjoyable experience. That is what we're here for! I'm responsible for far more than just the dish I planned, prepared and served. I rely on many other people and the actions of our servers, bartenders and hosts, who are all part of the package. A spotty glass or a stale cracker can be cause for complaint. This is a business, and the expectations of our customers cover the whole rainbow.

I am a firm believer in the proverb, "It's not what you say, It's how you say it."

I often hear people boasting that their husband, wife or significant other is a gourmet chef. I'm often tempted to ask, "Where did they study or apprentice? How many kitchens have they run? How many people did they supervise?"

I'm sure these people are excellent cooks in their own right, but they're not chefs. I hand out aspirin and Band-Aids all the time, but that doesn't make me a doctor. Have you ever mistakenly call a doctor, "Mister"? I guarantee you'll be corrected pronto. If you have ever seen the test given by the American Culinary Federation to people aspiring towards the title of Master Chef, you'll have a better appreciation of what that means. A cook is *not* a chef.

I have learned some great techniques from other people. If you don't open up your mind to new ideas and techniques you'll become a fossil, old before your time and stuck in your ways. Cooking is like music, fashion or cars. It's always changing.

You need to know the basics, but that's not enough anymore. From this point on, keep your eyes and ears open. And keep your mouth shut, at least until you can speak as an authority because you have been there and done it.

The most important advice I can give in closing is to never stop learning. I have learned so much from just observing and listening to other people. Opinions are butts. Everybody's got one, but some are bigger than others. I have told employees if they have a better way to do something, just show me. I base my opinions on knowledge and experience, but if you can show me a better way to do something, then go for it.

And last, but not least, listen to your mother. Look where it got me! I had lemons so I turned them into lemonade, lemon soufflé, lemon tart, lemon mousse, you name it, I've done it—and had a heck of a lot of fun in the process!

The Oley Valley Inn

I will close with some words of wisdom my friend Phil taught me when I opened my restaurant.

"Don't argue with a fool. Listeners can't tell who is who."

Despite the ups and downs this has all been a great adventure...and I wouldn't trade one minute of it!

Bon Appétit!
Chef Steve

Index

a

advice 92
Aiolli 116
Alaska 15, 19
Alma 30
almond 129
Amaretto 142
American Culinary Federation (ACF) 84, 85, 182
Amish 98
anchovy fillets 69
anniversary 82
apple 17, 18, 29, 152
Apple Dumplings Oley Valley Inn 152
apple peeler 90
architect 171
artichoke hearts 116
artist 108, 162
Asiago Polenta 71
aspic 60
Aunt Margie 15
Aunt Marie 135
Award Winning 156
awards 84, 156
award, Best Duckling Piece 84
award, Best in Show 82
award, First Place 84
award, Second Place 82, 84
award, Third Place 85

b

B & B 132, 160
Baby Spinach Salad with Warm Bacon Dressing 115
bacon 122

baking cheese 57
baker 33
baking 60, 135
Banana Surprise Muffins 141
bananas 138, 140, 141
Bananas Foster French Toast 140
Bananas Foster Oley Valley Inn 138
Barrie 132, 162, 174
basement 168
basics 77, 86
beans 126, 149
Beard, James 77
Béarnaise Sauce 147
Béchamel 60
bed and breakfast 132, 160
beef 21
Beef Braised in Beer and Onion 66
beet 125
Berks County 98, 110, 180
Berks County Mushroom Chowder 133
Berks-Lehigh Chef's Association 85
Bethlehem, Pennsylvania 12
Betsy 60, 64
Betty 166
Beurre Blanc 123
Beverly 174
birthdays 78
biscotti 129
Block, Thea 100, 110, introduction
blueberry 38
Bohemia 91
Bosler, Nelda 96
Boston butt 63
Bot Boi 99
bread 128
bread crumbs 116
Brewster 160
Brookside 52, 55, 58, 72, 74, 90, 96, 101, 110
Brookside Clubhouse 55
broth 26
budget 59
buffet 126

building 97
Bungalow 10
buns 136-7
burger 92
butternut squash 114
BYOB 96, 106, 110

c

cake 38, 39 55, 62, 82, 91, 156, 158, 179
Calistoga 161
carpet 171
catering 94
centerpieces 79
Charlie 104
chaud-froid 60
cheese 118, 125
cheeseburger 92
cheesecake 36, 90, 155
chef 52, 58, 180
Chef Albert Kumin 62
Chef Anthony Seta 59
Chef Arno Schmidt 64
Chef Cleefeld 59
Chef de Cuisine 74
Chef Eddie Bradley 60
Chef Eric Saucey 60, 182
Chef Fritz Sonnenschmidt 59, 85
Chef Patrick Gorey 58
Chef James Heywood 60
Chef Joe Mure 64
Chef Luigi 64
Chef Pat Gorey 74, 93
Chef Peter Van Erp 62
Chef Pierre Rausch 77
Chef Says 16, 65, 122
Chef Steven Beno 60
Chef Walter Schryer 62
Chef Wayne Almquist 62
Chef's Note 13, 65, 112, 133
Chef's Says Note 16, 65, 122
cherries 22

chestnuts 11
chicken 15, 30, 53, 61, 112, 149
Chicken Liver and Mushroom Pâté 112
children 8
chili 113, 127, 149
chocolate 34, 35, 129, 156-7, 158-9
Chocolate Almond Biscotti 129
Chocolate Cake 34, 35
Chocolate Chambord Torte Oley Valley Inn 158
Chocolate Fudge Cake with Peanut Butter 156
Chocolate Glaze 157
Christmas 110, 111
cider 22, 125
cinnamon 138
citrus 32
clam 12, 13
Clam Stew 13,
classes 58
clean 170
club 74
Coco Lopez® 153, 155
cocoa painting 82
Coconut Cream Cheesecake 155
Coconut Ice Cream 153
college 56
color striping 83
competitions 82
contractors 168
cooking, Shank Beef 16
cookbook 163
cookie 44, 90, 139
cooking 30, 93
corn 113, 126, 130
Country Club Cuisine 74
cover 162
crab 113, 130
Crab and Corn Fritters with Jalapeño Butter and Maple Syrup 113
Crab Crusted Flounder with Scalloped Corn 130
crabmeat 114, 130

cranberry 11
Cream of Coconut 153, 155
Cream Puff Pastry 154
critic 93
croquettes 26
Crowley, John Phillip "Phil" 96, 97, 100, 104, 105, 106, 108, 132
crumbly or dry 90
crust 15, 18, 40, 88, 89, 90
cuisine 76, 98, 180
culinary competition 52
Culinary Institute of America (CIA) 56
Culinary Salon 82
Curried Butternut Squash Soup with crabmeat 114
curry 114
custard 150
customer 175, 176

d

Dad 8, 9, 10, 12, 14, 19, 20, 103, 162
dandelion greens 12
David 104, 132, 160, 174
death 162
decorating 33, 110, 111
Delaware Valley Chef's Association 83, 84
Demi-Glace 57, 87
demolished 170
Dennis 52, 75, 96, 101
Derkhising, Mark 77
Dobson, Irene 162
dough 28, 60, 91
doughnut 42
dressing 115, 117, 125, 127
drink 23, 32
duckling 68
dumplings 67

e

Easy Hollandaise Sauce 145
education 58
eggs 30
Eggs "Inn Style" 144
Eggs Henry VIII 146
Tait, Elaine 93
Escoffier Room 62
Eskimo 19

f

family 101
farmers 99
Fastnachts 42, 43
fillets 123
fire 2, 107, 167,
flounder 130
flowers 162
food group 99
food order 106
forcemeat 83
Four Seasons 62
Frank 42
French restaurant 97
Fried Artichokes with Asiago and Zesty Lemon Aiolli 116
fritters 27, 29, 45, 113
frosting 33
Frozen Lemon Soufflé 109
Fudge 156
funeral 164
furniture 108, 161, 164

g

gala 54, 78
Garde Manger 59, 60
garden 22
garlic 118
German 8, 28, 67, 98
Gertrude 178, 179

girdle 25
glaze 41, 42, 68
Gorey, Pat 54, 56
Gourmet Magazine 180
Grace 52
graduated with honors 64
graduation 64
Graham Cracker 90
Grammy 14, 108
Grand Buffet 60
grandparents 8
Gremolata 69

h

herb butter 53
Hess's Department Store 40, 41, 85
Hog Maul 99
Holiday Buffet 55
Hollandaise Sauce 145
Honorable Mention 82, 85
humor 52

i

ice cream 138, 153
ice sculptor 54
Inn at Oley 96, 97, 100
instructor 86
interior 170
International Cuisine 59
Italian Egg Drop Soup 61

j

jalapeño 113
Jan 79, 106
Jarlsberg and Onion Fondue 118
Jayne 103, 104, 132, 160, 162, 174
Jeanette 30

Jerry 104
John 174
judge 85
juice 32

k

Kalbach, John 96
kielbasa 63
Kipfel 101
kitchen 4, 97, 168, 170
koi 4

l

Lace Cookies Almond Tuille 139
lamb 70
Larson, David 106, 108
leeks 122
legal requirement 95
lemon 32, 37
Lemon Curd 109, 154
Lemon Mousse 154
lemonade 23
lemongrass 127
Lenhartsville 9
lime 32
Linzer Torte 65
liquor license 96, 100, 106
lose 166
luau 52

m

Maiden Creek 9
market 25
marzipan 84
Master Chef 182
Master Chef Fritz Sonnenschmidt 180
Mennonites 98

Mensch, J.R. 99
mentor 132
meringue 37
Milos Country House 72
Milos, John 72
Mirepoix 68, 87
Mom 8, 9, 12, 20, 103, 162
Montreal 160
Moravian 91
Moravian College 12
Moravian Sugar Cake 91
Mother's Frozen Lemon Soufflé 109
muffins 24, 141, 143, 146
mushroom 112, 132
my own business 96

n

Newport 161
nuts, toasting 65

o

Oley 10
Oley Hotel 99
Oley Valley Community Fair 98
Oley Valley Hotel 96, 97
Oley Valley Inn 107, 110
Oley, Pennsylvania 98
Olympic coal stove 104
one-pot meals 99
Onion Soup 57
opening 106
Orange and Rosemary Roasted Pork Loin 120
OSHA 160
Osso Bucco 119
Osso Bucco with Gremolata 69
oven 62

p

painting 106, 160-1
pancakes 151
Panko, Japanese breadcrumbs 116
Pantry 59
parents 20
Partridge, Mr. 82, 90
party 79, 101
pastry 15, 18
pastry chef 62
Pasty 15
Pâté à Choux 154
Pâte Sucre 89
Pauline 52
Peanut Butter 156
Peanut Butter Filling 157
Pecan-Crusted Fillet of Red Snapper with Red Raspberry Beurre Blanc 123
pecans 123
Pennsylvania Dutch 28, 42, 98, 99
Penturelli, Ben 133
Phil 96, 97, 100, 104, 105, 106, 108, 132
philosophy 176
picnic 25
pie 17, 37, 40, 88
Pie Crust 88
plans 168
Polenta 71
Poppyseed Spätzle with Brown Butter 67
Pork Loin Roast 63
Pot Pie 26, 99
potato 17, 31, 43, 124, 136
Potato Milos 73
Pottstown, Pennsylvania 8
poultry 26
Profiteroles 154
pumpkin 148, 150, 151
Pumpkin Crème Brulee 150
Pumpkin Mushroom Soup 148
Pumpkin Pancakes Oley Valley Inn 151

r

raspberry 123
Ray 104, 180
recipes 132, 163
red snapper 123
relish 11
renovations 106, 164
rescue 2
restaurant operations 96
rice 119
risotto 119
Roast Duckling 68
Roasted Beet Salad with Chèvre and Walnut Croutons 125
Roasted Garlic Cheese Spread 118
Roasted Rack of Lamb 70
rolling pin 90
rolls 62
roof 103
roux 87, 133
Ruth Ann 103, 162, 174

s

Saffron Risotto 119
salad 115, 117, 125, 127
salmon 131
Salon of Culinary Arts 52
salsa 131
salvage 166
sauce 21, 71
sausage 63, 165
Sausage Scallopini 165
Savory Leek and Bacon Bread Pudding 122
Schlop Kuche 34
scholarship 56
Schultzie 52
Schwenksville, Pennsylvania 10, 20
Scalitino, Donna 164
scrapple 98
sculptures 52
sesame 131
Sesame-Crusted Salmon with Roasted Tomato and Papaya Salsa 131
settlement 103
shallots 112
short crust 15, 18
show 84
Shrove Tuesday 42
Simple Syrup 23, 142
sisters 39
Slatington, Pennsylvania 8
Slop Pie 34
Slurry 87
smoke 170
Smoked Trout Pâté 119
soot 167
soup 26, 28, 57, 61, 142
Sour Cream 143
Sour Cream Streusel Muffins 143
spätzle 67
spinach 115
spread 118
squash 114
Stella 42-44
stew 12
Stracciatela 61
strawberry 23, 24, 40, 142
Strawberry Soup with Amaretto 142
stuffing 11
Sunshine brand wood-burning stove 97, 104, 105
support 101
Sweet Potato Filling 121
syrup 43, 152

t

tart 65
teachers 59
teaching 12

test if there is enough butter 90
Thanksgiving Dinner 10
The Professional Chef 58
The Soul of a Chef 59
Thelma 52, 101
The Whitehouse Cookbook 163
to Sweat 87
Tokyo Twist 62
tomato 21, 117, 131, 165
too wet, pie crust 90
tools 90
trade school 86
trees 22
trends 77
trout 119
turkey 11, 26, 27, 28, 53
turnover 15

u

Uncle Earl 15, 19
upholsterer 161
USDA 167

v

vanilla bean 150
variations for pie crust 88
veal 53, 69
vegetarian 126
Vera 52
vinaigrette 117, 125

w

walnut 125, 128
Walnut Onion Bread 128
waste 98
water bath 87, 150, 155

weddings 78
White Chicken Chili 149
White House 62
wine racks 105

y

yams 121
Yeanish 8
Yeanish, Ray "Pappie" and Louise 8, 9
Yeanish, Ruth and Jay 8, 9

z

Zesty Lemongrass Dressing 127
zoning 160

*We've enjoyed sharing your celebrations.
Thanks for the memories.
It's been a heck of a lot of fun!*

A List of Recipes by Title

Apple Dumplings Oley Valley Inn 152

Asiago Polenta 71

Aunt Marie's Sticky Buns 135

Award Winning Oley Valley Inn Chocolate Cake 35

Baby Spinach Salad with Warm Bacon Dressing 115

Banana Surprise Muffins 141

Bananas Foster French Toast 140

Bananas Foster Oley Valley Inn 138

Beef Braised in Beer and Onions 66

Berks County Mushroom Chowder 133

Bérnaise Sauce 147

Bleu Cheese Dressing 49

Blueberry Streusel Coffee Cake 38

Canberry Relish 11

Chicken and Oyster Bisque with Shiitake Mushrooms 51

Chicken Française 53

Chilled Strawberry Soup with Amaretto 142

Chocolate Almond Biscotti 129

Chocolate Chambord Torte Oley Valley Inn 158

A List of Recipes by Title

Chocolate Fudge Cake with Peanut Butter 156

Cinnamon Ice Cream 138

Citrus Cooler 32

Coconut Cream Cheesecake 155

Coconut Ice Cream 153

Cookie or Graham Cracker Crust 90

Cornish Pasty 16

Country Chicken Liver and Mushroom Pâté 112

Crab and Corn Fritters with Jalapeño Butter and Maple Syrup 113

Crab Crusted Flounder with Scalloped Corn 130

Cranberry Orange Vinaigrette 13

Cranberry Relish 11

Curried Butternut Squash Soup with Crabmeat 114

Dad's Clam Stew 13

Easy Hollandaise Sauce 145

Eggs "Inn Style" 144

Eggs Henry VIII 146

Fastnacht Doughnut Glaze 42

For Lemon Mousse 154

Fresh Apple Tart 18

A List of Recipes by Title

Fresh Strawberry Pie 40-1

Fried Artichokes with Asiago and Zesty Lemon Aiolli 116

Grammy's Oven-Fried Chicken 15

Heirloom Tomato Salad 117

Jarlsberg and Onion Fondue 118

Kipfel 102

Lace Cookies Almond Tuille 139

Late Summer Succotash 126

Lemon Chiffon Meringue Pie 37

Lemon Curd 154

Lemon Mousse 154

Linzer Torte 65

Mary Lou's Cheesecake 36

Mom's Apple Fritters 29

Mom's Basic Red Sauce 21

Mom's Funny Paper Chocolate Cake 34

Moravian Sugar Cake 91

Mother's Frozen Lemon Soufflé 109

Oley Valley Onion Soup 57

Orange and Rosemary Roasted Pork Loin 120

A List of Recipes by Title

Osso Bucco with Gremolata 69

Oven-Fried Alaska Potatoes 17

Pâté à Choux 154

Pecan-Crusted Fillet of Red Snapper with Red Raspberry Beurre Blanc 123

Pie Crust 88

Poppyseed Spätzle with Brown Butter 67

Pork and Sauerkraut with Kielbasa 63

Potatoes Milos 73

Pumpkin Crème Brulee 150

Pumpkin Mushroom Soup 148

Pumpkin Pancakes Oley Valley Inn 151

Roast Duckling Oley Valley Inn 68

Roasted Beet Salad with Chèvre and Walnut Croutons 125

Roasted Garlic Cheese Spread 118

Roasted Rack of Lamb 70

Saffron Risotto 119

Sand Tarts 44

Sausage Scalitino 165

Savory Leek and Bacon Bread Pudding 122

Sesame-crusted Salmon with Roasted Tomato and Papaya Salsa 131

A List of Recipes by Title

Short Crust or Pâté Sucre 89

Sisters' Sour Cream Pound Cake 39

Smoked Trout Pâté 119

Snowy Cream Frosting 33

Sour Cream Streusel Muffins 143

Stella's Fastnachts 43

Sticky Buns 136-7

Stracciatela Italian Egg Drop Soup 61

Strawberry Lemonade 23

Strawberry Muffins 24

Sweet Potato Filling 121

Turkey and Chestnut Stuffing 11

Turkey Croquettes 27

Turkey Noodle Soup 26

Turkey Pot Pie 28

Twice-Baked Stuffed Potatoes 124

Walnut Onion Bread 128

Welsh Rarebit 50

White Chicken Chili 149

Zesty Lemongrass Dressing 127

198　　The Oley Valley Inn

Chef Steve's Stories

Advice to a Young Chef 92

After the Fire 167

Brookside Country Club 48

Brookside Country Club Chef de Cuisine 74

Brookside Crew 52

Brunch 134

Buying the Inn 100

Catering 101 94

Celebration Cakes 78

Charming Chickens 30

Chef Pat Gorey 54

Christmas at Oley Valley Inn 110

CIA Memories 59

Culinary Competitions 82

Culinary Institute of America 56

Dad 12

Demolishing the Kitchen 168

Chef Steve's Stories

Donna 164

Dutchy Sampling: 166

Furnishing the Inn 108

Grammy 14

Milos Country House Restaurant 72

Mom 20

Mom's Cookbook Collection 163

Mom's Garden 22

Mom's Passing 162

Mr. Partridge, "Mr. P" 90

My Family 8

My First Job 45

Oley, Pennsylvania Cuisine 98

Our Bed and Breakfast Begins 160

Perkiomen Bridge Hotel 47

Pumpkin Pancakes Anyone? 180

Queen of Shoppers 25

Chef Steve's Stories

Quirky customers 175

Rebuilding the Ruins 170

Reopening 174

Safari Party 79

Saying Good Bye 101

Searching for my own business 96

Setting up shop 103

Some Common Cooking Terms 87

Some of the Wreckage 6

Speaking Dutch 166

Stella 42

Studying at the Culinary Institute of America 58

Surveying the Damage 4

Teaching Teens 86

Thanksgiving Feasts at the Bungalow 10

We Have Been Part of Many Wonderful Events 178

Photo Credits

Our sincere thanks to:

The artist **Irene Dobson**
for allowing us to reproduce her beautiful
water color of the Oley Valley Inn on the front cover.

Cover Photographs by:
Barrie D. Frain
    Oley Valley Inn in Summer
    Oley Valley Inn at Christmas
    Details from the original ceiling of the Bar
Ineke Van Workhaven
    Gertrude Achatz's 90th Birthday Party

Interior Photographs:
Dennis Danko
    Steve and Barrie Dedication Page
Chris Young, Fleetwood Fire Company
    fire scenes
Steven A. Yeanish Archive
The Yeanish Family Collection
Collection of Barrie D. Frain

Special thanks to Thea and Natalie for their continual inspiration.

Visit our web site at www.oleyvalleyinn.com

Printed in the United States
119784LV00004B/249-298/P